Betty Crocker's

EAT AND LOSE WEIGHT

PRENTICE HALL

NEW YORK   LONDON   TORONTO   SYDNEY   TOKYO

Prentice Hall
15 Columbus Circle
New York, New York 10023

Published simultaneously in Canada by
Prentice Hall Canada Inc.

PRENTICE HALL and colophon are registered
trademarks of Simon & Schuster Inc.

BETTY CROCKER is a registered trademark
of General Mills, Inc.

Library of Congress Cataloging-in-Publication Data
Crocker, Betty.
[Eat and lose weight]
Betty Crocker's eat and lose weight.—1st ed.
p.   cm.
Includes index.
ISBN 0-13-074303-8
1. Reducing diets—Recipes.   I. Title.   II. Title: Eat and
lose weight.
RM222.2.C749   1990
641.5'635—dc19   89-3570
CIP

Manufactured in the United States of America

10 9 8 7 6 5 4 3 2

First Edition

On the cover:
Turkey with Chipotle Sauce (page 94)

CONTENTS

FOREWORD
4

INTRODUCTION
5

HOW TO USE *EAT AND LOSE WEIGHT*
6

APPETIZERS & SNACKS
20

FISH & SEAFOOD
36

POULTRY
68

MEATS
98

EGGS, CHEESE & LEGUMES
126

VEGETABLES
152

SALADS
174

BREADS, GRAINS & PASTA
196

DESSERTS
216

MENUS FOR FOUR WEEKS
240

THE *EAT AND LOSE WEIGHT* WORKBOOK
252

CALORIE CHART
260

INDEX
265

FOREWORD

Year after year, millions of Americans try to shed unwanted pounds. It is a fact that no matter how conscientiously weight-loss diets are followed, much of the weight is usually gained back, in many cases quickly. Does this mean that weight-loss programs are futile? Is it useless to try to lose weight? Not at all! The key to successful weight loss is learning to keep the weight off by making permanent, positive changes in eating and cooking habits—not just for a summer, or a year or two, but for a lifetime of well-being. *Eat and Lose Weight*'s Five-Point Program gives you that key. *Eat and Lose Weight* explains in simple terms how you can lose weight, then maintain your new weight so that you don't have to be overweight ever again.

Physical, mental and social well-being are the three components of a positive lifestyle approach to good health. Weight control is a very important part of this triangle. Betty Crocker's *Eat and Lose Weight* recipes are designed to help you lose weight by reducing the number and amounts of highly caloric ingredients and emphasizing appealing, nutritious foods. In addition, this book gives you a full month of delicious menus to help you learn how to maintain your ideal weight. And here is the most surprising part of all: When you share your *Eat and Lose Weight* recipes with friends and family, they will only know the food is fresh, satisfying and just a little bit more exciting.

THE BETTY CROCKER EDITORS

INTRODUCTION

You may wonder why you need another diet cookbook. The answer is that you don't, if you don't want to lose any weight, if your blood cholesterol is low, if you already eat a diet low in fat and high in fiber, and if you don't want to try new recipes that are nutritious and taste marvelous.

If you are serious about losing some weight, the Betty Crocker Five-Point Program will help you design a healthy lifestyle. The first step: You can follow a full month of 1200-calorie-a-day menus for gradual weight loss. The Five-Point Program is safe; it's not just another fad diet. It's a sensible eating plan for a lifetime. The bonus is that you can serve the very same food to your family and friends, just give them bigger portions.

Diets often don't provide recipes, and when they do, the recipes aren't very tasty. The 250 recipes in *Eat and Lose Weight* are in the Betty Crocker tradition of delicious eating. That makes this book one that you will want to use again and again—even after you lose weight—to help you keep the weight off. The recipes are healthier than traditional fare because they use less fat and less salt, have less cholesterol, are lower in calories and higher in dietary fiber. If your current diet is high in fat, cholesterol and salt and low in fiber, you may run an increased risk for such chronic diseases as diabetes, heart disease, hypertension, some forms of cancer and, of course, obesity.

One of my colleagues has found that the typical American family routinely prepares no more than ten different dinner entrées. My family is no different. If you can substitute one or two lower calorie, lower fat, lower salt, higher fiber recipes, it can help you and your loved ones to be more fit. I like to think that if I can find in a collection just one recipe that my family likes on a regular basis, that book is a success.

But, *Eat and Lose Weight* is more than just a cookbook. The Five-Point Program also includes strategies for making your lifestyle a healthier one. Pick the ones that suit you best.

Just whispering the word *Exercise* to dieters elicits moans and groans. If you are not physically active (most overweight people are not), it is very difficult to exercise. To try to be more positive about exercising, think of it as "playing." That means choosing several activities that you enjoy and varying them. Research shows that you'll lose weight faster if you burn at least an extra 1000 calories a week. If you weigh 150 pounds, that means walking 10 miles a week (1 mile = 100 calories). The more you weigh, the more calories you burn. The Five-Point Program not only gives you the number of calories burned for many different activities, it also provides tips to help you become more active.

Our research has revealed that women who successfully maintain a reduced weight exercise regularly. Increasing your level of physical activity can seem harder than cutting back on calories. So . . . don't forget to play!

When I graduated from high school a 4-H member and a champion cherry pie baker, I won the Betty Crocker Homemaker of Tomorrow Award. The award encouraged me, as a young college student, to learn more about food and nutrition. It is particularly fitting that I should have the honor of introducing the newest effort from Betty Crocker to help and encourage all of us on a path to good health. Here's to healthy, delicious eating!

JUDITH S. STERN, Sc.D.
Professor of Nutrition and Director of the
Food Intake Laboratory
University of California at Davis

How to Use
Eat and Lose Weight

To some people, the idea of trying to lose weight seems, at its best, a chore. To others, at its worst it seems an unattainable goal. But losing weight successfully—that means keeping the unwanted pounds from returning—is neither. With this book in hand, losing weight successfully isn't a losing proposition at all; it is methodical (it becomes habit), it can be fun and it certainly is rewarding. You can actually track your progress.

The *Eat and Lose Weight* plan is based on Betty Crocker's Five-Point Program. Our Five-Point Program teaches you how to:

1. Eat Smart
2. Exercise
3. Set Goals
4. Keep Good Records
5. Design Your Lifestyle

That sounds like a tall order, but the steps are simple. Perhaps the hardest part of losing weight is getting started.

In the following pages are more than 250 recipes that make taking that first step much easier. Once your scale registers an initial loss, you will be encouraged to continue your success. You will learn to recognize bad habits and exchange them for good ones. And, before you know it, you will have built a responsible lifetime program tailored to work exclusively for you.

Eat and Lose Weight recipes were developed with widely available foods. Most can be found at your local supermarket. These foods include some reduced-calorie products: margarine, mayonnaise, sour cream and salad dressing, for example. (Reduced-calorie products are always specified when called for.) This means that you can continue to use familiar kitchen techniques with some of the convenience foods that are habitual for you and your family.

Good-tasting reduced-calorie, low-fat and low-sodium products come onto the market daily. You can choose among them the products that address your personal concerns. If sodium is something you'd like to reduce in your diet, look for such low-sodium products as "light" soy sauce. If you like cheese but are worried about fat, try some of the low-fat cheeses. With the use of nonstick cooking spray and nonstick cookware in *Eat and Lose Weight* recipes, we've significantly reduced cooking fat (and cleanup is a breeze). A good nonstick skillet is one of the best efforts you can make to reduce dietary fat.

Everyone can use a bit of help in the willpower department, and it is never more challenging than when you are setting out to lose weight. For that reason, we show you recipe shortcuts, so that there's less temptation to nibble and pick while you cook. Try to find your own shortcuts where you can. A food processor is a great help in slicing, shredding, chopping and mixing. (While you're in the kitchen, go ahead and prepare ingredients for the next day, too.) Approximately one third of the *Eat and Lose Weight* recipes include microwave directions. The microwave oven is a boon to weight loss. It cooks with less added fat, and it cooks best those foods that are naturally lean and moist, such as fish and vegetables. All of the microwave recipes were tested using countertop microwave ovens with an output wattage of 625 to 650 watts. If using a microwave oven with a higher or lower wattage, cooking times may need to be adjusted; refer to your use and care manual for microwave techniques and safety.

Every *Eat and Lose Weight* recipe includes a per-serving nutritional analysis. To be sure of the calories consumed, keep serving sizes as close to the suggested serving amounts as possible. If you eat more, you will be increasing the total number of calories indicated in the nutritional analysis; if you eat less, you'll consume fewer calories than indicated. Some recipes offer alternatives to some ingredients. The nutritional analysis for recipes with alternate ingredients is figured on the use of the ingredient listed first. For example, Smoky Beef and Cheese Quiche calls for "½ cup shredded mozzarella or Monterey Jack cheese,"

SALAD BAR STRATEGY

Salad bars, whether at the greengrocer, supermarket, delicatessen or food co-op, are a great convenience. Some provide as many as fifteen or twenty fresh vegetables, washed, trimmed and cut into pieces. Most salad bars also stock such prepared salads as coleslaw, potato salad, Waldorf salad, gelatin-marshmallow molds and other combinations with higher fat contents. Help yourself to only a small amount of those with creamy dressings. Go easy on the cheese cubes, bacon bits, hard-cooked eggs, raisins and croutons, and concentrate on the crisp steamed beans and spinach. If coleslaw is what you're craving, pick up the shredded cabbage at the salad bar or in the produce section and make your own Creamy Coleslaw (page 186) at home!

and the nutritional analysis is based on the use of mozzarella. Many recipes are accompanied by serving suggestions, and these optional foods are not figured in the analysis.

THE FIVE-POINT PROGRAM

1.
EAT SMART

Eating smart means eating healthy, and it also means good eating habits. If you are overweight, you must learn to make some changes in your eating habits, and you must make an honest effort to make these changes permanent. The key issues here are variety and moderation. The Dietary Guidelines for Americans (published by the U.S. Department of Health and Human Services) recommends the following approach.

Eat a variety of foods. A well-balanced diet makes sense. No single food can satisfy all of your nutritional needs, so plan to select foods from each of these food groups every day: milk and dairy products (including yogurt and cheese); vegetables and fruits; cereals and grain-based foods (such as bread); meats (including fish, poultry and eggs); and dry beans and peas. Of course nutritional needs vary with age. Consult the Basic Food Groups Chart, on page 9.

Maintain a desirable weight. People who are considerably overweight are susceptible to numerous health problems. Those who are overweight are more likely to suffer from strokes, elevated blood fats and cholesterol, heart disease, high blood pressure, diabetes and some forms of cancer, among other ailments. To target your optimal weight range, consult the Height and Weight Tables on page 11. If you haven't been close to that range in years, consult with your doctor; together you may set intermediate goals.

Avoid too much fat, saturated fat and cholesterol. Why? Eating excess saturated fat and cholesterol will increase blood cholesterol levels in many people. However, those levels vary widely from person to person, due to heredity and the way individual bodies use cholesterol. It is clearly wise to be aware of the amounts of dietary cholesterol and saturated fats we ingest every day, and that can be tricky. Cholesterol and fat are sometimes "hidden" in foods, and restricting your intake means reading labels. Choose small amounts of lean meat, fish and poultry. Trimming excess fat and cooking without added fat decreases the amount of dietary cholesterol and saturated fat.

The American Heart Association recommends that daily cholesterol intake should not exceed 300 milligrams per day or 100 milligrams per 1000 calories, whichever is less. Glance over the cholesterol counts included with every *Eat and Lose Weight* recipe, so that you can plan your day sensibly. Authorities recommend limiting fat to a maximum of 30 to 35 percent of total calories.

Another compelling reason to restrict fat intake is this: By weight, fat has about twice as many calories (9 calories per gram) as carbohydrate or protein (4 calories per gram). Some people have the tendency to eat more of high-fat foods than low-fat foods in order to feel "satisfied," and in doing so, consume more calories. A considerable source of dietary fat (including saturated fat) is deep-fat fried foods that we commonly purchase: French fried potatoes, doughnuts, chicken and so forth. Cholesterol comes directly from foods of animal origin: meat, poultry, eggs and dairy

BASIC FOOD GROUPS CHART

Food Group	Recommended Daily Amounts	Equivalent of 1 Serving	Nutrient Contributions
Milk, Yogurt and Cheese	Children under 9 years: 3 servings Teenager 10 to 18 years: 4 servings Adults: 2 servings	1 cup milk or yogurt or 1 ounce cheese or ½ cup cottage cheese or ½ cup ice cream	Calcium Phosphorus Protein Riboflavin Vitamin A Vitamin D
Meat, Fish, Poultry and Legumes	2 servings	2–3 ounces cooked lean meat, fish or poultry or ½ cup cooked dried beans or 1 egg or 2 tablespoons peanut butter	Iron Niacin Phosphorus Protein Folic acid Vitamin B_6 Vitamin B_{12}*
Breads and Cereals (whole grain, enriched and fortified)	4 servings	1 slice bread or 1 ounce ready-to-eat cereal or ½ cup cooked cereal, rice or pasta	Carbohydrate Iron Niacin Riboflavin Thiamine Magnesium
Vegetables and Fruits	4 servings Include one good source of vitamin C daily. Frequently include deep yellow or dark green vegetables.	1 cup raw vegetables or ½ cup fruit, fruit juice or cooked vegetables or 1 medium or 2 small fruits	Carbohydrate Vitamin A Vitamin C
Combination Foods	Count as servings from the food groups from which they are made.	1 cup soup or 1 cup macaroni and cheese, lasagna, stew or ⅛ of a 15-inch pizza or 1 sandwich taco	Same nutrients as the foods they contain.
Fats, Sweets and Alcohol	Number of servings depends on the individual's calorie needs.		Fatty acids Vitamin E

....

Source: General Mills, Inc.
*Animal products only

products. As a rule of thumb, saturated fats tend to be solid at room temperature (with the exception of coconut and palm kernel oils). Lard, for example, contains saturated fat. Unsaturated fats tend to be liquid at room temperature. Vegetable oils (corn, safflower and cottonseed, for example) contain unsaturated fat. Wherever possible, substitute low-fat foods for fattier ones (skim milk for whole milk is a good substitution), trim fat off meats, and add a minimum of fat when cooking.

Eat food with adequate starch and fiber. Starches, like cereals and breads, are a kind of carbohydrate (complex). Sugars are carbohydrates, too (simple). Carbohydrates in general are attractive to people who want to lose weight because they are about half as caloric as fat. There are three persuasive reasons to choose complex carbohydrates over simple carbohydrates as a dietary mainstay. Complex carbohydrates have the nutritional advantage of vitamins and minerals; when metabolized they don't make blood sugar levels soar, then plummet (remember the energy spurt a sugary, midmorning doughnut gives, always followed by fatigue); and certain complex carbohydrates contain dietary fiber.

Fiber is the nondigestible portion of foods derived from plants. There are actually two kinds of dietary fiber: water-insoluble and water-soluble. The insoluble variety passes through the human body unchanged. Insoluble fiber promotes regularity and may reduce the risk of colon cancer. It is found in most vegetables and fruits, dried peas and beans, and wheat and corn bran.

Water-soluble fiber breaks apart when mixed with water and creates bulk. Soluble fiber slows the rate of food absorption; the stomach signals a "full" feeling and the desire to continue eating decreases. Studies have shown that soluble fiber in oat bran and beans lowers blood cholesterol in some individuals.

OILS

Oils for use in cooking contain mono-unsaturated, polyunsaturated and saturated fats. The term "saturation" is rather scientific; it describes the degree to which the fat molecules are loaded with hydrogen atoms. What it means to most of us is this: Research indicates that mono-unsaturated fats do not increase blood cholesterol levels, and polyunsaturated fats can actually lower them.

We rely on three oils for most of the *Eat and Lose Weight* recipes. Olive oil is primarily monounsaturated. The extra virgin and virgin olive oils may have a stronger olive flavor and are marvelous to dress salads and vegetables sparingly. Vegetable oil contains polyunsaturated fat. It has a high smoke point, so it is a good choice for high-temperature cooking. Sesame oil contains mostly polyunsaturated and monounsaturated fats. It ranges from pale yellow to brown in color and may be odorless or aromatic. As a light-colored oil pressed from raw seed, it has scant sesame flavor and is a nice, rather neutral vegetable oil. The darker oil is made from toasted seed, and it is used principally as a flavoring.

A high water-soluble fiber diet has been helpful in regulating blood sugar levels in some diabetics. Good sources of soluble fiber are barley and oat bran, apples and oranges, and kidney, navy and pinto beans.

Avoid too much sugar. The major health hazard from eating too much sugar is tooth decay. Dental problems are not simply a mat-

1983 METROPOLITAN
HEIGHT AND WEIGHT TABLES

WOMEN			
Height	**Small Frame**	**Medium Frame**	**Large Frame**
4'10"	102–111	109–121	118–131
4'11"	103–113	111–123	120–134
5'0"	104–115	113–126	122–137
5'1"	106–118	115–129	125–140
5'2"	108–121	118–132	128–143
5'3"	111–124	121–135	131–147
5'4"	114–127	124–138	134–151
5'5"	117–130	127–141	137–155
5'6"	120–133	130–144	140–159
5'7"	123–136	133–147	143–163
5'8"	126–139	136–150	146–167
5'9"	129–142	139–153	149–170
5'10"	132–145	142–156	152–173
5'11"	135–148	145–159	155–176
6'0"	138–151	148–162	158–179

Note: Weights at ages 25 to 59 based on lowest mortality. Weight in pounds according to frame (in indoor clothing weighing 3 pounds, shoes with 1-inch heels).

Source: Courtesy of Metropolitan Life Insurance Company Statistical Bulletin.

MEN			
Height	**Small Frame**	**Medium Frame**	**Large Frame**
5'2"	128–134	131–141	138–150
5'3"	130–136	133–143	140–153
5'4"	132–138	135–145	142–156
5'5"	134–140	137–148	144–160
5'6"	136–142	139–151	146–164
5'7"	138–145	142–154	149–168
5'8"	140–148	145–157	152–172
5'9"	142–151	148–160	155–176
5'10"	144–154	151–163	158–180
5'11"	146–157	154–166	161–184
6'0"	149–160	157–170	164–188
6'1"	152–164	160–174	168–192
6'2"	155–168	164–178	172–197
6'3"	158–172	167–182	176–202
6'4"	162–176	171–187	181–207

Note: Weights at ages 25 to 59 based on lowest mortality. Weight in pounds according to frame (in indoor clothing weighing 5 pounds, shoes with 1-inch heels).

Source: Courtesy of Metropolitan Life Insurance Company Statistical Bulletin.

ter of how much sugar you eat, but the frequency with which you eat sweets. Foods that contain a lot of sugar often also contain a lot of fat and are therefore high in calories. Because these foods are not rich in vitamins and minerals, they are not essential in the diet.

Avoid too much sodium. Sodium occurs naturally in foods, and it is used in pro-

cessing and preserving foods. For persons with high blood pressure, excessive sodium is a hazard. Sodium intake is but one of the factors known to affect blood pressure. Most Americans eat more sodium than they need. Reduce your intake by using less table salt, and eat sparingly those foods to which large amounts of sodium are added (pretzels, salted nuts, potato chips, mustard, garlic salt and soy sauce, to name a few).

If you drink alcoholic beverages, do so in moderation. Alcoholic beverages tend to be caloric and low in nutrients. Alcohol lowers inhibitions, making it that much easier to snack and overeat.

Be realistic. It's up to you to make smart food choices. Read the labels on prepared foods and know what it is you are paying for. Consult the Foods to Choose Chart on page 13 for an overview of foods to choose and foods to avoid.

To develop good habits, it makes sense to identify bad ones. The Daily Food Diary on page 259 is one of the worksheets designed to help you do just that, showing you how you spend both your calorie allowance and your time. You will be able to pinpoint problem areas and behavior patterns and take steps to change them by developing new coping skills. Your Record of Behavior Patterns and Coping Skills will help you (see page 256).

Positive lifestyle changes make the difference between being "on a diet" and shaping a delicious, reasonable eating plan for life. Be realistic about your weight-loss goals. It is easier to cut back on certain favorite foods high in calories and fat than to try to abstain from them altogether. When we feel deprived, sooner or later we binge. The *Eat and Lose Weight* 1200-calorie-a-day menus on pages 240–251 help you avoid backsliding because they satisfy with food that is varied and absolutely delicious.

You must add a modest exercise program to your day in order to lose weight efficiently and keep it off. Dropping pounds does nothing to improve body tone—only exercise will do that for you. Turn to pages 15–17 for some suggestions to get started safely. Regular exercise will be one of your best friends in maintaining your ideal weight.

Commercial weight-loss plans can be appealing. They promise results, but most of the weight lost so quickly on these diets is water, not fat. It is impossible to have adequate nutrition on a very low-calorie diet. Moreover, it has been shown that such diets cause the body to make metabolic changes in order to conserve weight! The fact is that in order to lose weight, you must consume fewer calories than you burn. And to keep weight off, you must develop an eating plan that you can live with. That is why crash diets fail. Before joining a commercial plan, make sure that it is run by credible nutritional professionals. Any plan that promises miraculous results will not be helpful in the long run.

In fact, it is important *not* to expect an enormous drop in weight quickly. Dramatic weight

WATER: THE FORGOTTEN NUTRIENT

About two-thirds of the human body is water. A fact just as surprising is that, even with all that water, our bodies need more water on a daily basis. Six to eight 8-ounce glasses of water are recommended every day. Other liquids may be counted toward that quota, but don't count coffee, tea or beverages containing alcohol; they have a dehydrating effect. Keeping the body well hydrated is an important step toward maintaining a healthy diet. If you tend to forget about water, keep a pitcher or thermos of cold water by you and help yourself to a glass now and then throughout the day.

FOODS TO CHOOSE CHART

· ·

MILK

Choose: Fortified skim, buttermilk, nonfat dry milk. Dry or low-fat creamed cottage cheese, farmer or pot cheese. Neufchâtel and other low-calorie cheeses. Nonfat and low-fat yogurt.

Avoid or eat sparingly: Whole milk, cream, ice cream, sour cream.

MEAT, POULTRY, FISH, EGGS

Choose: Very lean, well-trimmed meats. Extra-lean or low-fat ham and luncheon meats. Poultry and fish without skin. Broiled or baked foods.

Avoid or eat sparingly: Fatty meats, cold cuts, frankfurters. Panfried or deep-fat fried foods.

VEGETABLES

Choose: Fresh, plain frozen or canned (eat less often: corn, kidney and lima beans, peas, potatoes, winter squash).

Avoid or eat sparingly: Vegetables in sauces or deep-fat fried.

FRUITS

Choose: Fresh, unsweetened canned fruits or juices; fruits rich in vitamin C (oranges, grapefruit, strawberries, cantaloupes).

Avoid or eat sparingly: Fruits in heavy syrup, sweetened frozen fruit, fruit fritters.

CEREALS, BREADS

Choose: Whole grain, enriched, restored or fortified cereals and breads. Small muffins.

Avoid or eat sparingly: Rich or large muffins, pancakes, waffles, biscuits, doughnuts.

EXTRAS

Choose (only after you have your required servings in the preceding): Sugar-free gelatins, desserts made with skim milk, egg whites, low-calorie whips, cocoa powder, angel food cake, desserts in this book, popcorn without added fat, low-calorie jams, jellies, syrups. Reduced-calorie margarine, mayonnaise and sour cream.

Avoid or eat sparingly: Whipped cream, chocolate, fudge, caramels, most cakes, ordinary pies, cookies, fried or deep-fat fried snacks, jams, jellies, syrups, rich gravies, sauces, butter, margarine.

· ·

Source: General Mills, Inc.

Menu 1, Dinner (page 243)

loss is hard on your health, and any weight loss program should have your doctor's approval before you start. Be prepared to lose an average of one to two pounds a week. Research shows that weight loss at that rate is far more likely to be permanent than dramatic losses. It pays to be patient. Every body is different. You will have weeks when you lose more or less than two pounds. Just remember that you didn't gain that weight overnight, and it isn't going to go away overnight. Impossible goals will only set you up for disappointment. Setting goals along the way (pages 17–18) will keep you on track.

The amount of calories needed to maintain one's weight varies from person to person. Once you reach your ideal weight, with continued exercise you may be able to increase your daily calorie intake without gaining weight. Add 100 calories a day to find the intake at which *you* can maintain your weight.

2. EXERCISE

A moderate plan of exercise is practically essential to successful weight loss. Exercise improves muscle tone, which can only improve appearance and that, in turn, improves your outlook. Exercise relieves stress, too. A brisk daily walk can make a big difference, in your outlook and in your health.

If exercise still seems unappealing, think about this. The metabolism of an inactive person who reduces his or her caloric intake actually slows down, because the body recognizes that there's less "fuel" coming in and reacts to conserve energy. As a result, fewer

COPING

Most people find they have some trouble spots when trying to change habits.

- Eating too fast? Plan to give yourself a leisurely half hour, even if you are eating alone. Take small bites and chew slowly. Put your fork down between mouthfuls. Sit back and enjoy sips of flavored seltzer or a spritzer, if you are feeling festive.
- Nibbling on leftovers? Cover them and put them away as soon as you finish your meal. Or give them away. Or throw them out, if you must. Serve portions that seem skimpy on luncheon, not dinner, plates.
- Impulsive eating? Stick to a planned daily menu that "schedules" snacks. Before eating any "unplanned" food, drink a glass of water and make yourself wait ten minutes. Don't skip meals. Shop only from lists you've made out at home. Keep food out of sight. If someone is snacking and you are tempted, leave the room.
- Late-night snacking? Save your "scheduled" snacks until the evening comes around.
- Mindlessly snacking while watching television (or reading, or studying)? Limit your eating to one location, the dining room table, for example. Make it a rule not to munch while doing something else. If you don't think you can watch TV without eating, then turn off the television and do something else.
- Make use of your Behavior Patterns and Coping Skills Worksheet on page 256.

calories are burned, and weight loss is slowed or may even come to a halt. But here's good news: Even moderate exercise encourages the body to metabolize more quickly. Not only does it burn calories more efficiently during exercise, but some studies show that effect is sustained for as long as eight hours or longer after a thirty-minute workout.

A comforting word about exercise: There is at the very least one form of exercise that can accommodate your lifestyle, no matter how frenetic or how packed your schedule may seem. Exercise doesn't have to mean climbing up on a stationary bicycle (although that is good exercise). Exercise is many things to many people. It may be something done with others, like tennis; you may enjoy the support of a group activity (a great way to make new friends, too). Exercise may be done alone, like long, refreshing walks. In fact, one of the best ways to exercise is doing just that: walk-

METABOLISM

"Metabolism" is the term for the process by which the body turns food fuel into usable energy. Metabolic rates vary from person to person. Someone with a high rate of metabolism turns more food into energy than someone with a low rate of metabolism. Some people inherit a "slow" metabolism from their parents. This certainly does not mean that someone with a slow metabolism has an excuse for being fat. It does mean that he or she has additional, compelling reasons to pay attention to food intake, and to combine healthy eating habits with good exercise habits.

ing. Brisk walking (3.5 to 4 mph) has good aerobic effects.

The very word *exercise* makes most of us envision jump ropes and fitness gyms. Those things are certainly right for some people, but exercise options go far beyond. Bear two important things in mind: (1) Whatever form of exercise you choose, make sure it is something you enjoy doing; and (2) get the most benefit from exercise by doing it regularly. If you are serious about losing weight, exercise. If you have been sedentary for some time, exercise gradually at first.

How active are you? The Daily Exercise Diary on page 254 will help show you. You don't need to fill it out every single day for months on end, but you might keep it for a full week to start. Your Daily Exercise Diary will show you how the physical work your body does relates to the "fuel" you give it. You can refer to the Calories Burned in Various Physical Activities Chart on page 255.

A safe and effective exercise program has three phases: warm-up, cardiovascular (aerobic) activity and cool-down. (Walking, of course, is a sort of warm-up by itself.) To warm up, gentle stretching and some mild calisthenics are generally sufficient to prepare your body for aerobic exercise. Loosely defined, "aerobic exercise" is activity that maintains your heart rate for twenty to thirty minutes at 75 percent of its maximum potential. (To find your maximum heart rate, subtract your age from 220; if you smoke or have high blood pressure or high cholesterol, reduce that number by 10 percent for each.) To cool down, complete your workout with some more gentle stretching while your heart rate returns to normal.

Exercise that involves the whole body is the best aid to weight loss, and energetic walking does just that. If your schedule is a busy one, if you don't have time to go to the pool or if you don't want to buy any equipment, you can nevertheless exercise very effectively: Walk. Try for one mile at first and wear comfortable, supportive footwear. You'll soon be enjoying longer walks, and feeling more relaxed for it. Keep a date with your walking program every day.

3.
SET GOALS

When you set out to lose weight, think about the weight goal you wish to reach. You can help yourself attain that goal by setting "little" goals along the way. Achieving goals lets you relish your progress. Every time you reach a goal, set a new one. Examples of short-term goals might be losing two to three pounds in two weeks, or successfully following a week of 1200-calorie-a-day menus, or exercising five times a week for thirty minutes, or not *gaining* weight. Live one day at a time. You can tell yourself, "Today I will eat a piece of fruit instead of a doughnut during my break."

If you don't reach your short-term goal, don't berate yourself for it. Don't punish yourself today for yesterday's mistake; learn from mistakes and move forward. Rather than think, "I had six chocolate chip cookies yesterday, and I'll never make that up to myself," think, "Today I am going to put together a fresh, fun menu and enjoy a nice walk." Goals aren't just for weight loss. Maintaining your ideal weight is a goal in itself.

You can reward yourself every time you achieve a goal. You might make yourself a present of a luxurious bubble bath or a whole hour to read a good book without interruption. Be sure your rewards are not food rewards. Remember that you are losing weight to please yourself, not someone else. Having a family member or friend for moral support is another thing, and can be extremely helpful. (Beware of unintentional sabotage, though. When offered treats you want to avoid, say "No, thank you" rather than "No, I'm on a diet," and you won't hear "Another diet?" again.) Some people need more support than others, and they find it in group weight-loss programs, counseling or family and friends.

Weigh in regularly; you can take heart in your progress, and keep an alert for pounds creeping back. Make a serious contract with yourself to lose weight. You might even formalize your commitment on paper, stating your

CELLULITE

The fat that causes skin to take on a bumpy, orange-peel appearance is called "cellulite." The manufacturers of the numerous products that are sold to combat cellulite would have us believe it doesn't behave like other body fat. Cellulite is just fat. That dimpled look to the skin is an indication of poor muscle tone combined with inelastic skin.

The way to deal with cellulite is to exercise, with particular attention paid to the cellulite areas. Exercise won't directly reduce the amount of fat, but it will tone the muscles and improve the appearance. In women, thighs and buttocks seem to be the most popular trouble spots. Some people are more prone to it than others, and this may be in part genetic predisposition. That doesn't seem fair, but at least there is help: exercise.

behavior, weight and exercise goals, and have your best friend witness your contract. Even if your strongest support is within yourself, don't feel you must hide your commitment to losing weight. It has been shown that persons trying to lose weight are more successful when they have some active, outside support.

4.
KEEP GOOD RECORDS

Your Daily Food Diary will probably surprise you, because it is so easy to forget the little tidbits we pick up as the day goes on. For an overall picture of your food habits, it is wise to write down everything you eat for at least one full week. The Calorie Chart on pages 260–264 will help you figure total calories, and you may find a more comprehensive chart helpful, too, especially to keep you up-to-date on changes in commercial food products.

Track your progress in weight loss, in your measurements and in your changing habits. Watch the course of your weight (see the *Eat and Lose Weight* Progress Chart, page 258) over weeks and months. This will show you trends, and being able to point to progress will make you feel good. Tracking your loss gives you the opportunity to celebrate, too. Look forward to your rewards; you've earned them. As you lose weight, your measurements will change (see the Measurement Record, page 253) slowly but surely, and it is exciting to watch your "new" shape develop. Spend a few moments every week looking over your Daily Exercise Diary (page 254) and think about

FAST FOOD

Most people are willing to admit that they think fast food is "bad for you." Some fast-food choices, though, are better than others. Something to ask yourself before you walk through the door of a fast-food restaurant is this: Am I here because this is the only way I'll be able to eat breakfast/lunch/dinner quickly enough today, or am I here because I crave the taste of their burgers/pastries?

The best bet for lower calories and low fat is, of course, salads (with a tablespoon of dressing, at most); the salad bar is a boon to weight watchers. You can ask for low-calorie dressing or lemon wedges if they aren't offered. A plain roast beef sandwich (no sauce) is better than a fried hamburger. If you are determined to have only something fried, the best you can do is limit your portion. If ordering fried chicken, choose white meat and remove the skin. Hold the line at a "junior" burger rather than ordering a double·burger with sauce and fillings. And, common sense tells you that skim milk is wiser than one of the thick milk shakes. An up-to-date calorie count with nutritional information is usually available at fast-food restaurants.

what it tells you about your behavior. The power to change is in your hands.

5.
DESIGN YOUR LIFESTYLE

Everyone has eating patterns, whether they realize it or not. With the help of the Five-Point Program worksheets, you'll be able to recognize patterns and select those you want to change. Here again, it is important to be realistic. Family and work schedules can shake your resolve and make it difficult to keep to your agenda. Remember: Your weight-loss program is something you have decided to do for yourself, and you deserve the results.

An invaluable advantage of your move toward healthier eating habits is that the rest of your family will develop sensible habits, too. Children learn habits, both good and bad, at an early age, and behavior they learn as kids sets the pattern for their adult lives. If you have children, you have the opportunity to set an example.

Be flexible and keep your long-term goal in mind, remembering that slower progress ensures longer-lasting results. If you are accustomed to eating frequently in restaurants, you don't need to avoid them now. Choose the leaner foods on the menu and enjoy them (refresh your memory with a look at the Foods to Choose Chart, found on page 13). Sometimes it may seem your goals are being sabotaged. Special occasions focus on food; people celebrate by dining out and by baking cakes and other treats. We are accustomed to thinking of vacations as times to "let go" and indulge ourselves, a relaxing free-for-all. Holidays are nearly always marked with a cooking fronzy. How can anyone be expected to avoid food at times like these?

The answer is, you are not expected to do

SHOPPING SMART

- Never shop for groceries when you are hungry.
- Make out a grocery list before going to the store and stick to it.
- Limit "impulse" buying by treating yourself to fruits and vegetables, or such low-calorie treats as sesame rice cakes or reduced-calorie frozen desserts.
- Less time spent in the supermarket means less temptation to resist.
- Read food labels and know what it is you are paying for.
- If you don't buy it, you can't eat it.

---

anything of the sort. Make wise choices, and eat what you want *in moderation*. Be knowledgeable about what you put in your mouth so that there are no surprises when you stand on your scale. If you binge, if you gain weight, look forward rather than back, and decide what you are going to do about it *today*.

There may be times when, after steadily losing weight, you find that you hit a plateau and stay there no matter how conscientious you continue to be. A plateau doesn't mean you aren't making progress, but it does mean that you can't see it as easily. Your body is making adjustments. That can be discouraging, but persevere, and you will begin to see results again.

The *Eat and Lose Weight* recipes and menus that follow are your introduction to a lifetime of healthy eating. *Bon appétit!*

Friday Night Get-Together

·····································

Savory Stuffed Mushrooms (page 27)

Deviled Eggs with Vegetables (page 28)

Curried Meatballs with Chutney Sauce (page 26)

Herbed Yogurt Cheese (page 24) with Crackers

Pimiento Cheese Dip (page 23) with Crudités

Savory Popcorn Mix (page 31)

APPETIZERS & SNACKS

Pimiento Cheese Dip (page 23) and Herbed Yogurt Cheese (page 24)

HEALTHY HINTS

- A small, healthy snack between regular meals can help curb appetites. We recommend snacking on plain, hot-air-popped popcorn. With only 30 calories per cup, it compares favorably to 115 calories for ten potato chips, 210 calories for ¼ cup of peanuts or 110 calories for 1 ounce of pretzels. Sprinkle such herbs as oregano or dill weed over the popcorn for intriguing flavor.
- Crunchy rice or corn cakes make delicious snacks, with about 30 calories per cake. Use them instead of bread for sandwiches, or top with a pat of Herbed Yogurt Cheese (page 24) for a tangy, filling treat.
- Fresh fruit, whole grain bread and whole grain muffins pack a lot of nutrients and fewer calories than most snacks, and they are more filling. Their high-fiber, high-complex carbohydrate content means they take longer to digest so you feel "fuller" after eating them.
- Slice fresh fruit into bite-size pieces. It will take longer to eat than a whole piece of fruit.
- For a cold, refreshing treat, freeze melon pieces, banana slices and seedless grapes. Eat them in the summer instead of popsicles or in the winter as a sweet reminder of summer's harvest.
- Keep fresh, well-cleaned and ready-to-eat vegetables on hand in the refrigerator for easy, accessible snacks that have few calories.
- Blend fresh or frozen, unsweetened berries with skim milk for a filling shake. Use nonfat plain yogurt for a more enriched, frothy drink.
- Add sparkling water or club soda to fruit juice or white wine for a quenching cooler with fewer calories.

DELI COUNTERS

Supermarkets and specialty food stores cater to our need for high-quality, freshly prepared food by offering an assortment of sensational hors d'oeuvres, dips, spreads and tidbits. Choosing low-calorie treats can be easily managed by following some basic rules.

For party trays, select low-fat cheeses and meats, and avoid high-fat, high-sodium sausage, pepperoni and ham. Cooked turkey, roast beef and low-fat ham can be served in thinly sliced rolls or cut into cubes and served atop thinly sliced multigrain bread or melba toast. Purchase chicken wings and meatballs for appetizers, but not if they are fried or heavily sauced. Quick and easy dips can be made from marinated vegetable salads by draining the dressing, chopping the vegetables and mixing them with nonfat plain yogurt. Serve fresh vegetables as an accompaniment or use seafood sticks or rice crackers as dippers.

Per tablespoon:			
Calories	7	Fat	0 g
Protein	0 g	Cholesterol	0 mg
Carbohydrate	1 g	Sodium	8 mg

Mock Guacamole

This smooth dip tastes so rich that you'll swear it's made with creamy avocados.

1 can (14 ounces) asparagus cuts, drained
1 cup finely chopped seeded tomato (about 1 large)
1/3 cup chopped onion (about 1 medium)
2 tablespoons finely snipped fresh cilantro
2 tablespoons reduced-calorie mayonnaise or salad dressing
1 tablespoon lime juice
6 drops red pepper sauce
1 clove garlic, finely chopped
Dash of pepper

Place asparagus in workbowl of food processor fitted with steel blade or into blender container. Cover and process until smooth. Mix asparagus and remaining ingredients; cover and refrigerate at least 1 hour. Serve with Crisp Tortilla Chips (page 31) if desired.

ABOUT 2 CUPS DIP

Per tablespoon:			
Calories	10	Fat	0 g
Protein	1 g	Cholesterol	0 mg
Carbohydrate	2 g	Sodium	35 mg

Tangy Yogurt Dip

Serve crisp fresh vegetables or Crisp Tortilla Chips (page 31) with this dip.

1 cup nonfat plain yogurt
2 tablespoons chili sauce
1 to 2 teaspoons prepared horseradish

Mix all ingredients; cover and refrigerate at least 1 hour.

ABOUT 1 CUP DIP

Per tablespoon:			
Calories	20	Fat	1 g
Protein	2 g	Cholesterol	2 mg
Carbohydrate	1 g	Sodium	20 mg

Pimiento Cheese Dip

1 cup dry curd low-fat cottage cheese
1 cup nonfat plain yogurt
1 jar (4 ounces) pimientos, thoroughly drained
1 teaspoon onion powder
1/2 cup shredded sharp Cheddar cheese (2 ounces)

Place all ingredients except Cheddar cheese in workbowl of food processor fitted with steel blade or into blender container. Cover and process until smooth, about 1 minute. Add cheese; cover and process about 15 seconds longer. Cover and refrigerate at least 1 hour. Serve with fresh vegetables or pretzels if desired.

ABOUT 1¾ CUPS DIP

Per tablespoon:			
Calories	25	Fat	0 g
Protein	2 g	Cholesterol	0 mg
Carbohydrate	3 g	Sodium	140 mg

Per tablespoon:			
Calories	15	Fat	1 g
Protein	2 g	Cholesterol	5 mg
Carbohydrate	0 g	Sodium	20 mg

Herbed Yogurt Cheese

Homemade yogurt cheese, with half the calories of rich cream cheese, has the same smooth texture. It is delicious and versatile even without the dill weed and garlic. You can pack the cheese into a heart-shaped *coeur à la crème* mold rather than a strainer. Because these molds have fewer drainage holes, refrigerate the cheese for six hours longer.

4 cups nonfat plain yogurt
¼ cup snipped fresh dill weed or 1 tablespoon dried dill weed
1 teaspoon salt
2 cloves garlic, finely chopped

Line 6-inch strainer with coffee filter or double thickness cheesecloth. Place strainer over bowl. Mix all ingredients; pour into strainer. Cover strainer and bowl; refrigerate at least 12 hours. Unmold onto plate. Garnish with freshly ground pepper and additional dill weed if desired.

ABOUT 1¼ CUPS CHEESE SPREAD

Dilled Cucumber–Shrimp Spread

1 cup dry curd low-fat cottage cheese
½ package (8-ounce size) Neufchâtel cheese, softened
¼ cup nonfat plain yogurt
1 tablespoon snipped fresh dill weed or 1 teaspoon dried dill weed
1 teaspoon lemon juice
Freshly ground pepper
1 cup well-drained shredded seeded cucumber (about 1 medium)
1 can (4½ ounces) small shrimp, rinsed and drained

Place all ingredients except pepper, cucumber and shrimp in workbowl of food processor fitted with steel blade or in blender container. Cover and process until smooth, about 30 seconds. Spread mixture in shallow 9-inch serving plate; sprinkle with pepper. Top with cucumber and shrimp. Cover and refrigerate at least 2 hours. Serve with vegetable slices or crackers if desired.

ABOUT 2¼ CUPS SPREAD

Dilled Cucumber–Shrimp Spread

Per appetizer:

Calories	25	Fat	1 g
Protein	3 g	Cholesterol	7 mg
Carbohydrate	1 g	Sodium	30 mg

Curried Meatballs with Chutney Sauce

Chutney Sauce (below)
1 pound ground turkey
½ cup crushed cracker crumbs
⅓ cup evaporated skim milk
2 tablespoons finely chopped green onions
  (with tops)
1½ to 2 teaspoons curry powder
¼ teaspoon salt

Prepare Chutney Sauce. Heat oven to 400°. Mix remaining ingredients; shape into forty-eight 1-inch meatballs. Place in rectangular pan, 13 × 9 × 2 inches, sprayed with nonstick cooking spray. Bake uncovered until light brown and no longer pink inside, 10 to 15 minutes. Serve hot with Chutney Sauce and wooden picks.

4 DOZEN APPETIZERS

Chutney Sauce

½ cup nonfat plain yogurt
1 tablespoon finely chopped chutney
¼ teaspoon curry powder

Mix all ingredients; cover and refrigerate at least 1 hour.

MICROWAVE DIRECTIONS: Prepare Chutney Sauce and meatballs as directed. Place 24 meatballs in microwavable pie plate, 9 × 1¼ inches. Cover with waxed paper and microwave on high (100%) 3 minutes; rearrange meatballs. Cover and microwave until no longer pink inside, 2 to 4 minutes longer. Let stand covered 3 minutes; drain. Repeat with remaining meatballs. Serve hot with Chutney Sauce and wooden picks.

Per tablespoon:

Calories	2	Fat	1 g
Protein	1 g	Cholesterol	4 mg
Carbohydrate	2 g	Sodium	50 mg

Smoky Mushroom Spread

This may be the most versatile spread of all.

3 cups finely chopped mushrooms (about
  8 ounces)
½ cup finely chopped onion (about 1 medium)
1 clove garlic, finely chopped
1 tablespoon all-purpose flour
¼ teaspoon salt
⅛ teaspoon pepper
1 teaspoon Worcestershire sauce
¼ teaspoon liquid smoke
½ package (8-ounce size) Neufchâtel cheese,
  cut into cubes
½ cup nonfat plain yogurt
1 slice bacon, crisply cooked and finely
  crumbled

Spray 10-inch nonstick skillet with nonstick cooking spray; heat over medium heat until hot. Cook mushrooms, onion and garlic until onion is tender, about 2 minutes. Stir in flour, salt and pepper thoroughly. Stir in remaining ingredients except bacon. Heat until hot; sprinkle with bacon. Serve hot or cold with melba toast rounds if desired.

ABOUT 1½ CUPS SPREAD

Per appetizer:

Calories	25	Fat	1 g
Protein	1 g	Cholesterol	0 mg
Carbohydrate	4 g	Sodium	70 mg

Savory Stuffed Mushrooms

Serve six of these with slices of ripe tomato for a fresh, summertime lunch.

36 medium mushrooms (about 1 pound)
¼ cup chopped onion (about 1 small)
¼ cup chopped green bell pepper
2 tablespoons reduced-calorie margarine
1½ cups soft bread crumbs
½ teaspoon salt
½ teaspoon dried thyme leaves
¼ teaspoon ground turmeric
¼ teaspoon pepper

Remove stems from mushrooms; reserve caps. Finely chop enough stems to measure ⅓ cup. Cook and stir chopped mushroom stems, onion and bell pepper in margarine until tender, about 5 minutes; remove from heat. Stir in remaining ingredients.

Heat oven to 350°. Fill reserved mushroom caps with stuffing mixture; place mushrooms, filled sides up, in baking or broiler pan sprayed with nonstick cooking spray. Bake uncovered 15 minutes.

Set oven control to broil. Broil with tops 3 to 4 inches from heat until light brown, about 2 minutes. Serve hot.

36 APPETIZERS

MICROWAVE DIRECTIONS: Place chopped mushroom stems, onion, bell pepper and margarine in 1-quart microwavable casserole.

Cover tightly and microwave on high (100%) 1 minute; stir. Cover tightly and microwave until tender, 1 to 2 minutes longer. Continue as directed. Arrange mushroom caps, filled sides up (smallest mushrooms in center), on two 10-inch microwavable plates. Microwave one plate at a time uncovered on high (100%) 1 minute; rotate plate ½ turn. Microwave until hot, 30 to 60 seconds longer.

Per appetizer:

Calories	5	Fat	0 g
Protein	0 g	Cholesterol	0 mg
Carbohydrate	1 g	Sodium	2 mg

Spicy Carrots and Jícama

Jícama is becoming widely available. This large, scrubby root looks rather like a turnip and has the juicy crunch of water chestnut.

¼ cup lemon juice
2 teaspoons vegetable oil
½ teaspoon garlic powder
½ teaspoon chili powder
⅛ to ¼ teaspoon ground red pepper
4 medium carrots (about ½ pound)
½ pound jícama

Shake all ingredients except carrots and jícama in tightly covered container. Cut carrots lengthwise into fourths; cut each fourth crosswise into halves. Pare jícama; cut into 3 × ¼ × ¼-inch strips. Place vegetables in glass or plastic bowl or in heavy plastic bag. Pour lemon juice mixture over vegetables; toss well. Cover and refrigerate at least 2 hours, stirring occasionally. Drain before serving.

ABOUT 80 APPETIZERS

Per appetizer:			
Calories	20	Fat	1 g
Protein	1 g	Cholesterol	30 mg
Carbohydrate	1 g	Sodium	30 mg

Per serving:			
Calories	55	Fat	3 g
Protein	3 g	Cholesterol	140 mg
Carbohydrate	1 g	Sodium	210 mg

Peppery Minibites

Adjust the power of the green chilies in these miniature quiches to your taste.

½ cup chopped red or green bell pepper
¼ cup finely chopped green onions (with tops)
2 eggs
2 egg whites
½ cup shredded Cheddar cheese (2 ounces)
1 teaspoon chili powder
½ teaspoon ground cumin
⅛ teaspoon ground red pepper
1 can (4 ounces) chopped green chilies, well drained

Heat oven to 425°. Spray 10-inch nonstick skillet with nonstick cooking spray; heat over medium-high heat until hot. Cook bell pepper and onions until onions are tender, about 5 minutes. Beat eggs and egg whites slightly in medium bowl; stir in bell pepper mixture and remaining ingredients. Spoon 1 tablespoon mixture into small muffin cups, 1¾ × 1 inch, sprayed with nonstick cooking spray. Bake until centers are set, 8 to 10 minutes. Let cool 1 minute. Loosen edges with knife and remove from pan; serve immediately.

22 APPETIZERS

Deviled Eggs with Vegetables

Crunchy vegetables and important nutrients replace some of the egg yolks and their cholesterol in these scrumptious stuffed eggs. If using a food processor to prepare the vegetables, pat them dry after chopping.

4 hard-cooked eggs
2 tablespoons reduced-calorie sour cream
2 tablespoons finely chopped zucchini
1 tablespoon finely chopped celery
1 teaspoon snipped fresh dill weed or ¼ teaspoon dried dill weed
¼ teaspoon prepared mustard
¼ teaspoon salt
⅛ teaspoon pepper

Cut peeled eggs lengthwise into halves. Slip out yolks; mash 2 with fork (save remaining yolks for another purpose). Mix in remaining ingredients. Fill whites with yolk mixture, heaping it lightly. Garnish with pimientos and dill if desired. Cover and refrigerate up to 24 hours.

4 SERVINGS, 2 HALVES EACH

Curried Meatballs with Chutney Sauce (page 26) and
Deviled Eggs with Vegetables

Per cup:

Calories	90	Fat	4 g
Protein	1 g	Cholesterol	0 mg
Carbohydrate	13 g	Sodium	80 mg

Sweet Popcorn Mix

6 cups hot-air-popped popcorn
2 cups chocolate flavor frosted corn puff
  cereal
2 tablespoons margarine, melted
1 tablespoon sugar
¼ teaspoon ground cinnamon

Mix popcorn and cereal in large bowl. Drizzle margarine over popcorn mixture, tossing frequently to coat. Mix sugar and cinnamon; sprinkle on popcorn mixture, tossing frequently to coat evenly.

ABOUT 8 CUPS POPCORN MIX

Per appetizer:

Calories	10	Fat	0 g
Protein	0 g	Cholesterol	0 mg
Carbohydrate	3 g	Sodium	1 mg

Fruit Kabobs with Pineapple Dip

This recipe makes enough dip to serve on more than one occasion. Pineapple and cheese is a classic combination, served here with little fruit skewers—wonderful party food.

Pineapple Dip (below)
30 seedless green grapes
30 pineapple chunks, about ¾ inch each
  (¼ pineapple) or 1 can (8¼ ounces) sliced
  pineapple in juice, drained and each slice
  cut into eighths
30 mandarin orange segments or 1 can
  (11 ounces) mandarin orange segments,
  drained
15 strawberries, cut into halves

Prepare Pineapple Dip. Place any combination of 4 pieces of fruit on plastic or wooden picks. Serve with Pineapple Dip.

ABOUT 30 APPETIZERS

Per tablespoon:

Calories	20	Fat	1 g
Protein	1 g	Cholesterol	5 mg
Carbohydrate	2 g	Sodium	25 mg

Pineapple Dip

1 package (8 ounces) Neufchâtel cheese,
  softened
1 cup nonfat plain yogurt
2 tablespoons honey
2 teaspoons crushed gingerroot
1 can (8¼ ounces) crushed pineapple in juice,
  drained

Beat cheese, yogurt, honey and gingerroot until creamy. Fold in pineapple; cover and refrigerate at least 1 hour.

ABOUT 3 CUPS

Per cup:				
Calories	85	Fat		3 g
Protein	2 g	Cholesterol		0 mg
Carbohydrate	11 g	Sodium		160 mg

Per serving:				
Calories	75	Fat		3 g
Protein	1 g	Cholesterol		0 mg
Carbohydrate	11 g	Sodium		15 mg

Savory Popcorn Mix

Pop the corn without added oil, and you've got delicious popcorn without added calories. Because reduced-calorie margarine contains more water than ordinary margarine, we recommend using the regular item here so that the popcorn stays crisp and light.

6 cups hot-air-popped popcorn
2 cups pretzel sticks
2 cups tiny fish-shaped crackers
2 tablespoons margarine, melted
½ teaspoon garlic powder
½ teaspoon onion powder
½ teaspoon dried oregano leaves
½ teaspoon dried basil leaves
⅛ to ¼ teaspoon red pepper sauce

Heat oven to 300°. Mix popcorn, pretzel sticks and crackers in ungreased rectangular pan, 13 × 9 × 2 inches. Mix remaining ingredients. Drizzle over popcorn mixture; toss until evenly coated. Bake, stirring every 10 minutes, until toasted, about 30 minutes. Serve warm.

ABOUT 9 CUPS POPCORN MIX

MICROWAVE DIRECTIONS: Prepare as directed using large microwavable bowl. Microwave uncovered on high (100%), stirring every 2 minutes, until toasted, 4 to 6 minutes.

Crisp Tortilla Chips

Look for the thinnest tortillas to make the crispest chips. Cut them into irregular shapes (scissors are the easiest way) rather than wedges, which would be too long and narrow, cut from an 8-inch diameter.

4 flour tortillas (8-inches)
1 tablespoon reduced-calorie margarine, melted

Heat oven to 400°. Brush tortillas lightly with margarine; cut each into 12 pieces. Arrange in ungreased jelly roll pan, 15½ × 10½ × 1 inch. Bake uncovered until crisp and golden brown, 8 to 10 minutes. (Chips will become crisper as they cool.)

8 SERVINGS, 6 CHIPS EACH

Mushroom Pita Pizzas

Per serving:			
Calories	90	Fat	3 g
Protein	6 g	Cholesterol	8 mg
Carbohydrate	10 g	Sodium	80 mg

Per serving:			
Calories	80	Fat	2 g
Protein	2 g	Cholesterol	0 mg
Carbohydrate	14 g	Sodium	370 mg

Mushroom Pita Pizzas

As a main course, serve an entire round rather than a half. These pizzas are easily cut in half with scissors or a pizza wheel.

2 pita breads (6 inches in diameter)
2 cups sliced mushrooms* (about 5 ounces)
1 small red onion, thinly sliced and
   separated into rings
¼ cup chopped green bell pepper
2 tablespoons snipped fresh basil leaves or 2
   teaspoons dried basil leaves
1 cup finely shredded mozzarella cheese
   (4 ounces)
1 tablespoon grated Parmesan cheese

Heat oven to 425°. Split each bread into halves around edge with knife to make 4 rounds. Place rounds, cut sides up, on ungreased cookie sheet. Arrange mushrooms on bread rounds. Top with onion rings and bell pepper; sprinkle with basil and cheeses. Bake until cheese is melted, 8 to 10 minutes. Cut each round into 8 pieces.

8 SERVINGS, 4 PIECES OR ½ ROUND EACH

*1 can (4 ounces) mushroom stems and pieces, drained, can be substituted for fresh mushrooms.

Potato Snacks

Here is the wonderful flavor of French fried potatoes without all that fat. These homemade chips recall the famous Saratoga chips of days gone by.

3 medium unpared potatoes (about 1 pound)
Vegetable oil
1 teaspoon salt
½ teaspoon sugar
½ teaspoon paprika
¼ teaspoon dry mustard
⅛ teaspoon garlic powder

Set oven control to broil. Cut potatoes lengthwise into eighths. Place potatoes, cut sides down, in ungreased jelly roll pan, 15½ × 10½ × 1 inch. Brush lightly with oil. Mix remaining ingredients; sprinkle potatoes with half of the mixture. Broil potatoes with tops about 3 inches from heat until they bubble slightly, about 10 minutes. Turn; brush with oil and sprinkle with remaining salt mixture. Broil until golden brown and tender, about 5 minutes longer. Serve with reduced-calorie sour cream if desired.

6 SERVINGS, 4 PIECES EACH

Per square:			
Calories	25	Fat	1 g
Protein	0 g	Cholesterol	0 mg
Carbohydrate	4 g	Sodium	15 mg

Marshmallow Squares

Here is a satisfying, lower-calorie version of that old favorite. If you reach for a second one, don't forget to double the calories.

32 large marshmallows or 3 cups miniature marshmallows
¼ cup reduced-calorie margarine
½ teaspoon vanilla
5 cups crispy corn puff, toasted oat, cornflake or whole wheat flake cereal

Spray square pan, 9 × 9 × 2 inches, with nonstick cooking spray. Heat marshmallows and margarine in 3-quart saucepan over low heat until marshmallows are melted and mixture is smooth, stirring constantly; remove from heat. Stir in vanilla. Add half of the cereal at a time, stirring until evenly coated. Press in pan; cool. Cut into about 1½-inch squares.

36 SQUARES

Per serving:			
Calories	35	Fat	0 g
Protein	4 g	Cholesterol	0 mg
Carbohydrate	4 g	Sodium	790 mg

Hot Tomato Drink

2 cans (10½ ounces each) condensed beef broth (about 2½ cups)
1 cup tomato juice
1 cup water
1½ teaspoons prepared horseradish
½ teaspoon dried dill weed

Heat all ingredients to simmering; serve hot.

6 SERVINGS, ABOUT ¾ CUP EACH

MICROWAVE DIRECTIONS: Microwave all ingredients uncovered on high (100%) until hot, about 4 minutes.

Per serving:			
Calories	50	Fat	0 g
Protein	0 g	Cholesterol	0 mg
Carbohydrate	13 g	Sodium	15 mg

Lemony Apple Cider

1½ cups chilled unsweetened apple cider
1 can (12 ounces) sugar-free lemon-lime carbonated beverage

Mix ingredients; pour into ice-filled glasses. Garnish with lemon or apple wedges if desired.

4 SERVINGS, ABOUT ¾ CUP EACH

Peppery Minibites (page 28) and Lemony Apple Cider

Seafarer's Buffet

....

DILLED CUCUMBER–SHRIMP SPREAD (PAGE 24) WITH CRACKERS

MUSSELS WITH MUSTARD SAUCE (PAGE 62)

SMOKY CATFISH (PAGE 39)

PIMIENTO PASTA SALAD (PAGE 186)

EASY HERB ROLLS (PAGE 199) OR BREADSTICKS

ASSORTMENT OF FRESH VEGETABLES

CREAMY STRAWBERRY ANGEL CAKE (PAGE 219)

FISH & SEAFOOD

Clockwise from top: Smoky Catfish (page 39),
Pimiento Pasta Salad (page 186) and
Mussels with Mustard Sauce (page 62)

HEALTHY HINTS

- Prepare fish frequently, two or three times per week.
- There are many ways to prepare fresh or fresh frozen fish without adding fats and oils. Broil, bake or grill, or poach or microwave with a flavorful cooking liquid. Don't forget fresh herbs or a squeeze of fresh lemon at the end.
- To select fresh fish, make sure that the flesh is firm and elastic and springs back when pressed. Fresh fish should have no odor. For whole fish, look to see that the eyes are bright and clear, and that the scales are smooth and shiny.
- When buying frozen fish, make sure the package is tightly wrapped and that there is little or no airspace between the fish and the wrapping. The fish should be frozen solid and without discoloration (an indication of freezer burn) or odor.
- Overcooking renders fish dry and tough.

To test for doneness, place a fork at an angle into the thickest part of the flesh and twist gently. When done, the flesh will flake easily and look opaque. A thermometer inserted in the same area should read 160 degrees.

- Although fish is lower in cholesterol than either meat or poultry, it does contain measurable amounts of fat. According to the U.S. Department of Agriculture, fat contents vary widely among species and they are affected by season, locale and age. The National Fisheries Institute categorizes fish as lean, medium-fat and fatty (categories can overlap). Lean fish is less than 2.5 percent fat; medium-fat fish is 2.5 to 5 percent fat; and fatty fish is more than 5 percent fat. The list on page 39 can be used to guide you in choosing the proper fish for your dietary needs.

DELI COUNTERS

Cooked shellfish such as shrimp and crab legs is abundantly available in most deli sections and specialty shops. Served whole or in salads, shellfish is a wonderful addition to any meal. Imitation seafood sticks are a less expensive variation that can be used sparingly in salads, sandwiches and casseroles. Keep in mind, however, that both fresh and imitation seafood tend to be high in sodium, as is smoked fish of any kind. Choose a lean smoked fish when you indulge.

Lean Fish	Medium-fat Fish	Fatty Fish
Bass,	Anchovy	Butterfish
Sea	Bluefish	Carp
Striped	Catfish	Eel
Cod,	Croaker	Herring
Freshwater	Mullet	Mackerel,
Ocean	Porgy	Atlantic
Cusk	Redfish	Pacific
Flounder	Salmon, Pink	Spanish
Grouper	Shark	Pompano
Haddock	Swordfish	Sablefish
Halibut	Trout,	Salmon,
Lingcod	Rainbow	Chinook
Mackerel,	Sea	Coho
King	Tuna, Bluefin	Sockeye
Mahimahi	Turbot	Sardine
(Dolphin	Whitefish	Shad
Fish)		Tuna,
Monkfish		Albacore
Orange		Trout,
Roughy		Lake
Perch,		
Freshwater		
Ocean		
Pike,		
Northern		
Walleye		
Pollock		
Red Snapper		
Rockfish		
Scrod		
Smelt		
Sole		
Tilefish		
Tuna,		
Skipjack		
Yellowfin		
Whiting		

....
Source: General Mills, Inc.

Per serving:

Calories	110	Fat	3 g
Protein	19 g	Cholesterol	35 mg
Carbohydrate	1 g	Sodium	360 mg

Smoky Catfish

Liquid smoke can be found in the condiment or spice section of most supermarkets. Brush the fish once or twice with marinade while it refrigerates for more pronounced smoke flavor.

1 pound catfish or medium-fat fish fillets
2 tablespoons lemon juice
1 tablespoon soy sauce
1½ teaspoons liquid smoke
1 clove garlic, finely chopped
1 tablespoon snipped fresh chives

If fish fillets are large, cut into 4 serving pieces. Arrange pieces in rectangular baking dish, 12 × 7½ × 2 inches, sprayed with nonstick cooking spray. Mix remaining ingredients except chives; brush over fish. Cover and refrigerate about 30 minutes, brushing twice.

Heat oven to 400°. Bake uncovered until fish flakes easily with fork, 20 to 25 minutes. Sprinkle with chives.

4 SERVINGS

MICROWAVE DIRECTIONS: Arrange fish, thickest parts to outside edges, in rectangular microwavable dish, 12 × 7½ × 2 inches. Mix remaining ingredients except chives; brush over fish. Cover and refrigerate about 30 minutes, brushing twice. Cover tightly and microwave on high (100%) 3 minutes; rotate dish ½ turn. Microwave until fish flakes easily with fork, 3 to 5 minutes longer. Sprinkle with chives.

Per serving:			
Calories	140	Fat	4 g
Protein	21 g	Cholesterol	40 mg
Carbohydrate	5 g	Sodium	530 mg

Poached Fish Dijon

Milk added to the flavorful poaching liquid keeps white fish snowy white.

1 pound cod or firm lean fish fillets
2 cups water
⅓ cup skim milk
½ teaspoon salt
1 lemon, pared, thinly sliced and seeded
Dijon-Dill Sauce (below)

If fish fillets are large, cut into 4 serving pieces. Heat water, milk, salt and lemon slices to boiling in 10-inch skillet. Place fish in skillet. Heat to boiling; reduce heat. Simmer uncovered until fish flakes easily with fork, 8 to 10 minutes.

Prepare Dijon-Dill Sauce. Remove fish with slotted spatula; drain. Serve fish with sauce.

4 SERVINGS, WITH ABOUT 3 TABLESPOONS SAUCE EACH

Dijon-Dill Sauce

⅔ cup skim milk
1 tablespoon Dijon-style mustard
2 teaspoons cornstarch
1½ teaspoons snipped fresh dill weed or
   ½ teaspoon dried dill weed
⅛ teaspoon salt

Heat all ingredients to boiling over medium heat, stirring constantly. Boil and stir 1 minute.

MICROWAVE DIRECTIONS: Mix 1 cup hot water, the milk, salt and lemon slices in square microwavable dish, 8 × 8 × 2 inches. Cover with vented plastic wrap and microwave on high (100%) to boiling. Add fish with thickest parts to outside edges. Cover and microwave until fish flakes easily with fork, 5 to 7 minutes.

Mix all ingredients for Dijon-Dill Sauce in 2-cup microwavable measure. Microwave uncovered on high (100%), stirring every minute, until thickened, 2 to 3 minutes.

Per serving:			
Calories	155	Fat	6 g
Protein	19 g	Cholesterol	35 mg
Carbohydrate	7 g	Sodium	300 mg

Crunchy Baked Fish

When shopping for cheese-flavored crackers, check for the lowest calorie count available.

1 pound flounder or lean fish fillets
⅓ cup finely crushed cheese-flavored crackers
1 teaspoon parsley flakes
3 tablespoons reduced-calorie Russian
   dressing

Heat oven to 450°. If fish fillets are large, cut into 4 serving pieces. Mix crackers and parsley. Brush both sides of fish with Russian dressing; coat one side of fish with cracker mixture. Place fish, cracker side up, on cookie sheet sprayed with nonstick cooking spray. Bake uncovered until fish flakes easily with fork, 10 to 15 minutes.

4 SERVINGS

Per serving:

Calories	150	Fat	4 g
Protein	15 g	Cholesterol	25 mg
Carbohydrate	13 g	Sodium	300 mg

Per serving:

Calories	175	Fat	6 g
Protein	22 g	Cholesterol	40 mg
Carbohydrate	10 g	Sodium	360 mg

Catfish Stew

2 medium onions, sliced
1 clove garlic, finely chopped
2 teaspoons chili powder
2 teaspoons vegetable oil
1 can (28 ounces) whole tomatoes, undrained
1¾ cups water
½ cup uncooked long grain rice
1½ teaspoons snipped fresh oregano leaves
    or ½ teaspoon dried oregano leaves
1½ teaspoons snipped fresh thyme leaves or
    ½ teaspoon dried thyme leaves
½ teaspoon ground cumin
½ teaspoon red pepper sauce
1 package (10 ounces) frozen sliced okra
1 pound catfish or medium-fat fish fillets, cut
    into 1-inch pieces
½ cup chopped green bell pepper (about
    1 medium)

Cook and stir onions, garlic and chili powder
in oil in 4-quart nonstick Dutch oven over
medium heat until onions are tender, 2 to 3
minutes. Stir in tomatoes, water, rice, oregano, thyme, cumin and pepper sauce; break
up tomatoes. Heat to boiling; reduce heat.
Cover and simmer 20 minutes.

Rinse okra under running cold water to separate; drain. Stir okra, fish and bell pepper
into tomato mixture. Heat to boiling; reduce
heat. Cover and simmer, stirring occasionally, until fish flakes easily with fork and okra
is done, 5 to 10 minutes.

6 SERVINGS, ABOUT 1⅓ CUPS EACH

Baked Fish with Summer Vegetables

1 pound pollock or lean fish fillets
1 tablespoon lemon juice
Freshly ground pepper
1 cup thinly sliced zucchini or yellow squash
    (about 1 medium)
1 small onion, thinly sliced
1 tablespoon snipped fresh basil leaves or
    1 teaspoon dried basil leaves
1 can (8 ounces) stewed tomatoes, undrained
2 tablespoons grated Parmesan cheese

Heat oven to 350°. If fish fillets are large, cut
into 4 serving pieces. Place in ungreased rectangular baking dish, 11 × 7 × 1½ inches; sprinkle with lemon juice and pepper. Layer zucchini,
onion, basil and tomatoes over fish. Cover
and bake until fish flakes easily with fork,
about 30 minutes. Sprinkle with cheese.

4 SERVINGS

MICROWAVE DIRECTIONS: Arrange fish, thickest
parts to outside edges, in rectangular microwavable dish, 11 × 7 × 1½ inches. Continue as
directed. Cover tightly and microwave on high
(100%) 5 minutes; rotate dish ½ turn. Microwave until fish flakes easily with fork, 3 to 6
minutes longer. Sprinkle with cheese.

Per serving:			
Calories	165	Fat	7 g
Protein	20 g	Cholesterol	35 mg
Carbohydrate	6 g	Sodium	270 mg

Hot Salsa Cod

Prepare the spicy salsa ahead of time and serve it cold, if you like.

Hot Salsa (right)
1 pound cod or lean fish fillets
1 tablespoon reduced-calorie margarine, melted
1 tablespoon finely snipped fresh cilantro or 1 teaspoon dried cilantro leaves, if desired
¼ teaspoon salt
1 clove garlic, crushed

Prepare Hot Salsa. Set oven control to broil. If fish fillets are large, cut into 4 serving pieces. Place on rack sprayed with nonstick cooking spray in broiler pan. Mix margarine, cilantro, salt and garlic; brush half of the mixture over fish. Broil with tops about 4 inches from heat until light brown, about 6 minutes.

Turn fish carefully; brush with remaining margarine mixture. Broil until fish flakes easily with fork, 4 to 6 minutes longer. Serve with Hot Salsa; garnish with lime wedges if desired.

4 SERVINGS, WITH ABOUT ⅓ CUP SALSA EACH

Hot Salsa

1½ cups finely chopped tomatoes (about 2 medium)
½ cup chopped onion (about 1 medium)
1 tablespoon finely snipped fresh cilantro or 1 teaspoon dried cilantro leaves, if desired
1 tablespoon lemon juice
1 teaspoon vegetable oil
½ teaspoon dried oregano leaves
3 cloves garlic, crushed
1 canned jalapeño chili, seeded and finely chopped

Heat all ingredients over medium heat, stirring occasionally, until hot and bubbly, about 5 minutes.

MICROWAVE DIRECTIONS: Arrange fish, thickest parts to outside edges, in square microwavable dish, 8 × 8 × 2 inches. Mix margarine, cilantro, salt and garlic; brush over fish. Cover with vented plastic wrap and microwave on high (100%) 3 minutes; rotate dish ½ turn. Microwave until fish flakes easily with fork, 3 to 5 minutes longer. Let stand covered 3 minutes.

Mix all ingredients for Hot Salsa in 4-cup microwavable measure. Cover with vented plastic wrap and microwave on high (100%) 2 minutes; stir. Microwave until hot and bubbly, 2 to 3 minutes longer. Drain if desired. Serve with fish; garnish with lime wedges if desired.

Per serving:

Calories	210	Fat	11 g
Protein	22 g	Cholesterol	40 mg
Carbohydrate	5 g	Sodium	280 mg

Flounder with Mushrooms and Wine

1 pound flounder or lean fish fillets
½ teaspoon paprika
¼ teaspoon salt
⅛ teaspoon pepper
1½ cups sliced mushrooms* (about 4 ounces)
⅓ cup sliced leeks
1 tablespoon reduced-calorie margarine
⅓ cup dry white wine
¼ cup sliced almonds
1 tablespoon grated Parmesan cheese

Heat oven to 375°. If fish fillets are large, cut into 4 serving pieces. Arrange in ungreased square baking dish, 8 × 8 × 2 inches; sprinkle with paprika, salt and pepper. Cook and stir mushrooms and leeks in margarine until leeks are tender; stir in wine. Pour mushroom mixture over fish; sprinkle with almonds and cheese. Bake uncovered until fish flakes easily with fork, about 25 minutes.

4 SERVINGS

MICROWAVE DIRECTIONS: Decrease wine to ¼ cup. Arrange fish, thickest parts to outside edges, in square microwavable dish, 8 × 8 × 2 inches. Sprinkle with paprika, salt and pepper; set aside. Place mushrooms, leeks and margarine in 1-quart microwavable casserole. Cover tightly and microwave on high (100%) 2 minutes; stir and drain. Spoon mushroom mixture over fish; pour wine over top. Cover with vented plastic wrap and microwave 4 minutes; rotate dish ½ turn. Microwave until fish flakes easily with fork, 3 to 5 minutes longer. Sprinkle with almonds and cheese; cover and let stand 3 minutes.

*1 can (4 ounces) mushroom stems and pieces, drained, can be substituted for the mushrooms.

Per serving:

Calories	145	Fat	6 g
Protein	20 g	Cholesterol	40 mg
Carbohydrate	3 g	Sodium	180 mg

Parmesan Perch

This perch proves that a little Parmesan cheese can go a long way in flavor.

1 pound ocean perch or lean fish fillets
2 tablespoons dry bread crumbs
1 tablespoon grated Parmesan cheese
1 teaspoon dried basil leaves
½ teaspoon paprika
Dash of pepper
1 tablespoon reduced-calorie margarine, melted
2 tablespoons snipped parsley

Move oven rack to position slightly above middle of oven. Heat oven to 500°. If fish fillets are large, cut into 4 serving pieces. Mix remaining ingredients except margarine and parsley. Brush one side of fish with margarine; dip into crumb mixture. Place fish, uncoated sides down, in rectangular pan, 13 × 9 × 2 inches, sprayed with nonstick cooking spray. Bake uncovered until fish flakes easily with fork, about 10 minutes. Sprinkle with parsley.

4 SERVINGS

Per serving:

Calories	145	Fat	5 g
Protein	20 g	Cholesterol	110 mg
Carbohydrate	6 g	Sodium	35 mg

Orange Roughy with Red Peppers

For extra-crisp peppers when cooking this dish in the microwave, omit the step of cooking the peppers before adding the fish.

1 pound orange roughy or lean fish fillets
1 teaspoon olive or vegetable oil
1 small onion, cut into thin slices
2 red or green bell peppers, cut into julienne
  strips
1 tablespoon snipped fresh thyme leaves or
  1 teaspoon dried thyme leaves
¼ teaspoon pepper

If fish fillets are large, cut into 4 servings pieces. Heat oil in 10-inch nonstick skillet. Layer onion and bell peppers in skillet; sprinkle with half of the thyme and half of the pepper. Place fish over bell peppers and sprinkle with remaining thyme and pepper.

Cover and cook over low heat 15 minutes. Uncover and cook until fish flakes easily with fork, 10 to 15 minutes longer.

4 SERVINGS

MICROWAVE DIRECTIONS: Omit oil. Layer onion and bell peppers in rectangular microwavable dish, 12 × 7½ × 2 inches; sprinkle with half of the thyme and half of the pepper. Cover with vented plastic wrap and microwave on high (100%) 2 minutes. Arrange fish, thickest parts to outside edges, on bell peppers; sprinkle with remaining thyme and pepper. Cover with vented plastic wrap and microwave 4 minutes; rotate dish ½ turn. Microwave until fish flakes easily with fork, 3 to 5 minutes longer. Let stand covered 3 minutes.

Per serving:

Calories	130	Fat	4 g
Protein	20 g	Cholesterol	40 mg
Carbohydrate	4 g	Sodium	310 mg

Piquant Pike Fillets

The coarse-grained mustard you choose determines the flavor of these fillets. This creamy topping keeps the fish moist and luscious.

1 pound pike or lean fish fillets
2 tablespoons reduced-calorie sour cream
2 tablespoons coarse-grained mustard
2 tablespoons reduced-calorie Italian dressing
½ cup chopped onion (about 1 medium)

Heat oven to 400°. If fish fillets are large, cut into 4 serving pieces. Arrange fish in ungreased rectangular baking dish, 12 × 7½ × 2 inches. Mix remaining ingredients; spread over fish. Bake uncovered until fish flakes easily with fork, about 20 minutes.

4 SERVINGS

MICROWAVE DIRECTIONS: Arrange fish, thickest parts to outside edges, in microwavable dish, 12 × 7½ × 2 inches. Mix remaining ingredients; spread over fish. Cover with waxed paper and microwave on high (100%) 3 minutes; rotate dish ½ turn. Microwave until fish flakes easily with fork, 3 to 5 minutes longer. Let stand covered 3 minutes.

Fluffy Corn Bread (page 202), Crunchy Lemon
Rice (page 208) and
Orange Roughy with Red Peppers

Per serving:

Calories	125	Fat	4 g
Protein	20 g	Cholesterol	40 mg
Carbohydrate	2 g	Sodium	410 mg

Orange Roughy with Tarragon Sauce

1 pound orange roughy or lean fish fillets
¼ teaspoon salt
1 tablespoon lemon juice
½ teaspoon snipped fresh tarragon leaves or
⅛ teaspoon dried tarragon leaves
Paprika
Tarragon Sauce (below)

Set oven control to broil. If fish fillets are large, cut into 4 serving pieces. Place on rack sprayed with nonstick cooking spray in broiler pan; sprinkle with salt. Drizzle with lemon juice; sprinkle with tarragon and paprika. Broil with tops about 4 inches from heat until fish flakes easily with fork, 5 to 6 minutes. Prepare Tarragon Sauce; serve over fish.

4 SERVINGS, WITH ABOUT 2 TABLESPOONS SAUCE EACH

Tarragon Sauce

⅓ cup nonfat plain yogurt
1 tablespoon reduced-calorie mayonnaise or salad dressing
½ teaspoon snipped fresh tarragon leaves or
⅛ teaspoon dried tarragon leaves
Dash salt

Heat all ingredients just until hot (do not boil), stirring occasionally.

MICROWAVE DIRECTIONS: Arrange fish, thickest parts to outside edges, in square microwavable dish, 8 × 8 × 2 inches; sprinkle with salt. Drizzle with lemon juice; sprinkle with tarragon and paprika. Cover tightly and microwave on high (100%) 3 minutes; rotate dish ½ turn. Microwave until fish flakes easily with fork, 3 to 5 minutes longer. Mix Tarragon Sauce ingredients in 1-cup microwavable measure. Microwave uncovered on high (100%) stirring every 15 seconds, about 45 seconds.

Per serving:

Calories	190	Fat	4 g
Protein	22 g	Cholesterol	35 mg
Carbohydrate	16 g	Sodium	430 mg

Easy Fish and Vegetable Packets

4 frozen lean fish fillets (about 4 ounces each)
1 package (16 ounces) frozen broccoli, cauliflower and carrots
1 tablespoon snipped fresh dill weed or
1 teaspoon dried dill weed
½ teaspoon salt
¼ teaspoon pepper
4 tablespoons dry white wine

Heat oven to 450°. Place each frozen fish fillet on 12-inch square of aluminum foil. Top each fillet with ¼ of the vegetables; sprinkle with dill weed, salt and pepper. Pour 1 tablespoon wine over vegetables. Bring up sides of foil to make a tent; fold top edges over to seal. Fold in sides, making a packet; fold to seal. Place packets on ungreased cookie sheet. Bake until vegetables are crisp-tender and fish flakes easily with fork, about 40 minutes.

4 SERVINGS

Per serving:			
Calories	140	Fat	7 g
Protein	19 g	Cholesterol	35 mg
Carbohydrate	1 g	Sodium	160 mg

Per serving:			
Calories	175	Fat	6 g
Protein	22 g	Cholesterol	35 mg
Carbohydrate	9 g	Sodium	630 mg

Mediterranean Halibut

1 pound halibut or lean fish fillets
2 tablespoons lemon juice
1 tablespoon chopped onion
1 tablespoon chopped pimiento
1 tablespoon coarsely chopped pimiento-
    stuffed olives
1 tablespoon capers
1 tablespoon olive or vegetable oil

If fish fillets are large, cut into 4 serving pieces. Place in ungreased square baking dish, 8 × 8 × 2 inches. Mix remaining ingredients; spread over fish. Cover and refrigerate at least 30 minutes but no longer than 6 hours.

Heat oven to 350°. Cover and bake until fish flakes easily with fork, 20 to 30 minutes. Serve with freshly ground pepper if desired.

4 SERVINGS

MICROWAVE DIRECTIONS: Arrange fish, thickest parts to outside edges, in square microwavable dish, 8 × 8 × 2 inches. Continue as directed. Cover tightly and microwave on high (100%) 3 minutes; rotate dish ½ turn. Microwave until fish flakes easily with fork, 3 to 5 minutes longer. Let stand covered 3 minutes.

Halibut Stir-Fry

Fresh gingerroot and sesame oil give this stir-fry an Oriental twist. The darker the sesame oil, the more pronounced the toasted sesame flavor.

2 teaspoons sesame oil
1 pound halibut or lean fish steaks, cut into
    1-inch pieces
1 medium onion, thinly sliced
3 cloves garlic, finely chopped
1 teaspoon finely chopped gingerroot
1 package (10 ounces) frozen asparagus cuts,
    thawed and drained
1 can (4 ounces) sliced mushrooms, drained
1 medium tomato, cut into thin wedges
2 tablespoons soy sauce
1 tablespoon lemon juice

Heat oil in 10-inch nonstick skillet over medium-high heat. Add fish, onion, garlic, gingerroot and asparagus; stir-fry until fish almost flakes with fork, 2 to 3 minutes. Carefully stir in remaining ingredients; heat through. Serve with additional soy sauce if desired.

4 SERVINGS, ABOUT 2 CUPS EACH

Swordfish with Thyme-Apple Sauce and Zucchini in Wine (page 173)

Per serving:			
Calories	170	Fat	5 g
Protein	19 g	Cholesterol	35 mg
Carbohydrate	13 g	Sodium	240 mg

Swordfish with Thyme-Apple Sauce

Swordfish has a wonderful meaty quality that is very satisfying. Fresh thyme scents a sauce with apple slices.

Thyme-Apple Sauce (below)
1 pound swordfish or lean fish steaks, ½ to ¾ inch thick
2 tablespoons lemon juice

Prepare Thyme-Apple Sauce; keep warm.

Set oven control to broil. Place fish steaks on rack sprayed with nonstick cooking spray in broiler pan; brush with 1 tablespoon lemon juice. Broil with tops about 4 inches from heat 3 minutes. Turn; brush with remaining lemon juice. Broil until fish flakes easily with fork, 3 to 5 minutes longer. Serve with Thyme-Apple Sauce.

4 SERVINGS, WITH ABOUT ½ CUP SAUCE EACH

Thyme-Apple Sauce

2 tablespoon chopped onion
1 teaspoon vegetable oil
½ cup unsweetened apple juice
¼ cup water
1 tablespoon snipped fresh thyme leaves or ½ to 1 teaspoon dried thyme leaves
1½ teaspoons cornstarch
¼ teaspoon salt
Freshly ground pepper
1 large unpared red eating apple, thinly sliced

Cook and stir onion in oil in 2-quart nonstick saucepan over medium heat until onion is softened. Mix remaining ingredients except apple slices; stir into onion. Heat to boiling, stirring constantly. Boil and stir 1 minute. Stir in apple slices; heat until hot.

Per serving:			
Calories	195	Fat	8 g
Protein	24 g	Cholesterol	140 mg
Carbohydrate	6 g	Sodium	810 mg

Crustless Tuna Quiche

2 cans (6½ ounces each) tuna in water, drained
1 cup shredded Swiss cheese (4 ounces)
½ cup chopped onion (about 1 medium)
2 tablespoons all-purpose flour
2 eggs
2 egg whites
1 cup skim milk
¾ teaspoon salt
⅛ teaspoon red pepper sauce

Heat oven to 350°. Toss tuna, cheese and onion with flour. Spread in pie plate, 9 × 1¼ inches, sprayed with nonstick cooking spray. Beat eggs and egg whites slightly; beat in remaining ingredients. Pour egg mixture over tuna mixture. Bake uncovered until knife inserted in center comes out clean, 35 to 40 minutes. Let stand 10 minutes before cutting.

6 SERVINGS

Per serving:			
Calories	160	Fat	2 g
Protein	17 g	Cholesterol	30 mg
Carbohydrate	18 g	Sodium	590 mg

Per serving:			
Calories	180	Fat	4 g
Protein	19 g	Cholesterol	40 mg
Carbohydrate	17 g	Sodium	690 mg

Tuna-filled Tomatoes

Chewy bulgur makes this tuna salad special. Serve it on crisp, pretty lettuce leaves.

½ cup uncooked bulgur (cracked wheat)
½ cup cold water
2 cans (6½ ounces each) tuna in water, drained
¼ cup finely chopped onion (about 1 small)
2 tablespoons lemon juice
¼ teaspoon salt
½ teaspoon snipped fresh basil leaves or ¼ teaspoon dried basil leaves
½ teaspoon snipped fresh oregano leaves or ¼ teaspoon dried oregano leaves
4 drops red pepper sauce
6 large tomatoes
Lettuce leaves
2 tablespoons grated Parmesan cheese
12 pitted ripe olives

Cover bulgur with cold water. Let stand until bulgur is tender and water is absorbed, about 1 hour. Mix bulgur, tuna, onion, lemon juice, salt, basil, oregano and pepper sauce. Cover and refrigerate at least 3 hours.

Remove stem ends from tomatoes. Cut each tomato into 4 slices. Place the 2 end slices from each tomato, cut sides up, on lettuce leaves. Spoon about ¼ cup tuna mixture on each slice; sprinkle with Parmesan cheese. Top with remaining tomato slices; garnish with olives.

6 SERVINGS, 2 TOMATOES EACH

Southern Tuna Casserole

The corn in this casserole is strictly southern-style: pale, tender hominy (hulled kernels).

2 cans (6½ ounces each) tuna in water, drained
1 can (14½ ounces) hominy, drained
1 can (8 ounces) tomato sauce
1 cup chopped green bell pepper (about 1 medium)
¼ cup chopped onion (about 1 small)
½ teaspoon ground cumin
½ cup shredded Cheddar cheese (2 ounces)

Heat oven to 350°. Mix all ingredients except cheese in ungreased 1½-quart casserole; sprinkle with cheese. Bake uncovered until hot and cheese is melted, about 30 minutes.

6 SERVINGS, ABOUT ¾ CUP EACH

MICROWAVE DIRECTIONS: Mix all ingredients except cheese in 1½-quart microwavable casserole. Cover tightly and microwave on high (100%) 3 minutes; stir. Cover and microwave until hot, 4 to 6 minutes longer; sprinkle with cheese. Let stand covered until cheese melts, about 3 minutes.

Southern Tuna Casserole

Red Snapper Stew

Per serving:			
Calories	140	Fat	4 g
Protein	18 g	Cholesterol	30 mg
Carbohydrate	7 g	Sodium	630 mg

Per serving:			
Calories	215	Fat	9 g
Protein	13 g	Cholesterol	40 mg
Carbohydrate	20 g	Sodium	270 mg

Red Snapper Stew

1 medium onion, sliced
1 tablespoon reduced-calorie margarine
4 cups chicken broth
1 cup ¼-inch carrot slices (about 2 medium)
½ cup uncooked regular rice
1 tablespoon lemon juice
½ teaspoon salt
1 teaspoon snipped fresh dill weed or
    ¼ teaspoon dried dill weed
1 teaspoon snipped fresh thyme leaves or
    ¼ teaspoon dried thyme leaves
¼ teaspoon pepper
1 package (10 ounces) frozen baby Brussels
    sprouts
1½ pounds red snapper or lean fish fillets,
    cut into 1-inch pieces
1 cup sliced mushrooms (about 3 ounces)

Cook and stir onion in margarine in 4-quart nonstick Dutch oven over medium heat until onion is tender, about 5 minutes. Stir in chicken broth, carrots, rice, lemon juice, salt, dill weed, thyme and pepper. Heat to boiling; reduce heat. Cover and simmer until rice is tender, about 20 minutes.

Rinse Brussels sprouts under running cold water to separate; drain. Stir into rice mixture. Heat to boiling; reduce heat. Cover and simmer 5 minutes. Stir in fish and mushrooms; simmer until fish flakes easily with fork, 5 to 8 minutes longer.

8 SERVINGS, ABOUT 1 CUP EACH

Salmon-topped Rice Cakes

Puffy rice cakes come in many varieties. Use them in place of sliced bread, or snack on them all by themselves.

8 plain rice cakes
½ package (8-ounce size) Neufchâtel cheese,
    softened
⅓ cup nonfat plain yogurt
1 cup chopped celery (about 2 medium stalks)
¼ cup chopped onion (about 1 small)
1 can (7¾ ounces) salmon, drained and flaked

Set oven control to broil. Place rice cakes on ungreased cookie sheet. Mix cheese and yogurt; stir in remaining ingredients. Spread about ¼ cup mixture on each rice cake.

Broil with tops 5 to 6 inches from heat just until warm, 2 to 4 minutes. Serve immediately, and if desired, with freshly ground pepper.

4 SERVINGS, 2 RICE CAKES EACH

MICROWAVE DIRECTIONS: Prepare as directed. Microwave 4 rice cakes at a time on microwavable dinner plate uncovered on high (100%) 1 minute; rotate plate ½ turn. Microwave just until warm, 1 to 1½ minutes longer.

Steamed Grouper with Spinach

1 pound grouper or lean fish fillets
6 cloves garlic, thinly sliced
1 small onion, sliced
2 teaspoons olive or vegetable oil
½ teaspoon paprika
¼ teaspoon salt
¼ teaspoon pepper
⅓ cup dry white wine
2 packages (10 ounces each) frozen spinach, cooked and drained
½ lemon, cut into 4 wedges

If fish fillets are large, cut into 4 serving pieces. Cook and stir garlic and onion in oil in 10-inch nonstick skillet over medium heat until onion is softened. Arrange fish on onion; sprinkle with paprika, salt and pepper. Pour wine around fish. Heat to boiling; reduce heat. Cover and simmer until fish flakes easily with fork, 5 to 8 minutes.

Arrange spinach on deep platter. Carefully remove fish, garlic and onion with slotted spatula; place on spinach. Serve with lemon.

4 SERVINGS

MICROWAVE DIRECTIONS: Mix garlic, onion and oil in microwavable dish, 8 × 8 × 2 inches. Cover tightly and microwave on high (100%) until onion is softened, 1 to 2 minutes. Arrange fish, thickest parts to outside edges, on onion; sprinkle with paprika, salt and pepper. Pour wine around fish. Cover and microwave 4 minutes; rotate dish ½ turn. Microwave until fish flakes easily with fork, 3 to 5 minutes longer. Carefully remove fish, garlic and onion with slotted spatula; place on spinach. Serve with lemon wedges.

Zesty Red Snapper with Mushrooms

½ teaspoon paprika
1½ teaspoons snipped fresh tarragon leaves or ½ teaspoon dried tarragon leaves
1½ teaspoons snipped fresh oregano leaves or ½ teaspoon dried oregano leaves
½ teaspoon salt
⅛ teaspoon pepper
⅛ teaspoon red pepper
1 pound red snapper or lean fish fillets
2 tablespoons lemon juice
1 cup sliced mushrooms (about 3 ounces)

Heat oven to 400°. Mix paprika, tarragon, oregano, salt, pepper and red pepper. If fish fillets are large, cut into 4 serving pieces. Brush with 1 tablespoon of the lemon juice. Rub both sides of fish with herb mixture; arrange in ungreased rectangular baking dish, 12 × 7½ × 2 inches.

Cook and stir mushrooms in remaining lemon juice in 10-inch nonstick skillet over medium heat, about 2 minutes. Place mushrooms over fish. Cover and bake until fish flakes easily with fork, 15 to 20 minutes.

4 SERVINGS

Per serving:

Calories	120	Fat	4 g
Protein	20 g	Cholesterol	35 mg
Carbohydrate	1 g	Sodium	350 mg

Per serving:

Calories	275	Fat	6 g
Protein	21 g	Cholesterol	35 mg
Carbohydrate	34 g	Sodium	520 mg

Mustard Fish Steaks

Try this with a variety of mustards. The topping puffs and browns with cooking.

4 shark or medium-fat fish steaks, ½ inch thick (about 1 pound)
¼ teaspoon salt
⅛ teaspoon pepper
2 tablespoons lemon juice
2 egg whites
1 to 2 tablespoons Dijon-style mustard
2 tablespoons chopped green onions (with tops)

Set oven control to broil. Sprinkle fish steaks with salt and pepper. Place on rack sprayed with nonstick cooking spray in broiler pan; brush with 1 tablespoon lemon juice. Broil with tops about 4 inches from heat until light brown, about 5 minutes. Turn; brush with remaining lemon juice. Broil until fish flakes easily with fork, 3 to 5 minutes. Beat egg whites until stiff but not dry; fold in mustard and onions. Spread mixture over fish. Broil until golden brown, about 1½ minutes.

4 SERVINGS

Mahimahi with Pineapple Sauce

Pineapple Sauce (below)
1 pound mahimahi or lean fish fillets
1 tablespoon reduced-calorie margarine, melted
2 tablespoons flaked coconut
2 cups hot cooked rice

Prepare Pineapple Sauce; keep warm. Set oven control to broil. Score fish skin; place skin side up on rack sprayed with nonstick cooking spray in broiler pan. Broil with top about 4 inches from heat 4 minutes; turn. Brush with half of the margarine. Broil until fish flakes easily with fork, about 5 minutes. Brush with remaining margarine and sprinkle with coconut. Broil until coconut is golden brown, about 45 seconds. Top with Pineapple Sauce and serve with rice. Sprinkle with snipped parsley if desired.

4 SERVINGS, WITH ½ CUP RICE AND ABOUT 3 TABLESPOONS SAUCE EACH

Pineapple Sauce

1 can (8 ounces) crushed pineapple in juice, undrained
½ teaspoon ground ginger

Place pineapple and ginger in blender container. Cover and blend on high speed until smooth, about 15 seconds. Heat over medium heat until hot, stirring occasionally.

Per serving:			
Calories	125	Fat	3 g
Protein	19 g	Cholesterol	35 mg
Carbohydrate	5 g	Sodium	460 mg

Marinated Shark Steaks

1 pound shark or medium-fat fish steaks,
  ¾-inch thick
¼ cup orange juice
2 tablespoons snipped parsley
1 tablespoon snipped fresh basil leaves or 1
  teaspoon dried basil leaves
2 tablespoons chili sauce
1 tablespoon soy sauce
1 clove garlic, finely chopped
½ lemon, cut into 4 wedges

Place fish steaks in ungreased square baking dish, 8 × 8 × 2 inches. Mix remaining ingredients; pour over fish. Cover and refrigerate at least 1 hour but no longer than 6 hours, turning once.

Set oven control to broil. Place fish on rack sprayed with nonstick cooking spray in broiler pan; reserve marinade. Broil with tops about 4 inches from heat 5 minutes. Turn; brush with marinade. Broil until fish flakes easily with a fork, 5 to 7 minutes longer. Serve with lemon wedges.

4 SERVINGS

MICROWAVE DIRECTIONS: Arrange fish, thickest parts to outside edges, in square microwavable dish, 8 × 8 × 2 inches. Continue as directed. Cover with waxed paper and microwave on high (100%) 4 minutes; rotate dish ½ turn. Microwave until fish flakes easily with fork, 2 to 4 minutes longer. Let stand covered 3 minutes. Serve with lemon wedges.

Per serving:			
Calories	205	Fat	5 g
Protein	19 g	Cholesterol	40 mg
Carbohydrate	22 g	Sodium	390 mg

Apple-stuffed Sole

Crisp, crunchy apple slices, here with their skins, are a good source of fiber. Look for firm, flavorful apples. Granny Smiths are especially tart and fresh-tasting.

4 Dover sole or thin lean fish fillets (about
  1 pound)
½ teaspoon salt
¼ teaspoon pepper
4 cups ¼-inch slices unpared cooking apples
  (about 3 medium)
1 green onion (with top), cut lengthwise into
  fourths and into 3-inch pieces
½ cup unsweetened apple juice
¼ cup chopped green onions (with tops)
½ teaspoon ground cinnamon
¼ cup reduced-calorie sour cream

Heat oven to 350°. Sprinkle fish fillets with salt and pepper. Place 3 apple slices in the center of each fillet; top with green onion pieces. Fold fillets into thirds.

Mix remaining apples, apple juice, chopped green onions and cinnamon. Pour into ungreased square baking dish, 8 × 8 × 2 inches. Arrange fillets, seam sides down, over apples. Cover and bake until fish flakes easily with fork and apples are tender, 35 to 45 minutes.

Stir enough pan juices into sour cream until desired consistency; serve with fish. Sprinkle with additional ground cinnamon if desired.

4 SERVINGS

Marinated Shark Steaks and Spinach with Sprouts (page 184)

Per serving:			
Calories	210	Fat	4 g
Protein	20 g	Cholesterol	35 mg
Carbohydrate	24 g	Sodium	470 mg

Per serving:			
Calories	215	Fat	9 g
Protein	21 g	Cholesterol	35 mg
Carbohydrate	8 g	Sodium	450 mg

Sweet and Sour Fish

1 can (8 ounces) pineapple chunks in juice, drained (reserve juice)
3 tablespoons sugar
¼ cup vinegar
1 teaspoon soy sauce
¼ teaspoon salt
1 small clove garlic, finely chopped
2 tablespoons cornstarch
2 tablespoons cold water
1 small green bell pepper, cut into ½-inch strips
1 pound lean fish steaks, ½ to ¾ inch thick
¼ teaspoon salt
1 tomato, cut into 8 wedges

Heat oven to 350°. Add enough water to pineapple juice to measure 1 cup. Heat pineapple juice, sugar, vinegar, soy sauce, ¼ teaspoon salt and the garlic to boiling in 2-quart saucepan. Mix cornstarch and water; stir into sauce. Boil and stir 1 minute. Stir in pineapple chunks and bell pepper.

Place fish steaks in ungreased square baking dish, 8 × 8 × 2 inches; sprinkle with ¼ teaspoon salt. Pour pineapple mixture over fish. Bake uncovered until fish flakes easily with fork, 25 to 30 minutes. Add tomato wedges during the last 5 minutes of cooking.

4 SERVINGS

Sole Gratin

3 cups sliced mushrooms (about 8 ounces)
½ teaspoon salt
¼ teaspoon pepper
1 pound sole or lean fish fillets
¼ cup dry white wine
⅓ cup coarsely crushed zwieback
¼ cup sliced green onions (with tops)
3 tablespoons snipped fresh cilantro or 1 tablespoon dried cilantro leaves
2 tablespoons reduced-calorie margarine, melted

Heat oven to 425°. Place mushrooms in ungreased rectangular baking dish, 12 × 7½ × 2 inches; sprinkle with half the salt and pepper. Arrange fish on mushrooms; sprinkle with remaining salt and pepper. Pour wine around fish. Mix remaining ingredients; spread over top. Bake uncovered until fish flakes easily with fork, 15 to 20 minutes.

4 SERVINGS

MICROWAVE DIRECTIONS: Place mushrooms in rectangular microwavable dish, 12 × 7½ × 2 inches; sprinkle with half the salt and pepper. Arrange fish, thickest parts to outside edges, on top; sprinkle with remaining salt and pepper, the green onions and cilantro. Pour wine around fish. Cover with vented plastic wrap and microwave on high (100%) 4 minutes; rotate dish ½ turn. Uncover and microwave until fish flakes easily with fork, 2 to 4 minutes longer. Mix zwieback and margarine; sprinkle over fish.

Per serving:			
Calories	120	Fat	3 g
Protein	15 g	Cholesterol	30 mg
Carbohydrate	9 g	Sodium	880 mg

Per serving:			
Calories	125	Fat	4 g
Protein	19 g	Cholesterol	35 mg
Carbohydrate	4 g	Sodium	390 mg

Oriental Seafood Soup

1 small unpared cucumber
2 cans (10¾ ounces each) condensed chicken broth
2⅓ cups water
1 tablespoon soy sauce
⅛ teaspoon ground ginger
Dash of pepper
2 ounces uncooked vermicelli
½ pound firm lean fish fillets, cut into ½-inch slices
1 can (4½ ounces) tiny shrimp, rinsed and drained
1 cup sliced mushrooms* (about 3 ounces)
5 cups torn spinach (about 4 ounces)
¼ cup sliced green onions (with tops)

Cut cucumber lengthwise into halves; remove seeds. Cut each half crosswise into thin slices. Heat chicken broth, water, soy sauce, ginger and pepper to boiling in 3-quart nonstick saucepan; stir in vermicelli. Heat to boiling; cook uncovered just until vermicelli is tender, about 4 minutes. Stir in cucumber, fish, shrimp and mushrooms. Heat to boiling; reduce heat. Simmer uncovered until fish flakes easily with fork, about 1 minute. Stir in spinach until wilted. Sprinkle each serving with green onions.

6 SERVINGS, ABOUT 1 CUP EACH

*1 can (4 ounces) mushroom stems and pieces, drained, can be substituted for the fresh mushrooms.

Sole Steamed with Vegetables

4 sole or lean fish fillets (about 1 pound)
4 tablespoons lemon juice
½ teaspoon salt
¼ teaspoon pepper
½ cup coarsely shredded carrot
¼ cup finely chopped celery
½ cup coarsely shredded zucchini
¼ cup chopped onion (about 1 small)
½ teaspoon caraway seed

Heat oven to 400°. Place each fish fillet on 12-inch square piece of aluminum foil. Sprinkle with lemon juice, salt and pepper. Mix remaining ingredients; place on fish. Bring sides of foil up to make a tent; fold top edges over to seal. Fold in sides to form a packet; fold to seal. Bake packets on cookie sheet until vegetables are crisp-tender and fish flakes easily with fork, 20 to 25 minutes.

4 SERVINGS

MICROWAVE DIRECTIONS: Arrange fish, thickest parts to outside edges, in rectangular microwavable dish, 12 × 7½ × 2 inches. Continue as directed except decrease lemon juice to 2 tablespoons and omit salt and pepper. Cover with vented plastic wrap and microwave on high (100%) 4 minutes; rotate dish ½ turn. Microwave until fish flakes easily with fork, 2 to 4 minutes longer. Let stand covered 3 minutes.

Creamy Fish Chowder

Per serving:			
Calories	230	Fat	3 g
Protein	18 g	Cholesterol	20 mg
Carbohydrate	32 g	Sodium	1080 mg

Creamy Fish Chowder

This warming, full-flavored chowder gets its rich flavor from clam juice and evaporated skim milk.

2 cups cubed potatoes (about 2 medium)
1 cup ¼-inch carrot slices (about 2 medium)
½ cup chopped onion (about 1 medium)
1 cup clam juice
1 cup water
1 tablespoon reduced-calorie margarine
½ teaspoon salt
¼ teaspoon pepper
1 pound haddock or lean fish fillets, cut into 1-inch pieces
1 can (6½ ounces) whole clams, undrained
1 can (12 ounces) evaporated skim milk
2 tablespoons snipped fresh chives
1 teaspoon paprika

Heat potatoes, carrots, onion, clam juice, water, margarine, salt and pepper to boiling in 3-quart saucepan. Reduce heat; cover and simmer until potatoes are almost tender, 15 to 20 minutes.

Stir in fish and clams. Cover and heat to boiling. Reduce heat; simmer until fish flakes easily with fork, about 5 minutes. Stir in milk, chives and paprika; heat through.

8 SERVINGS, ABOUT 1 CUP EACH

MICROWAVE DIRECTIONS: Mix potatoes, carrots, onion, clam juice, water, margarine, salt and pepper in 3-quart microwavable casserole. Cover tightly and microwave on high (100%) 10 minutes, stirring after 5 minutes. Stir in fish and clams. Cover and microwave 5 minutes; stir in milk, chives and paprika. Cover and microwave until heated through, 3 to 5 minutes.

Per serving:			
Calories	170	Fat	8 g
Protein	19 g	Cholesterol	35 mg
Carbohydrate	5 g	Sodium	430 mg

Per serving:			
Calories	125	Fat	4 g
Protein	14 g	Cholesterol	14 mg
Carbohydrate	7 g	Sodium	125 mg

Fish with Green Chilies

1 pound lean fish fillets
1 medium onion, thinly sliced
1 tablespoon olive or vegetable oil
¼ teaspoon salt
¼ teaspoon coarsely ground pepper
1 can (4 ounces) chopped green chilies,
   drained
12 pimiento-stuffed olives
¼ cup dry white wine
1 tablespoon lemon juice
Lemon wedges

If fish fillets are large, cut into 4 serving pieces. Place onion in oil in 10-inch nonstick skillet. Place fish on onion; sprinkle with salt and pepper. Spoon chilies over fish; top with olives. Mix wine and lemon juice; pour over fish. Heat to boiling; reduce heat. Cover and simmer until fish flakes easily with fork, about 10 minutes. Serve with lemon wedges.

4 SERVINGS

MICROWAVE DIRECTIONS: Omit oil. Arrange onion in square microwavable dish, 8 × 8 × 2 inches; place fish on onion, thickest parts to outside edges. Sprinkle with salt and pepper. Spoon chilies over fish; top with olives. Mix 3 tablespoons wine and lemon juice; pour over fish. Cover with vented plastic wrap and microwave on high (100%) 4 minutes; rotate dish ½ turn. Microwave until fish flakes easily with fork, 3 to 5 minutes longer. Let stand covered 3 minutes. Serve with lemon wedges.

Mussels with Mustard Sauce

Mussels are quite easy to clean. Discard any with open or broken shells. Scrub the remaining mussels with a stiff brush under cold, running water. Remove the fibrous thread (the "beard").

2 cloves garlic, chopped
½ teaspoon cracked black pepper
1 teaspoon olive or vegetable oil
½ cup dry red wine
2 pounds mussels (about 8 dozen)
¼ cup snipped parsley
Mustard Sauce (below)

Cook and stir garlic and pepper in oil in 4-quart nonstick Dutch oven until garlic is softened. Add wine; heat to boiling. Add mussels and parsley. Cover and heat to boiling; reduce heat. Simmer until mussels open, 5 to 10 minutes. Stir to coat with liquid. Prepare Mustard Sauce; serve with mussels.

4 SERVINGS, ABOUT 24 MUSSELS AND 2 TABLESPOONS SAUCE EACH

Mustard Sauce

½ cup nonfat plain yogurt
2 tablespoons Dijon-style mustard
1 tablespoon reduced-calorie sour cream
1 teaspoon honey

Heat all ingredients, stirring occasionally, just until hot (do not boil).

Per serving:			
Calories	200	Fat	8 g
Protein	16 g	Cholesterol	170 mg
Carbohydrate	15 g	Sodium	630 mg

Seafood Pie with Rice Crust

This unusual rice casing is flecked with fresh chives. As soon as you slice the avocado, rub it with a cut lemon (or brush it with lemon juice) to prevent the flesh from browning.

1½ cups hot cooked rice
1 egg white
1 tablespoon snipped fresh chives
1 can (6 ounces) crabmeat, drained and cartilage removed
1 can (4½ ounces) tiny shrimp, rinsed and drained
⅓ cup finely chopped onion (about 1 medium)
1 jar (2 ounces) diced pimientos, drained
½ cup shredded mozzarella cheese (2 ounces)
3 eggs
1 egg yolk
1¼ cups skim milk
½ teaspoon salt
⅛ teaspoon red pepper
½ avocado, cut into 8 slices
4 cherry tomatoes, cut into halves

Heat oven to 350°. Mix rice, egg white and chives with fork; pour into pie plate, 9 × 1¼ inches, sprayed with nonstick cooking spray. Spread rice mixture evenly with rubber spatula on bottom and up side of pie plate (do not leave any holes). Bake uncovered 5 minutes.

Sprinkle crabmeat, shrimp, onion, pimientos and cheese in rice crust. Beat eggs, egg yolk, milk, salt and red pepper with hand beater until smooth. Pour over seafood mixture. Bake until knife inserted 1 inch from edge comes out clean, 25 to 30 minutes. Immediately run knife around edge to loosen crust. Let stand 10 minutes before cutting. Top each serving with avocado slice and cherry tomato half.

8 SERVINGS

Per serving:			
Calories	230	Fat	5 g
Protein	16 g	Cholesterol	210 mg
Carbohydrate	30 g	Sodium	490 mg

Stir-fried Garlic Shrimp

2 large cloves garlic, finely chopped
2 teaspoons vegetable oil
1 pound frozen, peeled and deveined medium-size raw shrimp, thawed
3 cups sliced mushrooms (about 8 ounces)
1 cup 1-inch pieces green onions (with tops)
¼ cup dry white wine
2 cups hot cooked rice

Cook and stir garlic in oil in 10-inch nonstick skillet over medium-high heat 1 minute. Add shrimp; stir-fry 1 minute. Stir in mushrooms, onions and wine; stir-fry until shrimp are pink and vegetables are hot, about 2 minutes longer. Serve over rice.

4 SERVINGS, ABOUT ¾ CUP SHRIMP MIXTURE AND ½ CUP RICE EACH

Stir-fried Garlic Shrimp (page 63) and Seafood Pie
with Rice Crust (page 63)

Per serving:			
Calories	315	Fat	3 g
Protein	22 g	Cholesterol	40 mg
Carbohydrate	50 g	Sodium	700 mg

Per serving:			
Calories	260	Fat	7 g
Protein	20 g	Cholesterol	80 mg
Carbohydrate	29 g	Sodium	850 mg

Curried Scallop Kabobs

1½ pounds sea scallops
12 whole large mushrooms
2 medium green bell peppers, cut into 1½-inch squares
1 package (9 ounces) frozen artichoke hearts, thawed and drained
½ cup unsweetened orange juice
½ to 1 teaspoon curry powder
¼ teaspoon salt
⅛ teaspoon pepper
2 medium unpared red eating apples, cut into sixths
1 tablespoon orange marmalade
3 cups hot cooked rice
2 tablespoons chopped toasted almonds

Place scallops, mushrooms, bell peppers and artichoke hearts in glass or plastic bowl. Mix orange juice, curry powder, salt and pepper; pour over scallops and vegetables. Cover and refrigerate at least 2 hours but no longer than 6 hours, stirring occasionally.

Set oven control to broil. Alternate scallops, vegetables and apple slices on each of six 15-inch metal skewers; reserve marinade. Place kabobs on rack sprayed with nonstick cooking spray in broiler pan. Mix ¼ cup marinade with orange marmalade; brush kabobs. Broil kabobs about 4 inches from heat, turning and brushing once with marinade mixture, until scallops are white in center, about 5 minutes. Serve with rice; sprinkle with almonds.

6 SERVINGS, 1 KABOB AND ½ CUP RICE EACH

Scallop Pizza

Instead of the traditional flour crust, we've put tender scallops and cheese on an herb-flavored rice crust.

3 cups cooked rice
¼ cup reduced-calorie Italian dressing
1 egg
1 egg white
1 tablespoon snipped fresh basil leaves or 1 teaspoon dried basil leaves
1 tablespoon snipped fresh oregano leaves or 1 teaspoon dried oregano leaves
¾ pound bay scallops*
1 ounce sliced pepperoni, cut into ½-inch strips (about ¼ cup)
½ cup chopped green onions (with tops)
½ cup shredded mozzarella cheese (2 ounces)

Heat oven to 425°. Mix rice, Italian dressing, egg, egg white, basil and oregano. Spread mixture in 12-inch pizza pan sprayed with nonstick cooking spray. Bake until knife inserted in center comes out clean and top is light brown, 20 to 25 minutes. Layer scallops, pepperoni, onions and cheese on crust; bake until scallops are white, 10 to 12 minutes. Cut into 12 pieces. Run knife around edge to loosen before removing pieces.

6 SERVINGS, 2 PIECES EACH

*Sea scallops, cut into ½-inch pieces, can be substituted for bay scallops.

Per serving:				
Calories	360	Fat		9 g
Protein		16 g	Cholesterol	195 mg
Carbohydrate		54 g	Sodium	1760 mg

Seafood Pasta with Vegetables

½ cup chopped onion (about 1 medium)
2 cloves garlic, finely chopped
2 teaspoons vegetable oil
2 tablespoons cornstarch
1¾ cups clam- and tomato-flavored cocktail
½ pound bay scallops*
1 pound frozen, peeled and deveined,
    medium-size raw shrimp, thawed
2 cups ¼-inch slices yellow squash (about
    2 small)
1 medium green bell pepper, cut into ¼-inch
    strips
2 tablespoons snipped fresh basil leaves or
    2 teaspoons dried basil leaves
1 teaspoon salt
¼ teaspoon pepper
6 ounces rotini or spiral macaroni, cooked
    and drained
1 cup 1-inch tomato pieces (about 1 medium)
2 tablespoons snipped parsley

Cook and stir onion and garlic in oil in 4-quart nonstick Dutch oven over medium heat until onion is tender. Mix cornstarch and clam- and tomato-flavored cocktail; stir into onion mixture. Cook and stir until thickened and bubbly. Stir scallops, shrimp, squash, bell pepper, basil, salt and pepper into onion mixture. Cover and cook until seafood is done and vegetables are crisp-tender, about 5 minutes. Stir in rotini, tomato and parsley; heat through.

8 SERVINGS, ABOUT 1¼ CUPS EACH

*Sea scallops, cut into ½-inch pieces, can be substituted for bay scallops.

Summer's End

....

Chicken with Fruit and Cheese (page 87) or

Chili-stuffed Peppers (page 91)

Broccoli with Mushrooms and Thyme (page 158)

Sliced Oranges with Julienne Beets and
Honey-Mustard Dressing (page 192)

Bread Pudding with Brown Sugar Meringue (page 228)

POULTRY

Clockwise from top: Broccoli with Mushrooms and Thyme (page 158),
Chicken with Fruit and Cheese (page 87) and Chili-stuffed Peppers (page 91)

HEALTHY HINTS

- Most of the chicken recipes in this chapter call for skinned chicken. We keep the skin intact for whole roast chicken because the skin keeps it moist during the longer cooking time.
- The white meat of poultry is lower in fat and cholesterol. Certain parts, such as the gizzard, heart and liver, are high in cholesterol but can be enjoyed occasionally.
- Removing the skin from poultry reduces the fat content by more than half. To reduce the total fat and saturated fat content of poultry to its lowest, serve skinless white meat only.
- Chicken breasts may be conveniently purchased skinned and boned. Two pounds of small chicken breasts with skin and bones are equivalent to about 1¼ pounds of chicken breast meat.
- When eating out, order only half a chicken breast. If you are served a whole chicken breast (or a quarter of a chicken, or more), take the remainder home for another meal.

DELI COUNTERS

Turkey and chicken lend themselves to many delicious deli meals; they are even used as substitutes in many processed foods, such as frankfurters and smoked luncheon meats. Turkey "ham" and turkey frankfurters are lower in calories than either the pork or beef preparations. When buying turkey for sandwiches, order it shaved rather than sliced. The shavings offer more volume per weight, and it's easier to make yourself a more modest sandwich. When a hot meal is in order, baked or roasted chicken is preferable to fried chicken, because it is lower in fat; light meat is preferable to dark meat for the same reason. When fried chicken is the only choice, remove the skin before eating.

Per serving:			
Calories	245	Fat	14 g
Protein	28 g	Cholesterol	90 mg
Carbohydrate	2 g	Sodium	80 mg

Lemon-Basil Chicken

Covering the chicken during the first hour of baking makes for a moist bird and keeps the basil from turning black.

3-pound broiler-fryer chicken
1 lemon
1 clove garlic, thinly sliced
½ cup snipped fresh basil leaves or 1 table-
    spoon dried basil leaves
½ teaspoon garlic powder

Heat oven to 375°. Remove excess fat from chicken; fasten neck skin of chicken to back with skewer. Fold wings across back with tips touching. Grate 2 teaspoons lemon peel; reserve. Cut lemon into halves; rub chicken with juice from 1 lemon half. Place garlic, 2 tablespoons of the fresh basil (1 teaspoon dried basil leaves) and remaining lemon half in cavity. Rub chicken with reserved lemon peel; sprinkle garlic powder and remaining basil over chicken.

Place chicken, breast side up, on rack in shallow rectangular roasting pan. Cover and bake 1 hour. Uncover and bake until drumstick meat feels very soft when pressed between fingers, about 30 minutes longer.

4 SERVINGS

Per serving:			
Calories	275	Fat	10 g
Protein	25 g	Cholesterol	70 mg
Carbohydrate	22 g	Sodium	520 mg

Chicken with Peppers and Onions

If you like, substitute 2 cups of homemade spaghetti sauce for the jarred sauce suggested.

3-pound broiler-fryer chicken, cut up and
    skinned
1 teaspoon Italian seasoning
¼ teaspoon salt
¼ teaspoon pepper
2 medium green bell peppers, cut into ¼-inch
    strips
2 medium onions, thinly sliced
1 jar (4 ounces) mushroom stems and pieces,
    drained
1 jar (15½ ounces) spaghetti sauce

Heat oven to 375°. Remove excess fat from chicken. Place chicken, meaty sides up, in rectangular pan, 13 × 9 × 2 inches. Sprinkle with Italian seasoning, salt and pepper. Mix remaining ingredients; spread over chicken. Cover and bake 30 minutes. Spoon sauce over chicken. Bake uncovered, spooning sauce over chicken occasionally, until thickest pieces are done, about 45 minutes longer.

6 SERVINGS, WITH ABOUT ⅓ CUP SAUCE EACH

Chicken-Vegetable Soup and Popovers (page 201)

Per serving:			
Calories	170	Fat	5 g
Protein	19 g	Cholesterol	45 mg
Carbohydrate	13 g	Sodium	1010 mg

Per serving:			
Calories	170	Fat	2 g
Protein	21 g	Cholesterol	50 mg
Carbohydrate	15 g	Sodium	850 mg

Chicken-Vegetable Soup

The chicken is skinned for a low-fat broth. To lower sodium, use low-sodium bouillon.

3 cups tomato-vegetable juice
2 cups water
5 cups finely chopped cabbage
1 medium onion, sliced
2 cups ¼-inch carrot slices (about 4 medium)
1 cup chopped celery (about 2 medium stalks)
2 tablespoons instant chicken bouillon
¼ teaspoon pepper
3-pound broiler-fryer chicken, cut up and skinned
½ teaspoon salt
½ teaspoon paprika
2 tablespoons reduced-calorie margarine

Heat tomato-vegetable juice, water, cabbage, onion, carrots, celery, bouillon (dry) and pepper to boiling in 4-quart nonstick Dutch oven; reduce heat. Cover and simmer 30 minutes.

Remove excess fat from chicken; cut each chicken breast half into halves; sprinkle chicken with salt and paprika. Heat margarine in 10-inch skillet over medium heat until hot. Cook chicken in margarine until light brown on all sides, 15 to 20 minutes. Add chicken to soup. Heat to boiling; reduce heat.

Cover and simmer until chicken is done, about 30 minutes longer. Place chicken in soup bowls; pour soup over chicken.

8 SERVINGS, ABOUT 1 CUP EACH

Chicken Soup with Leeks

3-pound broiler-fryer chicken, cut up and skinned
4 cups water
½ cup uncooked barley
½ cup sliced carrot (about 1 medium)
½ cup sliced celery (about 1 medium stalk)
2 teaspoons salt
2 teaspoons instant chicken bouillon (dry)
¼ teaspoon pepper
1 bay leaf
1½ cups sliced leeks (with tops)

Remove excess fat from chicken. Heat all ingredients except leeks to boiling in 4-quart nonstick Dutch oven; reduce heat. Cover and simmer 30 minutes.

Stir in leeks. Heat to boiling; reduce heat. Cover and simmer until thickest pieces of chicken are done, about 15 minutes. Remove chicken; cool slightly. Remove meat from bones; cut into 1-inch pieces. Skim fat from broth; remove bay leaf. Add chicken to broth; heat until hot, about 5 minutes.

6 SERVINGS, ABOUT 1 CUP EACH

Per serving:			
Calories	360	Fat	13 g
Protein	28 g	Cholesterol	70 mg
Carbohydrate	32 g	Sodium	860 mg

Chicken Satay

3-pound broiler-fryer chicken, cut up and
   skinned
⅓ cup peanut butter
1 tablespoon honey
3 tablespoons lime juice
2 tablespoons soy sauce
½ teaspoon ground cumin
½ teaspoon ground coriander
¼ teaspoon red pepper sauce
3 cups hot cooked rice
2 tablespoons sliced green onion tops or
   1 tablespoon snipped parsley

Remove excess fat from chicken. Mix peanut butter and honey; gradually stir in lime juice and soy sauce. Mix in cumin, coriander and pepper sauce. Place chicken, meaty sides down, in rectangular baking dish, 13 × 9 × 2 inches. Brush about half of the peanut butter mixture over chicken. Turn chicken pieces; brush with the remaining mixture. Cover and refrigerate at least 2 hours.

Heat oven to 375°. Cover and bake 30 minutes; spoon sauce over chicken. Cover and bake until thickest pieces are done, about 20 minutes longer. Serve chicken over rice. Skim fat from drippings and spoon drippings over chicken. Sprinkle with onion tops.

6 SERVINGS, WITH ABOUT ½ CUP RICE AND 2 TABLESPOONS SAUCE EACH

MICROWAVE DIRECTIONS: Prepare chicken as directed except arrange meaty sides up, thickest parts to outside edges, in rectangular microwavable dish, 12 × 7½ × 2 inches. Cover with waxed paper and microwave on high (100%) 10 minutes; rotate dish ½ turn. Microwave until thickest pieces are done, 4 to 8 minutes longer. Serve chicken over rice. Skim fat from drippings and spoon drippings over chicken. Sprinkle with onion tops.

Per serving:			
Calories	145	Fat	2 g
Protein	23 g	Cholesterol	60 mg
Carbohydrate	7 g	Sodium	70 mg

Chutney Chicken

Chutney is a chunky, sweet-sour Indian condiment. The most popular commercial variety is made with mango.

3-pound broiler-fryer chicken, cut up and
   skinned
¼ cup chopped chutney
¼ cup lime juice
2 tablespoons finely chopped onion
2 tablespoons nonfat plain yogurt
½ teaspoon curry powder
¼ teaspoon dry mustard
1 lime, cut into wedges

Remove excess fat from chicken. Mix all ingredients except chicken and lime wedges in glass or plastic bowl or heavy plastic bag. Add chicken, turning to coat. Cover and refrigerate at least 2 hours.

Heat oven to 375°. Remove chicken from marinade; reserve marinade. Place chicken, meaty sides up, in rectangular pan, 13 × 9 × 2 inches. Pour reserved marinade over chicken.

Cover and bake 30 minutes; spoon pan juices over chicken. Bake uncovered until thickest pieces are done, about 30 minutes longer. Arrange on serving platter; pour sauce over chicken. Serve with lime wedges.

6 SERVINGS

MICROWAVE DIRECTIONS: Prepare chicken as directed. Arrange chicken, meaty sides up, thickest parts to outside edges, in rectangular microwavable dish, 12 × 7½ × 2 inches. Pour reserved marinade over chicken. Cover with waxed paper and microwave on high (100%) 10 minutes; spoon pan juices over chicken. Rotate dish ½ turn. Cover and microwave until thickest pieces are done, 6 to 10 minutes longer. Serve with lime wedges.

Per serving:			
Calories	205	Fat	5 g
Protein	23 g	Cholesterol	60 mg
Carbohydrate	17 g	Sodium	430 mg

Apricot Chicken

3-pound broiler-fryer chicken, cut up and
 skinned
2 tablespoons soy sauce
2 tablespoons honey
1 tablespoon vegetable oil
1 tablespoon chili sauce
½ teaspoon ground ginger
⅛ teaspoon ground red pepper
1 can (16 ounces) apricot halves in juice,
 drained

Heat oven to 375°. Remove excess fat from chicken. Place chicken, meaty sides up, in rectangular pan, 13 × 9 × 2 inches. Mix remaining ingredients except apricots; brush over chicken, turning pieces to coat. Bake uncovered, brushing with soy mixture occasionally, until thickest pieces are done, 50 to 60 minutes. About 5 minutes before chicken is done, arrange apricots around chicken; brush chicken and apricots with soy mixture. Bake until apricots are hot, about 5 minutes.

6 SERVINGS

MICROWAVE DIRECTIONS: Prepare soy mixture as directed. Arrange chicken, meaty sides up, thickest parts to outside edges, in rectangular microwavable dish, 12 × 7½ × 2 inches. Brush chicken with soy mixture, turning pieces to coat. Cover tightly and microwave on high (100%) 10 minutes. Brush with soy mixture; rotate dish ½ turn. Cover tightly and microwave until thickest pieces are done, 6 to 10 minutes longer. Arrange apricots around chicken; brush chicken and apricots with soy mixture. Microwave uncovered until apricots are hot, about 1 minute.

Per serving:			
Calories	315	Fat	16 g
Protein	35 g	Cholesterol	100 mg
Carbohydrate	8 g	Sodium	390 mg

Cold Poached Chicken with Two Sauces

Here is an elegant, do-ahead recipe that is ideal for entertaining. The two southwestern sauces—bright red pepper and pale avocado—are very festive. Serve the chicken and sauces hot if preferred.

4 small chicken breast halves (about 2 pounds), skinned and boned
¼ cup water
1 tablespoon lemon juice
¼ teaspoon salt
Pepper Sauce (right)
Avocado Sauce (right)

Remove excess fat from chicken. Place chicken, water, lemon juice and salt in 10-inch nonstick skillet. Heat to boiling; reduce heat. Cover and simmer until chicken is done, about 10 minutes. Refrigerate until cold, at least 2 hours.

Prepare Pepper Sauce and Avocado Sauce. For each serving, place ¼ cup Pepper Sauce on plate; top with chicken breast half and 2 tablespoons Avocado Sauce.

4 SERVINGS

Pepper Sauce

2 large red bell peppers
1 jalapeño chili, seeded
1 tablespoon lemon or lime juice
1 tablespoon olive or vegetable oil
¼ teaspoon salt
⅛ teaspoon pepper

Set oven control to broil. Broil peppers with tops 4 to 5 inches from heat, turning frequently until skin blisters and browns, about 10 minutes. Wrap in towels and let stand 5 minutes, or place in plastic bag and let stand 15 to 20 minutes. Remove skin, stems, seeds, and membrane from peppers. Place peppers along with remaining ingredients in blender container. Cover and blend on high speed until smooth, about 15 seconds. Cover and refrigerate.

Avocado Sauce

⅓ cup nonfat plain yogurt
1 tablespoon reduced-calorie sour cream
1 teaspoon lemon juice
½ avocado

Place all ingredients in blender container. Cover and blend on high speed, scraping sides of blender container occasionally, until smooth, about 60 seconds. Cover and refrigerate.

Cold Poached Chicken with Two Sauces

Per serving:

Calories	150	Fat	3 g
Protein	23 g	Cholesterol	60 mg
Carbohydrate	8 g	Sodium	220 mg

Per serving:

Calories	385	Fat	7 g
Protein	37 g	Cholesterol	85 mg
Carbohydrate	42 g	Sodium	790 mg

Plum-barbecued Chicken

3-pound broiler-fryer chicken, cut up and
    skinned
1 can (16 ounces) purple plums in juice,
    drained and pitted
¼ cup chopped onion (about 1 small)
¼ cup chili sauce
2 tablespoons lemon juice
1 tablespoon prepared mustard

Heat oven to 375°. Remove excess fat from chicken. Place chicken, meaty sides up, in rectangular plan, 13 × 9 × 2 inches, sprayed with nonstick cooking spray. Place remaining ingredients into workbowl of food processor fitted with steel blade or into blender container. Cover and blend on medium speed until well blended. Pour over chicken. Cover and bake 30 minutes; spoon pan juices over chicken. Bake uncovered until thickest pieces are done, about 20 minutes longer. Remove chicken to platter. Stir pan juices; spoon over chicken.

6 SERVINGS

MICROWAVE DIRECTIONS: Prepare sauce as directed. Arrange chicken, meaty sides up, thickest parts to outside edges, in rectangular microwavable dish, 12 × 7½ × 2 inches. Pour sauce over chicken. Cover with waxed paper and microwave on high (100%) 10 minutes. Spoon sauce over chicken; rotate dish ½ turn. Cover and microwave until thickest pieces are done, 6 to 10 minutes longer. Stir juices; spoon over chicken.

Spicy Curried Chicken with Couscous

4 small chicken breast halves (about 2 pounds),
    skinned and boned
2 teaspoons vegetable oil
¼ teaspoon salt
⅛ teaspoon ground red pepper
1 teaspoon vegetable oil
1 cup chopped unpared green apple (about
    1 medium)
½ cup chopped onion (about 1 medium)
1 clove garlic, finely chopped
2 teaspoons curry powder
2 teaspoons grated orange peel
1 cup chicken broth or water
¼ cup raisins
1 tablespoon cornstarch
¼ cup cold water
2 cups hot cooked couscous or rice

Remove excess fat from chicken; cut chicken into 1-inch pieces. Heat 2 teaspoons oil in 10-inch nonstick skillet until hot. Cook and stir chicken, salt and red pepper in oil over medium heat until chicken is done, about 5 minutes; remove chicken. Add 1 teaspoon oil, the apple, onion, garlic, curry powder and orange peel; cook and stir until apple is tender, about 7 minutes.

Stir in chicken broth, raisins and chicken. Heat to boiling, stirring constantly. Mix cornstarch and water; stir into chicken mixture. Boil and stir 1 minute. Serve over couscous.

4 SERVINGS, ABOUT ¾ CUP CURRIED CHICKEN AND ½ CUP COUSCOUS EACH

Per serving:			
Calories	190	Fat	7 g
Protein	23 g	Cholesterol	60 mg
Carbohydrate	9 g	Sodium	210 mg

Garlic Chicken Kiev

3 tablespoons reduced-calorie margarine, softened
1 tablespoon snipped fresh chives or parsley
⅛ teaspoon garlic powder
6 small chicken breast halves (about 3 pounds), skinned and boned
2 cups cornflakes, crushed (about 1 cup)
2 tablespoons snipped parsley
½ teaspoon paprika
¼ cup buttermilk or skim milk

Mix margarine, chives and garlic powder; shape into rectangle, 3 × 2 inches. Cover and freeze until firm, about 30 minutes. Remove excess fat from chicken; flatten each chicken breast half to ¼-inch thickness between waxed paper or plastic wrap.

Heat oven to 425°. Cut margarine mixture crosswise into 6 pieces. Place 1 piece on center of each chicken breast. Fold long sides over margarine; fold up ends and secure with wooden pick. Mix cornflakes, parsley and paprika. Dip chicken into buttermilk; lightly and evenly coat with cornflake mixture. Place chicken breasts, seam sides down, in square pan, 9 × 9 × 2 inches, sprayed with nonstick cooking spray. Bake uncovered until chicken is done, about 35 minutes.

6 SERVINGS

MICROWAVE DIRECTIONS: Prepare chicken as directed. Arrange coated chicken breasts, seam sides down, on microwavable rack in microwavable dish. Microwave uncovered on high (100%) 4 minutes; rotate dish ½ turn. Microwave until chicken is done, 4 to 6 minutes longer. Let stand uncovered 5 minutes.

Chicken and Asparagus Roulades

Per serving:			
Calories	265	Fat	10 g
Protein	36 g	Cholesterol	145 mg
Carbohydrate	7 g	Sodium	420 mg

Chicken and Asparagus Roulades

This dish is a taste of spring anytime of the year. Slice the roulades crosswise and arrange the slices in a shallow pool of sauce.

4 small chicken breast halves (about 2 pounds), skinned and boned
¼ teaspoon salt
¼ teaspoon onion powder
¼ teaspoon dried dill weed
1 package (10 ounces) frozen asparagus spears, thawed and drained
½ medium red bell pepper, cut into ¼-inch strips
Mock Hollandaise Sauce (page 133)

Heat oven to 375°. Remove excess fat from chicken; flatten each chicken breast half to ¼-inch thickness between plastic wrap or waxed paper. Mix salt, onion powder and dill weed; sprinkle over chicken. Place ¼ of asparagus spears and pepper strips crosswise on large end of each chicken breast half. Roll tightly and secure with wooden picks. Place chicken, seam sides down, in square pan, 8 × 8 × 2 inches, sprayed with nonstick cooking spray. Cover and bake until chicken is done, about 30 minutes.

Prepare Mock Hollandaise Sauce; serve with chicken. Garnish with snipped fresh dill weed if desired.

4 SERVINGS, WITH ABOUT 3 TABLESPOONS SAUCE EACH

MICROWAVE DIRECTIONS: Prepare chicken as directed. Place in square microwavable dish, 8 × 8 × 2 inches. Cover with waxed paper and microwave on high (100%) 3 minutes; rotate dish ½ turn. Microwave until chicken is done, 4 to 6 minutes longer. Let stand covered 3 minutes.

Per serving:			
Calories	270	Fat	7 g
Protein	46 g	Cholesterol	120 mg
Carbohydrate	2 g	Sodium	230 mg

Chicken Breasts Dijon

6 small chicken breast halves (about 3 pounds), skinned and boned
¼ cup Dijon-style mustard
1 teaspoon vegetable oil
2 tablespoons dry white wine
Freshly ground pepper
2 tablespoons mustard seed

Heat oven to 400°. Remove excess fat from chicken. Place chicken, meaty sides up, in rectangular pan, 13 × 9 × 2 inches, sprayed with nonstick cooking spray. Mix mustard, oil and wine; brush over chicken. Sprinkle with pepper and mustard seed. Bake uncovered until chicken is done, about 30 minutes. Sprinkle with snipped parsley if desired.

6 SERVINGS

Waldorf Chicken

This is an unusual variation on the popular salad that turns chicken into a masterpiece.

6 small chicken breast halves (about 3 pounds),
   skinned and boned
1 cup unsweetened apple juice
1 tablespoon lemon juice
¼ teaspoon salt
¼ teaspoon ground ginger
1 tablespoon cornstarch
2 cups coarsely chopped unpared red apples
   (about 2 medium)
1 cup diagonally cut celery slices (about
   2 medium stalks)
3 tablespoons raisins
1 tablespoon sliced green onion (with top)

Remove fat from chicken. Place chicken, ½ cup of the apple juice, the lemon juice, salt and ginger in 10-inch nonstick skillet. Heat to boiling; reduce heat. Cover and simmer until done, about 20 minutes. Remove chicken; keep warm.

Mix remaining apple juice and the cornstarch; add to hot liquid. Heat to boiling, stirring constantly. Boil and stir 1 minute. Stir in remaining ingredients; heat through. For each serving, diagonally slice chicken breast, overlapping slices. Top with sauce.

6 SERVINGS, WITH ABOUT ⅓ CUP SAUCE EACH

MICROWAVE DIRECTIONS: Decrease apple juice to ¾ cup. Place chicken, ½ cup of the apple juice, the lemon juice, salt and ginger in 3-quart microwavable casserole. Cover tightly and microwave on high (100%) 6 minutes; rotate casserole ½ turn. Microwave until chicken is done, 6 to 8 minutes longer. Remove chicken; keep warm. Mix remaining apple juice and the cornstarch; add to hot liquid. Microwave uncovered, stirring every minute until thickened, 3 to 4 minutes. Stir in remaining ingredients and microwave until hot, 2 to 3 minutes. Continue as directed.

Waldorf Chicken

Chicken with Vegetables

4 small chicken breast halves (about 2 pounds), skinned and boned
1 egg white
1 teaspoon cornstarch
1 teaspoon soy sauce
¼ teaspoon salt
3 medium zucchini
2 tablespoons cornstarch
2 tablespoons cold water
2 tablespoons vegetable oil
1 medium onion, thinly sliced
2 large cloves garlic, finely chopped
1 teaspoon finely chopped gingerroot
3 cups sliced mushrooms (about 8 ounces)
½ cup chicken broth
2 tablespoons soy sauce

Cut chicken into strips, 2 × 1 inch. Mix egg white, 1 teaspoon cornstarch, 1 teaspoon soy sauce and the salt in medium bowl; stir in chicken. Cover and refrigerate 20 minutes.

Cut zucchini lengthwise into halves; cut diagonally into ¼-inch slices. Mix 2 tablespoons cornstarch and the water; reserve. Heat oil in 12-inch skillet or wok over high heat until hot. Add chicken; stir-fry until chicken is done, about 3 minutes. Remove chicken. Add onion, garlic and gingerroot; stir-fry until garlic is brown. Add zucchini and mushrooms; stir-fry 2 minutes. Stir in chicken, chicken broth and 2 tablespoons soy sauce; heat to boiling. Stir in cornstarch mixture. Boil and stir 1 minute.

6 SERVINGS, ABOUT 1 CUP EACH

Sherried Orange Chicken

4 small chicken breast halves (about 2 pounds), skinned and boned
2 tablespoons sherry
2 tablespoons soy sauce
1 tablespoon packed brown sugar
1 teaspoon snipped fresh oregano leaves or ¼ teaspoon dried oregano leaves
2 cloves garlic, finely chopped
1 can (11 ounces) mandarin orange segments, drained (reserve juice)
1 teaspoon vegetable oil
2 teaspoons cornstarch
2 tablespoons raisins
2 cups hot cooked rice
1 tablespoon snipped fresh chives

Remove excess fat from chicken. Place chicken breasts in glass or plastic bowl or heavy plastic bag. Mix sherry, soy sauce, brown sugar, oregano, garlic and ¼ cup of the reserved mandarin orange juice; pour over chicken. Cover and refrigerate 1 hour, turning once.

Heat oil in 10-inch nonstick skillet until hot. Cook chicken in oil over medium heat until lightly browned on both sides; add sherry mixture. Reduce heat; cover and cook until chicken is done, about 10 minutes. Remove chicken; keep warm. Mix cornstarch and remaining juice; stir into hot liquid. Heat to boiling, stirring constantly. Boil and stir 1 minute. Stir in orange segments and raisins; heat through. Serve chicken and sauce over rice; sprinkle with chives.

4 SERVINGS, WITH ABOUT ⅓ CUP SAUCE EACH

MICROWAVE DIRECTIONS: Place chicken, meaty sides down, thickest parts to outside edge, in 2-quart microwavable casserole. Prepare sherry mixture as directed; pour over chicken. Cover and refrigerate 1 hour, turning once.

Microwave covered on high (100%) 5 minutes; rotate casserole ½ turn. Microwave until chicken is done, 6 to 9 minutes longer. Remove chicken; keep warm. Mix cornstarch and 2 tablespoons of the remaining juice; stir into hot liquid. Microwave uncovered, stirring every minute until thickened, 5 to 7 minutes. Strain sauce; stir in raisins and orange segments. Serve chicken and sauce over rice; sprinkle with chives.

Per serving:			
Calories	230	Fat	6 g
Protein	33 g	Cholesterol	85 mg
Carbohydrate	1 g	Sodium	200 mg

Lemon Chicken

6 small chicken breast halves (about 3 pounds), skinned and boned
2 tablespoons reduced-calorie margarine
½ cup dry white wine
1 tablespoon lemon juice
¼ teaspoon salt
¼ teaspoon snipped fresh dill weed or
    ⅛ teaspoon dried dill weed
½ lemon, thinly sliced
2 tablespoons sliced green onions (with tops)

Remove excess fat from chicken. Cook chicken in margarine in 10-inch nonstick skillet over medium heat, turning once, until light brown, about 10 minutes. Mix wine, lemon juice, salt and dill weed; pour over chicken. Place lemon slices on chicken. Heat to boiling; reduce heat. Cover and simmer until chicken is done, 10 to 15 minutes. Remove chicken; keep warm. Heat wine mixture to boiling; cook until reduced by half, about 3 minutes. Pour over chicken; sprinkle with onions.

6 SERVINGS

MICROWAVE DIRECTIONS: Decrease wine to ¼ cup. Place margarine in 3-quart microwavable casserole. Microwave uncovered on high (100%) until melted, about 1½ minutes. Arrange chicken in margarine, thickest parts to outside edges. Cover tightly and microwave 4 minutes. Mix wine, lemon juice, salt and dill weed; pour over chicken. Place lemon slices on chicken; rotate casserole ½ turn. Cover tightly and microwave until chicken is done, 4 to 6 minutes longer. Let stand covered 5 minutes; sprinkle with onions.

Spicy Drumsticks with Blue Cheese Sauce

Per serving:

Calories	310	Fat	18 g
Protein	33 g	Cholesterol	110 mg
Carbohydrate	4 g	Sodium	320 mg

Spicy Drumsticks with Blue Cheese Sauce

It is hard to believe these drumsticks are guilt-free. The Blue Cheese Sauce makes a superb dip for vegetables or salad dressing.

Blue Cheese Sauce (below)
1 tablespoon vegetable oil
1 tablespoon vinegar
1 to 2 teaspoons red pepper sauce
¼ teaspoon salt
12 chicken drumsticks (about 2 pounds)

Prepare Blue Cheese Sauce. Mix oil, vinegar, pepper sauce and salt in glass or plastic bowl or heavy plastic bag; add drumsticks and toss until evenly coated. Cover and refrigerate at least 1 hour.

Set oven control to broil. Place chicken on rack sprayed with nonstick cooking spray in broiler pan. Broil with tops about 6 inches from heat 20 minutes. Turn; broil until chicken is done, 15 to 20 minutes longer. Serve with Blue Cheese Sauce.

6 SERVINGS, 2 DRUMSTICKS WITH ABOUT 2 TABLE-SPOONS SAUCE EACH

Blue Cheese Sauce

1 cup nonfat plain yogurt
2 tablespoons finely crumbled blue cheese (1 ounce)
2 tablespoons reduced-calorie mayonnaise or salad dressing
½ teaspoon celery seed

Mix all ingredients; cover and refrigerate 1 hour.

Per serving:

Calories	350	Fat	8 g
Protein	36 g	Cholesterol	90 mg
Carbohydrate	32 g	Sodium	450 mg

Chicken with Fruit and Cheese

Sweet pear, tart cranberry and creamy-salty feta are an irresistible combination.

4 small chicken breast halves (about 2 pounds), skinned and boned
1 tablespoon reduced-calorie margarine
1 tablespoon water
1 jar (4½ ounces) strained pears (baby food)
⅔ cup fresh or frozen cranberries
2 cups hot cooked brown rice
1 tablespoon sliced green onion (with top)
2 tablespoons crumbled feta cheese (1 ounce)

Remove excess fat from chicken. Heat margarine in 10-inch nonstick skillet until hot. Cook chicken in margarine until brown on both sides; add water. Spoon pears over chicken. Heat to boiling; reduce heat. Cover and simmer 10 minutes. Sprinkle cranberries over chicken. Cover and simmer until chicken is done, about 5 minutes longer. Serve over rice; sprinkle with onion and cheese.

4 SERVINGS, WITH ABOUT ½ CUP RICE EACH

Clockwise from top: Ginger Chicken on Skewers (page 90),
Italian Chicken Stir-Fry (page 90) and Chicken Breasts Dijon (page 81)

Per serving:			
Calories	290	Fat	10 g
Protein	37 g	Cholesterol	95 mg
Carbohydrate	10 g	Sodium	370 mg

Per serving:			
Calories	155	Fat	5 g
Protein	23 g	Cholesterol	60 mg
Carbohydrate	5 g	Sodium	50 mg

Italian Chicken Stir-Fry

Pepperoni cut into strips rather than left in slices makes that marvelous flavor go further.

1 pound skinless boneless chicken breasts
1 tablespoon olive or vegetable oil
¼ cup ¼-inch strips thinly sliced pepperoni (about 1 ounce)
2 cloves garlic, finely chopped
2 large bell peppers, cut into 1-inch squares
1 medium onion, thinly sliced
2 cups ¼-inch zucchini slices (about 2 medium)
¼ cup dry red wine
1 teaspoon snipped fresh thyme leaves or ½ teaspoon dried thyme leaves
1 teaspoon snipped fresh rosemary leaves or ½ teaspoon dried rosemary leaves
¼ teaspoon salt
⅛ teaspoon pepper
1 tablespoon grated Parmesan cheese

Remove excess fat from chicken; cut chicken into 2-inch pieces. Heat oil in 10-inch nonstick skillet or wok over medium-high heat. Add chicken, pepperoni and garlic; stir-fry until chicken is almost done, 3 to 4 minutes. Remove chicken mixture from skillet; keep warm.

Heat remaining ingredients except cheese to boiling in skillet; stir-fry until vegetables are crisp-tender, 3 to 4 minutes. Stir in chicken; heat through. Sprinkle with Parmesan cheese.

4 SERVINGS, ABOUT 1¼ CUPS EACH

Ginger Chicken on Skewers

These savory kabobs are delicious served over a bed of Pineapple Rice (pages 208–209).

1 teaspoon grated lime peel
¼ cup lime juice
1 tablespoon olive or vegetable oil
2 teaspoons finely chopped gingerroot
¼ teaspoon pepper
1 clove garlic, finely chopped
4 small chicken breast halves (about 2 pounds), skinned and boned
12 whole medium mushrooms
1 medium green bell pepper, cut into eighteen 1-inch squares
½ large red onion, cut into twelve ½ × 1-inch pieces

Mix lime peel, lime juice, oil, gingerroot, pepper and garlic in glass or plastic bowl or heavy plastic bag. Remove excess fat from chicken; cut chicken into 1-inch pieces. Stir chicken, mushrooms and bell pepper into lime mixture. Cover and refrigerate at least 3 hours, stirring occasionally.

Set oven control to broil. Alternate chicken, mushrooms, bell pepper and onion on each of six 11-inch metal skewers; reserve lime mixture. Place skewers on rack sprayed with nonstick cooking spray in broiler pan. Broil with tops 3 to 4 inches from heat, turning and brushing vegetables once with lime mixture, until chicken is done, 8 to 10 minutes.

6 SERVINGS

Per serving:			
Calories	175	Fat	7 g
Protein	13 g	Cholesterol	110 mg
Carbohydrate	15 g	Sodium	410 mg

Chili-stuffed Peppers

3 large bell peppers, (green, red or yellow)
½ pound ground turkey, cooked and drained
1 cup cooked rice
¼ cup chopped onion (about 1 small)
1 teaspoon ground cumin
½ teaspoon salt
¼ teaspoon pepper
2 eggs
2 cloves garlic, finely chopped
1 can (4 ounces) chopped green chilies
1 jar (2 ounces) diced pimientos, drained
½ cup shredded Monterey Jack cheese

Heat oven to 350°. Cut bell peppers lengthwise into halves. Remove seeds and membranes; rinse peppers. Cook 2 minutes in enough boiling water to cover; drain. Mix remaining ingredients except cheese; loosely stuff each pepper half. Arrange peppers in rectangular baking dish, 12 × 7½ × 2 inches, sprayed with nonstick cooking spray. Cover and bake until rice mixture is hot, about 30 minutes. Uncover; sprinkle with cheese. Bake until cheese is melted, about 5 minutes longer.

6 SERVINGS

MICROWAVE DIRECTIONS: Prepare peppers as directed. Cover with vented plastic wrap and microwave on high (100%) 6 minutes; rotate dish ½ turn. Sprinkle with cheese. Microwave uncovered until rice mixture is hot and cheese is melted, 1 to 3 minutes longer.

Per serving:			
Calories	165	Fat	3 g
Protein	28 g	Cholesterol	75 mg
Carbohydrate	4 g	Sodium	350 mg

Turkey with Wine

1 tablespoon reduced-calorie margarine
1 clove garlic, finely chopped
1 pound boneless turkey breast slices, cutlets or turkey tenderloin steaks (¼ to ½ inch thick)
Salt
½ cup dry red wine
1 tablespoon tomato paste
3 cups sliced mushrooms (about 8 ounces)
2 tablespoons chopped green onions (with tops)

Heat margarine and garlic in 10-inch nonstick skillet over medium heat until hot. Lightly sprinkle turkey slices with salt; cook until no longer pink, turning once, 8 to 10 minutes. Remove turkey; keep warm. Mix wine and tomato paste in skillet; stir in mushrooms. Cook uncovered, stirring occasionally, until mushrooms are tender, 3 to 5 minutes. Serve mushrooms over turkey; sprinkle with onions.

4 SERVINGS, WITH ABOUT ¼ CUP MUSHROOMS EACH

NOTE: If turkey pieces are more than ½ inch thick, flatten between plastic wrap or waxed paper.

Per serving:			
Calories	200	Fat	6 g
Protein	24 g	Cholesterol	55 mg
Carbohydrate	13 g	Sodium	510 mg

Turkey-Vegetable Chili

½ cup chopped green bell pepper
¼ cup chopped onion (about 1 small)
2 cloves garlic, finely chopped
2 teaspoons olive or vegetable oil
3 cups cut-up cooked turkey or chicken
½ cup water
1 tablespoon snipped fresh oregano leaves
    or 1 teaspoon dried oregano leaves
1 tablespoon chili powder
1 teaspoon ground cumin
½ teaspoon salt
1 can (16 ounces) whole tomatoes, undrained
1 package (10 ounces) frozen mixed vegetables
2 cups ½-inch zucchini slices (about 2 medium)

Cook and stir bell pepper, onion and garlic in oil in 3-quart saucepan over medium heat until onion is tender, about 3 minutes. Stir in remaining ingredients except frozen vegetables and zucchini; break up tomatoes. Heat to boiling; reduce heat. Cover and simmer 1 hour, stirring occasionally.

Stir in frozen vegetables and zucchini. Heat to boiling; reduce heat. Simmer uncovered, stirring occasionally, until zucchini is crisp-tender, about 5 minutes.

6 SERVINGS, ABOUT 1 CUP EACH

MICROWAVE DIRECTIONS: Mix bell pepper, onion, garlic and oil in 3-quart microwavable casserole. Cover tightly and microwave on high (100%) 3 minutes. Stir in remaining ingredients except frozen vegetables and zucchini; break up tomatoes. Cover and microwave 15 minutes. Stir in frozen vegetables; cover and microwave 10 minutes. Stir in zucchini; cover and microwave until zucchini is crisp-tender, 3 to 6 minutes longer.

Per serving:			
Calories	240	Fat	10 g
Protein	23 g	Cholesterol	140 mg
Carbohydrate	14 g	Sodium	320 mg

Turkey Pie

2 cups cut-up cooked turkey or chicken
1 jar (4½ ounces) sliced mushrooms, drained
½ cup sliced green onions
1 cup shredded natural Swiss cheese (4 ounces)
1⅓ cups skim milk
¾ cup variety baking mix
2 eggs
2 egg whites

Heat oven to 400°. Sprinkle turkey, mushrooms, onions and cheese in pie plate 10 × 1½ inches, sprayed with nonstick cooking spray. Beat remaining ingredients until smooth, 15 seconds in blender on high speed or 1 minute with hand beater. Pour into pie plate. Bake until golden brown and knife inserted halfway between center and edge comes out clean, 30 to 35 minutes. Let stand 5 minutes before cutting.

6 SERVINGS

Per serving:			
Calories	315	Fat	12 g
Protein	29 g	Cholesterol	60 mg
Carbohydrate	22 g	Sodium	125 mg

Turkey Pasta with Pesto

Use a flavorful olive oil to make this pesto. Calories have been cut dramatically here, but the wonderful, distinctive flavor remains.

Pesto (below)
2 cups uncooked rigatoni macaroni (about 4 ounces)
2 cups ¼-inch zucchini slices (about 2 medium)
⅓ cup chopped onion
1 medium carrot, cut into julienne strips
2 teaspoons olive or vegetable oil
3 cups cut-up cooked turkey or chicken

Prepare Pesto. Cook macaroni as directed on package; drain.

Cook and stir zucchini, onion and carrot in oil in 10-inch nonstick skillet over medium heat until zucchini is crisp-tender, 3 to 4 minutes. Stir in turkey; heat just until turkey is hot, about 3 minutes. Stir in macaroni and Pesto; toss until well coated. Heat until hot.

6 SERVINGS, ABOUT 1 CUP EACH

Pesto

2 tablespoons olive oil
1 tablespoon nonfat plain yogurt
2 teaspoons lemon juice
¼ cup grated Parmesan cheese
1 tablespoon pine nuts
2 to 3 cloves garlic
1 cup firmly packed fresh basil leaves

Place all ingredients in blender container in order listed. Cover and blend on medium speed, stopping blender occasionally to scrape sides, until almost smooth, about 2 minutes.

Per serving:			
Calories	235	Fat	6 g
Protein	19 g	Cholesterol	40 mg
Carbohydrate	26 g	Sodium	490 mg

Turkey-Pasta Primavera

1 cup chopped broccoli
⅓ cup chopped onion
2 cloves garlic, finely chopped
1 medium carrot, cut into julienne strips
1 tablespoon vegetable oil
2 cups cut-up cooked turkey or chicken
1 teaspoon salt
2 cups chopped tomatoes (about 2 medium)
4 cups hot cooked spaghetti or fettuccine
⅓ cup freshly grated Parmesan cheese
2 tablespoons snipped parsley

Cook and stir broccoli, onion, garlic and carrot in oil in 10-inch nonstick skillet over medium heat until broccoli is crisp-tender, about 10 minutes. Stir in turkey, salt and tomatoes; heat just until turkey is hot, about 3 minutes. Spoon turkey mixture over spaghetti; sprinkle with cheese and parsley.

6 SERVINGS, WITH ABOUT ⅔ CUP TURKEY MIXTURE AND ⅔ CUP SPAGHETTI EACH

Per serving:			
Calories	215	Fat	7 g
Protein	31 g	Cholesterol	75 mg
Carbohydrate	6 g	Sodium	180 mg

Turkey with Chipotle Sauce

Chipotle chilies are ripened, dried and smoked jalapeño chilies. These wrinkled, brown chilies have a smoky flavor and can be purchased in specialty food shops and in the gourmet section of many supermarkets.

Chipotle Sauce (right)
2 teaspoons vegetable oil
1 pound boneless turkey breast slices, cutlets or turkey tenderloin steaks (¼ to ½ inch thick)
¾ cup chopped seeded tomato (about 1 medium)
2 tablespoons sliced green onion tops

Prepare Chipotle Sauce; keep warm. Heat oil in 10-inch nonstick skillet over medium-high until hot. Cook turkey in oil, turning once, until no longer pink, 8 to 10 minutes. Arrange on serving plate; top with Chipotle Sauce. Sprinkle with tomato and green onion tops.

4 SERVINGS, WITH ABOUT 3 TABLESPOONS SAUCE EACH

Chipotle Sauce

½ cup nonfat plain yogurt
2 tablespoons chopped green onions
1 to 2 tablespoons chopped, seeded and drained canned chipotle chilies in adobo sauce
2 tablespoons creamy peanut butter
⅛ teaspoon salt

Place all ingredients in blender container. Cover and blend on medium speed, stopping blender occasionally to scrape sides, until well blended, about 20 seconds. Heat sauce over low heat until hot, stirring occasionally.

NOTE: If turkey pieces are more than ½ inch thick, flatten between plastic wrap or waxed paper.

MICROWAVE DIRECTIONS: Prepare Chipotle Sauce as directed; pour into 1-cup microwavable measure. Omit oil; arrange turkey slices on microwavable serving plate. Cover with waxed paper and microwave on medium-high (70%) 4 minutes; rotate plate ½ turn. Microwave until no longer pink, 4 to 6 minutes longer. Microwave Chipotle Sauce uncovered on high (100%), stirring every 15 seconds, until hot, about 1½ minutes. Continue as directed.

Turkey with Chipotle Sauce

Herbed Cornish Hens

Per serving:

Calories	250	Fat	5 g
Protein	29 g	Cholesterol	100 mg
Carbohydrate	22 g	Sodium	590 mg

Curried Cornish Hens with Apples

Kitchen shears make cutting the hens in half simple work.

2 Rock Cornish hens (about 1 pound each),
   split lengthwise
¼ cup sherry
¼ cup unsweetened apple juice
2 tablespoons soy sauce
½ to 1 teaspoon curry powder
¼ teaspoon dry mustard
2 cloves garlic, crushed
2 cups thinly sliced unpared apples (about
   2 medium)

Place hens, skin sides down, in rectangular baking dish, 12 × 7½ × 2 inches, or heavy plastic bag. Mix remaining ingredients except apples; pour marinade over hens. Cover and refrigerate, turning hens occasionally, at least 6 hours.

Heat oven to 350°. Remove hens from marinade. Arrange apples in marinade in baking dish; place hens, skin sides up, on apples. Cover and bake 30 minutes; spoon juices over top. Bake uncovered until hens are done, about 30 minutes longer.

4 SERVINGS, ½ HEN WITH ABOUT ⅓ CUP APPLES EACH

MICROWAVE DIRECTIONS: Prepare Rock Cornish hens as directed. Cover with waxed paper and microwave on high (100%) 10 minutes; spoon juices over top. Sprinkle with paprika. Cover and microwave until hens are done, 6 to 10 minutes longer.

Per serving:

Calories	210	Fat	8 g
Protein	29 g	Cholesterol	100 mg
Carbohydrate	6 g	Sodium	300 mg

Herbed Cornish Hens

3 Rock Cornish hens (about 1 pound each)
1 cup herb-seasoned croutons
¼ cup sliced ripe olives
2 tablespoons lemon juice
2 tablespoons vinegar
1 tablespoon vegetable oil
1 teaspoon snipped fresh thyme leaves or
   ¼ teaspoon dried thyme leaves
¼ teaspoon salt
1 clove garlic, crushed

Heat oven to 350°. Dry cavities of hens (do not rub cavities with salt). Mix croutons and olives. Stuff each hen loosely with ⅓ cup stuffing; fasten openings with skewers and lace shut with string. Place hens, breast sides up, in shallow baking pan.

Mix remaining ingredients; pour over hens. Roast uncovered until hens are done, spooning lemon mixture over hens every 20 minutes, about 2 hours. To serve, cut hens into halves along backbone from tail to neck.

6 SERVINGS

Fiesta Fare

....

Mock Guacamole (page 23) with Crisp Tortilla Chips (page 31)

Mexican Flank Steak (page 101)
or Pork Fajitas (page 115)

Beans and Rice (page 142)

Gazpacho Mold (page 190)

Maple Custard (page 227)

MEATS

Clockwise from top: Pork Fajitas (page 115), Mexican Flank Steak (page 101),
Mock Guacamole (page 23), Crisp Tortilla Chips (page 31)
and Beans and Rice (pages 142–143)

Healthy Hints

- The recommended daily allowance of protein for men and women is about six ounces daily. One way to meet this requirement is to divide portions between two or three meals. We recommend accompanying meat with whole grain bread, grains, fresh fruit and vegetables to enhance the value of protein and add other nutrients to the balanced meal.

- Meat loses about 25 percent of its weight during cooking. To get three ounces of cooked meat, start with about four ounces of raw, boneless meat. Plan on about ½ pound per person for small to medium meat cuts with bones.

- Proper cooking methods are important when cooking lean meats. A good way to cook lean meat, without drying it, is to braise it or use it in stews. You can refrigerate braised or stewed meat overnight to solidify the fat. Remove the hardened fat before reheating to serve.

- In general, the higher the grade of meat, the more marbling of fat within the muscle tissue. Cuts and grades of meat vary in calorie content. As an example, three ounces of cooked sirloin have approximately 180 calories; the same amounts of cooked round steak and flank steak have 165 and 210 calories, respectively.

- Increase the amount of fresh vegetables or legumes in stir-fries or casseroles to stretch the servings, lower the calories and reduce the fat content. With these additions, one pound of beef or pork will serve six.

- Enjoy high-fat, high-sodium organ meats such as liver, sausage and heart only occasionally.

Deli Counters

Buy extra-lean, at least 95 percent fat-free luncheon meat and ham. Select roast beef instead of sausage, bologna or other meats high in fat and sodium. Have meats sliced or shaved because they "go further," and add fewer calories than thick slices.

Per serving:			
Calories	240	Fat	6 g
Protein	23 g	Cholesterol	50 mg
Carbohydrate	24 g	Sodium	250 mg

Dilled Steak with Vegetables

1½-pound lean beef bone-in round or chuck
  steak, about ½ inch thick
2 tablespoons all-purpose flour
½ teaspoon salt
⅛ teaspoon pepper
1 tablespoon vegetable oil
½ cup water
2 teaspoons vinegar
½ teaspoon dried dill weed
12 small new potatoes (about 1½ pounds)
3 medium zucchini, cut into 1-inch slices
¼ cup cold water
2 tablespoons all-purpose flour
½ cup nonfat plain yogurt

Trim fat from beef steak. Mix 2 tablespoons flour, the salt and pepper. Sprinkle 1 side of beef with half of the flour mixture; pound in. Turn beef and pound in remaining flour mixture. Cut beef into 6 serving pieces. Heat oil in 4-quart nonstick Dutch oven. Cook beef in oil over medium heat until brown, about 15 minutes. Mix ½ cup water, the vinegar and dill weed; pour over beef. Heat to boiling; reduce heat. Cover and simmer until beef is just tender, about 45 minutes. Add potatoes; cover and simmer 15 minutes. Add zucchini; cover and simmer until vegetables are tender, 10 to 15 minutes. Remove beef and vegetables; keep warm.

Add enough water to cooking liquid to measure 1 cup. Shake ¼ cup water and 2 tablespoons flour in tightly covered container; gradually stir into cooking liquid. Heat to boiling, stirring constantly. Boil and stir 1 minute. Stir in yogurt; heat just until hot. Serve with beef and vegetables.

6 SERVINGS, WITH ABOUT ½ CUP VEGETABLES AND 3 TABLESPOONS SAUCE

Per serving:			
Calories	125	Fat	5 g
Protein	17 g	Cholesterol	50 mg
Carbohydrate	3 g	Sodium	220 mg

Mexican Flank Steak

1 pound lean beef flank steak
1 can (4 ounces) chopped green chilies (undrained)
⅓ cup lime juice
¼ cup chopped onion (about 1 small)
2 cloves garlic, finely chopped
1 teaspoon vegetable oil
½ teaspoon salt

Trim fat from beef steak; cut both sides of beef into diamond pattern ⅛ inch deep. Place in glass or plastic bowl or heavy plastic bag. Mix remaining ingredients; pour over beef, turning beef to coat both sides. Cover and refrigerate at least 8 hours but no longer than 24 hours, turning occasionally.

Set oven control to broil. Drain and scrape marinade off of beef; reserve. Broil beef with top 2 to 3 inches from heat until brown, about 5 minutes. Turn beef; broil 5 minutes longer. Cut beef diagonally across grain at slanted angle into thin slices; keep warm. Heat reserved marinade to boiling; serve over beef.

6 SERVINGS, WITH ABOUT 2 TABLESPOONS SAUCE EACH

Indian Beef with Cucumber Rice

Per serving:

Calories	330	Fat	10 g
Protein	32 g	Cholesterol	85 mg
Carbohydrate	28 g	Sodium	650 mg

Indian Beef with Cucumber Rice

Here are many of the classic flavors of far-away India: cardamom, clove, nutmeg, ginger, coriander, cumin and turmeric. The Indians love their cooling *raita*, yogurt with cucumber. We've stirred crunchy cucumber right into the rice.

1½ pounds lean beef boneless chuck roast
1 cup nonfat plain yogurt
1 teaspoon cardamom seeds (removed from pods), crushed
¼ teaspoon ground cloves
⅛ teaspoon ground nutmeg
1 tablespoon reduced-calorie margarine
2 cups chopped onions (about 2 large)
1 tablespoon grated gingerroot
2 cloves garlic, finely chopped
¾ teaspoon coriander seed, crushed
½ teaspoon cumin seed
¼ teaspoon ground turmeric
¾ teaspoon salt
Cucumber Rice (right)
¼ cup cold water
1 tablespoon cornstarch
1 tablespoon all-purpose flour
¼ cup nonfat plain yogurt
Snipped fresh cilantro

Trim fat from beef roast; cut beef into 1-inch cubes. Mix 1 cup yogurt, the cardamom, cloves and nutmeg in glass or plastic bowl or heavy plastic bag; stir in beef. Cover and refrigerate at least 4 hours.

Heat margarine in 10-inch nonstick skillet over medium heat until melted. Cook and stir onions, gingerroot and garlic about 2 minutes. Stir in beef mixture, coriander, cumin, turmeric and salt. Heat to boiling; reduce heat. Cover and cook, stirring occasionally, until meat is tender, about 1½ hours.

Prepare Cucumber Rice. Shake water, cornstarch and flour in tightly covered container; gradually stir into beef mixture. Heat to boiling, stirring constantly. Boil and stir 1 minute. Serve beef mixture over Cucumber Rice; drizzle with yogurt and sprinkle with cilantro.

6 SERVINGS, ABOUT ½ CUP BEEF MIXTURE AND ½ CUP RICE EACH

Cucumber Rice

2 cups hot cooked rice
1 cup chopped seeded cucumber (about 1 medium)
2 tablespoons lemon juice

Mix all ingredients; heat if necessary.

Per serving:			
Calories	280	Fat	6 g
Protein	20 g	Cholesterol	50 mg
Carbohydrate	35 g	Sodium	540 mg

Per serving:			
Calories	285	Fat	5 g
Protein	28 g	Cholesterol	70 mg
Carbohydrate	30 g	Sodium	950 mg

Garlicky Beef with Peppers

1 pound lean beef boneless round steak, about ½ inch thick
1 tablespoon reduced-calorie margarine
¼ cup chopped onion (about 1 small)
4 cloves garlic, finely chopped
1 to 2 tablespoon snipped fresh thyme leaves or 1 to 2 teaspoons dried thyme leaves
¼ teaspoon salt
¼ teaspoon pepper
2 bell peppers, cut into ¼-inch strips
¼ cup dry red wine
2 tablespoons cornstarch
1 cup cold beef broth
3 cups hot cooked rice

Trim fat from beef steak; cut beef with grain into 2-inch strips. Cut strips diagonally across grain into ¼-inch slices. (For ease in cutting, partially freeze beef, about 1½ hours.) Heat margarine in 10-inch nonstick skillet until melted. Add onion, garlic, thyme, salt and pepper; cook and stir over medium-high heat until onion is tender, about 3 minutes. Stir in beef and bell peppers; cook and stir until beef is no longer pink, about 4 minutes.

Stir in wine; reduce heat. Cover and simmer 5 minutes. Stir cornstarch into beef broth until dissolved; stir into beef mixture. Cook and stir over medium-high heat until thickened. Serve over rice.

6 SERVINGS, ABOUT ½ CUP BEEF MIXTURE AND ½ CUP RICE EACH

Beef with Pea Pods

2 pounds lean beef boneless round steak, ¾ to 1 inch thick
1 clove garlic, finely chopped
½ teaspoon salt
Dash of pepper
1 can (10½ ounces) condensed beef broth
2 tablespoons cornstarch
¼ cup water
1 tablespoon soy sauce
¼ teaspoon crushed gingerroot or ⅛ teaspoon ground ginger
1 package (7 ounces) frozen Chinese pea pods
4 cups hot cooked rice

Trim fat from beef steak; cut beef with grain into 2-inch strips. Cut strips diagonally across grain into ¼-inch slices. (For ease in cutting, partially freeze beef, about 2 hours.) Cook and stir beef and garlic in 10-inch nonstick skillet or wok over medium-high heat until beef is brown. Sprinkle with salt and pepper; stir in beef broth. Heat to boiling; reduce heat. Simmer uncovered until beef is tender, 10 to 15 minutes. (Add water if necessary.)

Mix cornstarch, water and soy sauce; stir into beef mixture. Cook until mixture thickens and boils, stirring constantly. Boil and stir 1 minute. (Gravy will be thin.) Stir in gingerroot and pea pods. Cook, stirring occasionally, until pea pods are crisp-tender, about 5 minutes. Serve over rice.

8 SERVINGS, ABOUT ½ CUP BEEF MIXTURE AND ½ CUP RICE EACH

Per serving:			
Calories	230	Fat	6 g
Protein	22 g	Cholesterol	65 mg
Carbohydrate	21 g	Sodium	330 mg

Per serving:			
Calories	265	Fat	10 g
Protein	14 g	Cholesterol	35 mg
Carbohydrate	29 g	Sodium	255 mg

Beef Stroganoff

1 pound lean beef boneless round steak, about ½ inch thick
1 tablespoon reduced-calorie margarine
½ cup chopped onion (about 1 medium)
1 clove garlic, finely chopped
3 cups sliced mushrooms (about 8 ounces)
¼ cup dry red wine
2 tablespoons cornstarch
1 cup condensed beef broth
¼ teaspoon pepper
¾ cup nonfat plain yogurt
2 cups hot cooked noodles or rice
2 tablespoons snipped parsley

Trim fat from beef steak; cut beef with grain into 2-inch strips. Cut strips diagonally across grain into ¼-inch slices. (For ease in cutting, partially freeze beef, about 1½ hours.) Heat margarine in 10-inch nonstick skillet until melted. Add onion and garlic; cook and stir over medium-high heat until onion is tender. Stir in beef and mushrooms; cook and stir until beef is no longer pink. Stir in wine; reduce heat. Cover and simmer 10 minutes.

Stir cornstarch into beef broth until dissolved; stir into beef mixture. Cook and stir over medium-high heat until thickened; remove from heat. Stir in pepper and yogurt; reduce heat. Cover and simmer, stirring occasionally, until beef is tender, about 30 minutes. Serve over noodles; sprinkle with parsley.

6 SERVINGS, ABOUT ⅔ CUP BEEF MIXTURE AND ½ CUP NOODLES EACH

Easy Beef Casserole

1½ cups cut-up cooked lean beef
1½ cups uncooked elbow macaroni (about 6 ounces)
1 cup sliced celery (about 2 medium stalks)
½ cup skim milk
¼ cup chopped onion (about 1 small)
1½ teaspoons dried basil leaves
½ teaspoon garlic powder
⅛ teaspoon pepper
1 jar (8 ounces) mushroom stems and pieces, undrained
1 can (8 ounces) tomato sauce

Heat oven to 350°. Mix all ingredients in ungreased 2-quart casserole. Cover and bake 30 minutes; stir. Cover and bake until macaroni is tender, about 20 minutes longer.

6 SERVINGS, ABOUT ¾ CUP EACH

MICROWAVE DIRECTIONS: Mix all ingredients in 3-quart microwavable casserole; pour ½ cup water over top. Cover tightly and microwave on high (100%), stirring every 6 minutes, until macaroni is tender, 15 to 18 minutes. Let stand covered 5 minutes.

Meatballs in Dijon Sauce

Per serving:				
Calories	310	Fat	14 g
Protein	20 g	Cholesterol	55 mg
Carbohydrate	26 g	Sodium	400 mg

Meatballs in Dijon Sauce

660 1 pound lean ground beef

60 1 slice whole wheat bread, crumbled

¼ cup finely chopped onion (about 1 small)

1 tablespoon Dijon-style mustard

¼ teaspoon salt

¼ teaspoon pepper

Dijon Sauce (right)

270 3 cups hot cooked noodles *2 oz*

930

Heat oven to 400°. Mix all ingredients except Dijon Sauce and noodles; shape into twenty-four 1¼-inch meatballs. Place on rack sprayed with nonstick cooking spray in broiler pan. Bake uncovered until done and light brown, 20 to 25 minutes.

Prepare Dijon Sauce; add meatballs, stirring gently, until meatballs are hot. Serve over noodles.

6 SERVINGS, 4 MEATBALLS AND ½ CUP NOODLES EACH

Dijon Sauce

3 tablespoons all-purpose flour *100*

1 tablespoon cornstarch

1½ teaspoons instant beef bouillon *5*

1 cup water

1 cup skim milk *90*

3 tablespoons finely snipped chives

2 tablespoons Dijon-style mustard

¼ teaspoon pepper *195*

1 teaspoon lemon juice

Mix flour, cornstarch, bouillon (dry) and water in 2-quart saucepan; stir in remaining ingredients. Cook over medium heat until mixture thickens and boils, stirring constantly. Boil and stir 1 minute.

MICROWAVE DIRECTIONS: Prepare meatballs as directed and place in rectangular microwavable dish, 12 × 7½ × 2 inches. Cover with waxed paper and microwave on high (100%) 3 minutes; rearrange meatballs. Cover and microwave until no longer pink inside, 4 to 6 minutes longer. Let stand covered 3 minutes; drain. Mix all ingredients for Dijon Sauce in 2-quart microwavable casserole. Microwave uncovered, stirring every minute until thickened, 4 to 6 minutes. Stir in meatballs; serve over noodles.

930
200
1030

÷2 = 515

Per serving:

Calories	315	Fat	16 g
Protein	22 g	Cholesterol	65 mg
Carbohydrate	20 g	Sodium	680 mg

Beef and Bulgur Casserole

Bulgur is also known as cracked wheat, parboiled wheat or wheat pilaf. To make bulgur, whole wheat is cooked and dried. Then, part of the bran is removed and the remaining grain is cracked into coarse, angular pieces that retain their shape after cooking.

1½ pounds lean ground beef
1 cup chopped onion (about 1 large)
1 cup uncooked bulgur (cracked wheat)
2 cups chopped tomatoes (about 2 medium)
2 cups water
3 tablespoons snipped parsley
2 teaspoons instant beef bouillon (dry)
1½ teaspoons salt
1 teaspoon snipped fresh oregano leaves or
 ½ teaspoon dried oregano leaves
¼ teaspoon instant minced garlic
¼ teaspoon pepper
½ cup grated Parmesan cheese

Heat oven to 350°. Cook and stir ground beef and onion in 10-inch nonstick skillet until beef is brown; drain. Stir in remaining ingredients except cheese. Pour into ungreased 2-quart casserole or rectangular dish, 12 × 7½ × 2 inches. Cover and bake until bulgur is tender, about 45 minutes. Stir in cheese. Sprinkle with snipped parsley if desired.

8 SERVINGS, ABOUT ¾ CUP EACH

MICROWAVE DIRECTIONS: Crumble ground beef into 3-quart microwavable casserole; add onion. Cover with waxed paper and microwave on high (100%) 5 minutes; break up and stir. Cover and microwave until very little pink remains, 4 to 6 minutes longer; drain. Stir in remaining ingredients except cheese. Cover and microwave 10 minutes; stir. Cover and microwave until bulgur is tender, 10 to 14 minutes longer. Stir in cheese. Sprinkle with snipped parsley if desired.

Per serving:

Calories	235	Fat	14 g
Protein	18 g	Cholesterol	100 mg
Carbohydrate	9 g	Sodium	440 mg

Oriental Vegetable Meat Roll

Water chestnuts add crunch to this unusual meat roll. To reduce sodium, use "light" soy sauce.

1 pound lean ground beef
1 cup soft whole wheat bread crumbs (about 2 slices bread)
1 egg
⅓ cup coarsely chopped green onions (with tops)
2 tablespoons soy sauce
1 teaspoon ground ginger
¼ teaspoon pepper
1 can (8 ounces) water chestnuts, chopped
1 jar (2.5 ounces) mushroom stems and pieces, drained
1 jar (2 ounces) diced pimientos, drained

Heat oven to 350°. Mix all ingredients except water chestnuts, mushrooms and pimientos. Shape mixture into a 12 × 10-inch rectangle on waxed paper. Mix remaining ingredients.

Spread over beef mixture to within 1 inch of edges; press into beef mixture. Roll up, beginning at narrow end, using waxed paper to help roll. Pinch edges and ends of roll to seal. Place roll, seam side down, on rack sprayed with nonstick cooking spray in broiler pan. Bake uncovered until done, 1 to 1¼ hours. Let stand 10 minutes before slicing.

6 SERVINGS, ABOUT 1½-INCH SLICE EACH

Per serving:			
Calories	200	Fat	4 g
Protein	17 g	Cholesterol	35 mg
Carbohydrate	24 g	Sodium	85 mg

Roast Beef Pocket Sandwiches

These are terrific take-along sandwiches when the yogurt mixture is packed separately and added just before serving.

1 cup nonfat plain yogurt
1½ teaspoons snipped fresh dill weed or ½ teaspoon dried dill weed
1 teaspoon prepared mustard
1 cup chopped bell pepper (about 1 medium)
2 pita breads (6-inches), cut into halves
⅓ pound thinly sliced lean roast beef
1 cup alfalfa sprouts

Mix yogurt, dill weed and mustard; stir in bell pepper. Fill each pita bread half with ⅓ cup yogurt mixture and ¼ of the beef and alfalfa sprouts.

4 SERVINGS

Per serving:			
Calories	150	Fat	9 g
Protein	18 g	Cholesterol	290 mg
Carbohydrate	6 g	Sodium	310 mg

Liver Italiano

1 medium onion, sliced
1 tablespoon olive or vegetable oil
1 pound beef liver, about ½ inch thick
2 tablespoons water
1 teaspoon ground coriander
1 teaspoon fennel seed
½ teaspoon salt
½ teaspoon ground cumin
2 cups ¼-inch zucchini or yellow summer squash slices (about 2 small)

Cook and stir onion in oil in 10-inch nonstick skillet over medium heat until onion is tender, about 5 minutes. Remove onion with slotted spoon; reserve. Cut beef liver into 6 serving pieces if necessary. Cook liver in same skillet over medium-high heat until brown, 2 to 3 minutes on each side. Drizzle water over liver. Mix coriander, fennel, salt and cumin; sprinkle over liver. Arrange onion and zucchini on liver. Cover and cook over low heat until zucchini is crisp-tender, 6 to 8 minutes.

6 SERVINGS

Per serving:			
Calories	360	Fat	21 g
Protein	21 g	Cholesterol	65 mg
Carbohydrate	24 g	Sodium	520 mg

Pork Chops with Vegetables

This is a nice way to satisfy the desire for fresh corn-on-the-cob.

4 lean pork loin or rib chops, about ½ inch thick
1 teaspoon garlic powder
¼ teaspoon ground sage
1 medium onion, thinly sliced
½ cup chicken broth
½ teaspoon salt
⅛ teaspoon pepper
2 ears corn, cut into 2-inch pieces
2 medium zucchini, cut into 1-inch pieces
2 tablespoons snipped parsley

Trim fat from pork chops. Rub pork on both sides with garlic powder and sage. Cook pork in 10-inch nonstick skillet over medium heat until brown on both sides. Place onion on pork. Mix chicken broth, salt and pepper; pour around pork. Heat to boiling; reduce heat. Cover and simmer 30 minutes. Add corn and zucchini; spoon juices over vegetables. Cover and simmer until pork is tender and zucchini is crisp-tender, 10 to 15 minutes longer. Sprinkle with parsley.

4 SERVINGS

MICROWAVE DIRECTIONS: Decrease chicken broth to ¼ cup. Arrange pork chops, narrow ends toward center, in square microwavable dish, 8 × 8 × 2 inches. Place onion on pork. Mix chicken broth, salt and pepper; pour around pork. Cover with vented plastic wrap and microwave on medium (50%) 7 minutes; rotate dish ½ turn. Microwave 7 minutes longer. Arrange corn and zucchini on pork. Cover with vented plastic wrap and microwave, rotating dish ½ turn every 7 minutes, until pork is done and zucchini is crisp-tender, 14 to 16 minutes longer. Sprinkle with parsley.

Per serving:			
Calories	330	Fat	20 g
Protein	19 g	Cholesterol	65 mg
Carbohydrate	18 g	Sodium	510 mg

Pork with Squash and Onions

4 lean pork loin or rib chops, about ½ inch thick
1 teaspoon dried sage leaves
½ teaspoon salt
¼ teaspoon pepper
2 cloves garlic, finely chopped
2 medium onions, cut into ¼-inch slices
½ cup chicken broth
1 acorn squash (about 1½ pounds)

Trim fat from pork chops. Cook pork in 10-inch nonstick skillet over medium heat until brown on both sides. Mix sage, salt, pepper and garlic; sprinkle half of mixture on pork. Place onions on pork. Pour chicken broth around pork; cover and simmer 15 minutes.

Cut squash crosswise into 1-inch slices; remove seeds and fibers. Cut each slice into fourths. Place on pork; sprinkle with remaining sage mixture. Cover and simmer until pork is done and squash is tender, about 15 minutes.

4 SERVINGS

Pork Chops with Vegetables

Pork Chops with Rhubarb Sauce

Per serving:			
Calories	285	Fat	19 g
Protein	17 g	Cholesterol	65 mg
Carbohydrate	10 g	Sodium	320 mg

Pork Chops with Rhubarb Sauce

Red rhubarb gives the sauce a bold, pink color. Chop the rhubarb well; if the pieces are too large, the sauce will be stringy.

4 lean rib or loin pork chops, about ½ inch thick
1 teaspoon dried rosemary leaves
½ teaspoon salt
¼ teaspoon pepper
2 cups chopped rhubarb (about 6 medium stalks)
¼ cup unsweetened apple juice
1 tablespoon packed brown sugar
1 tablespoon cornstarch
2 tablespoons cold water

Set oven control to broil. Trim fat from pork chops. Mix rosemary, salt and pepper; rub over pork. Place pork on rack sprayed with nonstick cooking spray in broiler pan. Broil pork with tops 3 to 5 inches from heat 10 minutes; turn pork. Broil until done, 5 to 10 minutes longer.

Heat rhubarb, apple juice and brown sugar to boiling; reduce heat. Cover and simmer until rhubarb is tender, about 10 minutes. Mix cornstarch and water; stir into rhubarb. Heat to boiling; boil and stir until thickened, about 1 minute. Serve with pork chops.

4 SERVINGS, WITH ABOUT ⅓ CUP SAUCE EACH

MICROWAVE DIRECTIONS: Decrease apple juice to 3 tablespoons. Prepare pork chops as directed. Arrange pork, narrow ends toward center, in square microwavable dish, 8 × 8 × 2 inches. Cover with vented plastic wrap and microwave on medium (50%), rotating dish ¼ turn every 5 minutes until pork is done, 20 to 23 minutes. Let stand covered 5 minutes. Mix apple juice, brown sugar, cornstarch and water in 4-cup microwavable measure; stir in rhubarb. Cover and microwave on high (100%), stirring every 2 minutes, until thickened, 4 to 6 minutes. Serve with pork chops.

Per serving:			
Calories	290	Fat	21 g
Protein	18 g	Cholesterol	90 mg
Carbohydrate	7 g	Sodium	370 mg

Pretzel Pork with Sauerkraut Relish

Here is a dish with rich German flavor, yet it is quite low in calories. The crushed pretzel coating helps keep the pork chops juicy.

Sauerkraut Relish (below)
6 lean pork rib chops, about ½ inch thick
1 egg, slightly beaten
2 tablespoons water
½ teaspoon garlic powder
½ cup crushed pretzels
2 teaspoons reduced-calorie margarine

Prepare Sauerkraut Relish. Trim fat from pork chops and remove ribs; pound pork until ¼ inch thick. Mix egg, water and garlic powder. Dip pork into egg mixture; coat with crushed pretzels. Heat 1 teaspoon of the margarine in 10-inch nonstick skillet over medium heat until melted. Cook 3 pieces pork, turning once, until done, about 8 minutes. Remove pork from skillet; keep warm. Repeat with remaining margarine and pork. Serve pork with Sauerkraut Relish.

6 SERVINGS, WITH ABOUT ⅓ CUP RELISH EACH

Sauerkraut Relish

1 can (8 ounces) sauerkraut, rinsed and drained
¼ cup chopped red or green bell pepper
2 tablespoons finely chopped onion
½ teaspoon caraway seed
1 to 2 teaspoons sugar

Mix all ingredients; cover and refrigerate at least 1 hour.

Per serving:			
Calories	305	Fat	19 g
Protein	17 g	Cholesterol	65 mg
Carbohydrate	16 g	Sodium	590 mg

Pineapple Pork Chops

4 lean pork loin or rib chops, about ½ inch thick
Salt
1 can (8 ounces) pineapple slices in juice, drained (reserve juice)
2 tablespoons packed brown sugar
¼ teaspoon ground nutmeg

Heat oven to 350°. Trim fat from pork chops. Lightly sprinkle both sides of pork with salt. Place pork in ungreased square pan or baking dish, 8 × 8 × 2 inches. Mix 2 tablespoons of the reserved pineapple juice with the brown sugar and nutmeg; spoon half of the mixture over pork. Top with pineapple slices; spoon remaining mixture over pineapple. Cover and bake 30 minutes. Uncover and bake, spooning sauce over pork occasionally, until done, 15 to 20 minutes longer. Garnish with snipped chives if desired.

4 SERVINGS

MICROWAVE DIRECTIONS: Prepare pork chops as directed. Arrange pork, narrow ends toward center, in square microwavable dish, 8 × 8 × 2 inches. Mix 2 tablespoons of the reserved pineapple juice with the brown sugar and nutmeg; spoon half of the mixture over pork. Cover with vented plastic wrap and microwave on medium (50%) 10 minutes. Arrange pineapple slices over pork; spoon remaining mixture over pineapple and pork. Cover and rotate dish ½ turn. Microwave until pork is done, 10 to 15 minutes longer. Let stand covered about 3 minutes. Garnish with snipped chives if desired.

Per serving:

Calories	300	Fat	12 g
Protein	19 g	Cholesterol	50 mg
Carbohydrate	30 g	Sodium	330 mg

Pork Fajitas

Tortillas vary in size, weight and, of course, calories. When buying them by weight, select the package with the most tortillas; they'll be thinner and have fewer calories.

¾ pound lean pork tenderloin
1 tablespoon vegetable oil
2 tablespoons lime juice
2 cloves garlic, sliced
2 teaspoons chili powder
1 teaspoon garlic powder
½ teaspoon salt
¼ teaspoon pepper
4 flour tortillas (8-inch)
1 medium onion, sliced
1 medium green or red bell pepper, cut into ¼-inch strips
¾ cup chopped seeded tomato (about 1 medium)
¼ cup reduced-calorie sour cream

Trim fat from pork tenderloin; cut pork with grain into 2-inch strips. Cut strips across grain into ¼-inch slices. (For ease in cutting, partially freeze pork, about 1½ hours.) Mix 1 tablespoon oil, the lime juice, garlic, chili powder, garlic powder, salt and pepper in glass or plastic bowl or heavy plastic bag. Place pork in bowl, tossing to coat. Cover and refrigerate at least 8 hours but no longer than 24 hours, turning pork occasionally.

Heat oven to 350°. Wrap tortillas in aluminum foil and heat until warm, about 15 minutes. Remove from oven; keep tortillas wrapped. Remove pork from marinade.

Heat 10-inch nonstick skillet or wok over medium-high heat until 1 or 2 drops water bubble and skitter when sprinkled in skillet. Add pork; stir-fry 4 minutes. Add onion and bell pepper; stir-fry until vegetables are crisp-tender, 4 to 5 minutes longer.

For each serving, place ¼ of the pork mixture, chopped tomato and sour cream in center of tortilla. Fold tortilla over filling; serve with lime wedges if desired.

4 SERVINGS

Per Serving:

Calories	230	Fat	15 g
Protein	13 g	Cholesterol	45 mg
Carbohydrate	5 g	Sodium	650 mg

Pork and Broccoli Risotto

The method below is a shortcut to the time-consuming traditional one, where broth is added very gradually. This risotto still achieves a slightly firm texture, just as it should. The grains of Arborio rice are shorter and fatter than those of ordinary rice.

1 pound lean pork boneless loin or leg
2 teaspoons vegetable oil
3 cups broccoli flowerets
1 cup chopped red bell pepper
2 cloves garlic, finely chopped
1 teaspoon salt
½ cup chopped onion (about 1 medium)
1 tablespoon reduced-calorie margarine
1 cup uncooked long grain or Arborio rice
¼ cup dry white wine
1 cup beef broth
1¼ cups water
¼ cup skim milk
2 tablespoons grated Parmesan cheese

Trim fat from pork loin; cut pork into slices, 2 × 1 × ¼ inch. Heat vegetable oil in 10-inch nonstick skillet over medium heat. Cook and stir pork, broccoli, bell pepper, garlic and salt in oil until pork is done and vegetables are crisp-tender, about 5 minutes. Remove from skillet; keep warm.

In same skillet, cook onion in margarine until onion is tender, about 3 minutes. Stir in rice and wine; cook and stir until wine is absorbed, about 30 seconds. Stir in broth and water; heat to boiling. Reduce heat; cover

and cook until rice is almost tender and mixture is creamy, about 15 minutes. Stir in milk and reserved pork mixture; heat through. Sprinkle with Parmesan cheese.

6 SERVINGS, ABOUT ¾ CUP EACH

Per serving:

Calories	215	Fat	12 g
Protein	13 g	Cholesterol	40 mg
Carbohydrate	13 g	Sodium	270 mg

Savory Pork Stew

1 pound lean pork boneless shoulder
1 cup chopped onion (about 1 large)
1 teaspoon snipped fresh rosemary leaves or
   ½ teaspoon dried rosemary leaves
1 tablespoon snipped fresh basil leaves or
   1 teaspoon dried basil leaves
¼ teaspoon pepper
½ cup water
2 cups 1-inch carrot slices (about 6 medium)
1 large green bell pepper, cut into 1-inch pieces
3 cups halved mushrooms (about 8 ounces)
½ cup Burgundy or other dry red wine
1 can (8 ounces) tomato sauce

Trim fat from pork shoulder; cut into 1-inch cubes. Spray 3-quart nonstick saucepan with nonstick cooking spray. Cook and stir pork over medium heat until brown. Stir in onion, rosemary, basil, pepper and water. Heat to boiling; reduce heat. Cover and simmer until pork is almost tender, about 1 hour.

Stir in remaining ingredients. Cover and simmer until vegetables are tender, stirring occasionally, about 30 minutes.

6 SERVINGS, ABOUT 1 CUP EACH

Savory Pork Stew

Per serving:

Calories	165	Fat	8 g
Protein	16 g	Cholesterol	40 mg
Carbohydrate	8 g	Sodium	340 mg

Pork Florentine

Imagine a Swiss Cheese Sauce with no added fat! Fresh spinach makes a difference here, just quickly wilted and freshened with a squeeze of lemon.

¾ pound lean pork tenderloin, cut into 6 slices
2 teaspoons reduced-calorie margarine
2 teaspoons olive or vegetable oil
Swiss Cheese Sauce (right)
½ cup chopped onion (about 1 medium)
1 clove garlic, finely chopped
1 tablespoon reduced-calorie margarine
½ teaspoon salt
¼ teaspoon pepper
¼ teaspoon ground nutmeg
1 pound fresh spinach
1 tablespoon lemon juice
Ground nutmeg

Pound pork tenderloin slices until ¼ inch thick. Heat 1 teaspoon of the margarine and 1 teaspoon of the oil in 4-quart nonstick Dutch oven over medium-low heat until hot. Cook 3 slices pork in oil mixture, turning once, until done, about 10 minutes. Remove pork from skillet; keep warm. Repeat with remaining margarine, oil and pork.

Prepare Swiss Cheese Sauce. Cook and stir onion and garlic in 1 tablespoon margarine in 4-quart nonstick Dutch oven over medium heat until onion is tender, about 3 minutes. Stir in salt, pepper and nutmeg. Add spinach; toss just until spinach is wilted. Drizzle with lemon juice. Arrange spinach on serving platter; place pork over spinach. Serve with Swiss Cheese Sauce. Sprinkle with nutmeg.

6 SERVINGS, WITH ABOUT ¼ CUP SPINACH AND 2 TABLESPOONS SAUCE EACH

Swiss Cheese Sauce

1 tablespoon cornstarch
¾ cup skim milk
2 tablespoons nonfat plain yogurt
½ cup shredded Swiss cheese (2 ounces)
¼ teaspoon ground nutmeg

Mix cornstarch and milk. Cook over medium heat until mixture thickens and boils, stirring constantly. Boil and stir 1 minute; remove from heat. Stir in cheese and nutmeg; heat until cheese melts.

Per serving:

Calories	260	Fat	13 g
Protein	13 g	Cholesterol	45 mg
Carbohydrate	24 g	Sodium	420 mg

Ginger Pork on Pineapple

1 pineapple
1 pound lean ground pork
¼ cup chopped onion (about 1 small)
1 tablespoon packed brown sugar
1 tablespoon vinegar
1 teaspoon ground ginger
½ teaspoon salt
¼ teaspoon pepper
1 medium green bell pepper, cut into 1-inch pieces
1 can (8 ounces) tomato sauce
1 can (8 ounces) sliced water chestnuts, drained

Pare pineapple; cut crosswise into 6 slices. Place pineapple on rack sprayed with nonstick cooking spray in broiler pan.

Cook and stir ground pork and onion in 10-inch nonstick skillet over medium heat until pork is light brown; drain. Stir in remaining ingredients. Heat to boiling; reduce heat. Simmer uncovered, stirring occasionally, until bell pepper is crisp-tender, about 10 minutes.

Set oven control to broil. Broil pineapple with tops 4 to 5 inches from heat 5 minutes; turn. Broil until hot and bubbly, 3 to 5 minutes longer. Serve pork mixture over pineapple.

6 SERVINGS, ABOUT ⅔ CUP PORK MIXTURE AND 1 SLICE PINEAPPLE EACH

MICROWAVE DIRECTIONS: Prepare pineapple as directed. Arrange pineapple slices in deep round microwavable platter. Cover with waxed paper. Crumble pork and onion in 2-quart microwavable casserole. Cover tightly and microwave on high (100%) 3 minutes; stir. Cover and microwave until pork is done, 3 to 5 minutes longer; drain. Stir in remaining ingredients. Cover tightly and microwave 5 minutes; stir. Cover and microwave until bell pepper is crisp-tender, 3 to 5 minutes longer. Let stand covered 5 minutes. Microwave pineapple until hot, about 4 minutes. Serve pork mixture over pineapple slices.

Per serving:			
Calories	335	Fat	23 g
Protein	20 g	Cholesterol	65 mg
Carbohydrate	13 g	Sodium	380 mg

Pork and Pasta Stir-Fry

1¼ pounds lean pork boneless loin or leg
1 teaspoon cornstarch
1 teaspoon soy sauce
¼ teaspoon salt
⅛ teaspoon pepper
2 tablespoons vegetable oil
2 large cloves garlic, finely chopped
¼ to ½ teaspoon crushed red pepper
1 cup ¼-inch diagonally cut celery slices
1 small green or red bell pepper, cut into
   1-inch pieces
2 cups bean sprouts (about 4 ounces)
1½ cups sliced mushrooms (about 4 ounces)
2 cups cooked vermicelli
¼ cup sliced green onions (with tops)
1 tablespoon soy sauce

Trim fat from pork loin; cut pork with grain into 2-inch strips. Cut strips across grain into ⅛-inch slices. (For ease in cutting, partially freeze pork, about 1½ hours.) Toss pork, cornstarch, 1 teaspoon soy sauce, the salt and pepper in glass or plastic bowl or heavy plastic bag. Cover and refrigerate 20 minutes.

Heat oil in 12-inch nonstick skillet or wok over high heat until hot. Add pork, garlic and red pepper; stir-fry until pork is no longer pink, about 5 minutes. Add celery and bell pepper; stir-fry 2 minutes. Add bean sprouts and mushrooms; stir-fry 2 minutes. Add vermicelli, green onions and 1 tablespoon soy sauce; toss until thoroughly mixed and hot.

6 SERVINGS, ABOUT 1 CUP EACH

Beef with Pea Pods (page 104) and Pork and Pasta Stir-Fry (page 119)

Per serving:			
Calories	190	Fat	8 g
Protein	21 g	Cholesterol	60 mg
Carbohydrate	8 g	Sodium	500 mg

Per serving:			
Calories	220	Fat	5 g
Protein	18 g	Cholesterol	25 mg
Carbohydrate	25 g	Sodium	670 mg

Oriental Pork and Cabbage

1 pound lean pork tenderloin
2 teaspoons soy sauce
1 teaspoon sesame oil
1 teaspoon cornstarch
1 teaspoon sugar
½ teaspoon salt
⅛ teaspoon pepper
2 cloves garlic, finely chopped
3 teaspoons vegetable oil
2 cups coarsely shredded cabbage (about 8 ounces)
1 medium bell pepper, cut into ¼-inch strips
1 cup 1-inch green onion pieces (with tops)
1 tablespoon toasted sesame seed

Trim fat from pork tenderloin; cut pork with grain into 2-inch strips. Cut strips across grain into ¼-inch slices. (For ease in cutting, partially freeze pork, about 1½ hours.) Toss pork with soy sauce, sesame oil, cornstarch, sugar, salt, pepper and garlic in glass or plastic bowl or heavy plastic bag. Cover and refrigerate 30 minutes.

Heat 1 teaspoon vegetable oil in 10-inch nonstick skillet over medium-high heat. Add pork; stir-fry until pork is brown, 4 to 5 minutes. Remove pork.

Add 2 teaspoons vegetable oil to skillet. Add cabbage, bell pepper and green onions; stir-fry 2 minutes. Stir in pork; heat until hot. Sprinkle with sesame seed.

4 SERVINGS, ABOUT 1 CUP EACH

Ham- and Swiss-topped Potatoes

3 medium baking potatoes
2 tablespoons cornstarch
2 cups skim milk
1 tablespoon Dijon-style mustard
¼ teaspoon pepper
½ cup shredded Swiss cheese (2 ounces)
2 cups cut-up fully cooked smoked extra-lean ham (about 8 ounces)
1 package (10 ounces) frozen asparagus cuts, thawed and drained

Heat oven to 375°. Prick potatoes with fork. Bake until tender, about 1 hour.

Mix cornstarch and milk in 2-quart nonstick saucepan. Cook over medium heat until mixture thickens and boils, stirring constantly. Stir in mustard, pepper and cheese. Cook and stir until cheese is melted. Stir in ham and asparagus; heat through.

To serve, cut potatoes lengthwise into halves. Score cut sides of potatoes ½-inch deep. Push ends to open potato. Serve sauce over potato halves.

6 SERVINGS, ½ POTATO AND ABOUT ⅔ CUP SAUCE EACH

MICROWAVE DIRECTIONS: Prick potatoes with fork; arrange about 2 inches apart in circle in microwave. Microwave uncovered on high (100%) until tender, 10 to 13 minutes. Let stand 5 minutes. Decrease milk to 1¾ cups. Mix cornstarch and milk in 2-quart microwavable casserole. Microwave uncovered, stirring every minute, until thickened, 4 to 6 minutes. Stir in mustard, pepper and cheese until cheese is melted. Stir in ham and asparagus. Microwave until heated through, 4 to 6 minutes. Serve as directed.

Per serving:			
Calories	225	Fat	6 g
Protein	19 g	Cholesterol	30 mg
Carbohydrate	23 g	Sodium	820 mg

Creamy Smoked Ham

The addition of crisp-crunchy zucchini strips makes this creamy dish lighter and more fun. Look for at least 95 percent fat-free ham.

1 medium onion, thinly sliced
1 tablespoon reduced-calorie margarine
3 cups cut-up fully cooked smoked extra-lean ham (about 12 ounces))
4 small zucchini (about 1 pound), cut into ¼-inch strips
1 green bell pepper, cut into ¼-inch slices
⅛ teaspoon pepper
½ cup reduced-calorie sour cream
1 teaspoon poppy seed
3 cups hot cooked noodles

Cook and stir onion in margarine in 10-inch nonstick skillet until onion is tender. Stir in ham, zucchini, bell pepper and pepper. Cover and cook over medium heat, stirring occasionally, until vegetables are crisp-tender, about 8 minutes. Stir in sour cream and poppy seed; heat just until hot. Serve over noodles.

6 SERVINGS, ABOUT 1 CUP HAM MIXTURE AND ½ CUP NOODLES EACH

Per serving:			
Calories	270	Fat	16 g
Protein	10 g	Cholesterol	5 mg
Carbohydrate	23 g	Sodium	600 mg

Italian Sausage and Vegetables

You don't have to swear off sausage entirely. Here it is served over a bed of spaghetti squash strands. Bulk Italian sausage may be used instead of links.

1 spaghetti squash (about 3 pounds)
1 pound Italian sausage, casing removed and crumbled, or bulk Italian sausage
½ cup chopped onion (about 1 medium)
1 cup coarsely chopped zucchini (about 1 medium)
¼ cup snipped parsley
1 large clove garlic, crushed
1 tablespoon dried basil leaves
3 cups coarsely chopped tomatoes (about 4 medium)
⅓ cup grated Parmesan cheese
½ teaspoon salt
¼ teaspoon pepper

Heat oven to 400°. Prick squash with fork. Bake until tender, about 1 hour. Cook and stir sausage and onion in 10-inch nonstick skillet over medium heat until sausage is done, about 10 minutes; drain. Stir in zucchini, parsley, garlic and basil. Cover and cook 3 minutes. Stir in tomatoes and cheese. Cut squash into halves; remove seeds and fibers. Remove spaghettilike strands with 2 forks; toss with salt and pepper. Serve sausage mixture over squash.

6 SERVINGS, ABOUT 1¾ CUPS EACH

Lamb Patties with Fresh Mint Sauce

Fresh Mint Sauce (below)
1 pound lean ground lamb
⅔ cup soft bread crumbs
⅓ cup dry red wine
½ teaspoon salt
¼ teaspoon dried rosemary leaves, crushed
2 small cloves garlic, finely chopped

Prepare Sauce. Set oven control to broil. Mix remaining ingredients. Shape lamb mixture into 4 patties, each about 1 inch thick. Place patties on rack sprayed with nonstick cooking spray in broiler pan. Broil with tops about 3 inches from heat, until desired doneness, 5 to 7 minutes on each side for medium. Serve with Fresh Mint Sauce. Garnish with mint leaves and sliced kiwifruit if desired.

4 SERVINGS, WITH 1½ TABLESPOONS SAUCE EACH

Fresh Mint Sauce

¼ cup mashed pared kiwifruit (about 1 medium)
1 tablespoon snipped fresh mint leaves or ½ teaspoon dried mint leaves, crushed
2 teaspoons sugar
2 teaspoons lime juice

Mix all ingredients.

MICROWAVE DIRECTIONS: Prepare Fresh Mint Sauce and lamb patties. Place patties on microwavable rack in microwavable dish. Cover with vented plastic wrap and microwave on high (100%) 3 minutes; rotate dish ½ turn. Microwave until patties are almost done, 3 to 4 minutes longer. Let stand covered 3 minutes. Serve with Fresh Mint Sauce. Garnish with mint leaves and sliced kiwifruit if desired.

Lamb Paprikash

1 pound lean lamb boneless shoulder or leg
1 can (6 ounces) tomato paste
1 can (16 ounces) tomatoes, drained (reserve ⅓ cup liquid)
8 ounces mushrooms, cut into fourths
1 medium onion, thinly sliced
1 medium green bell pepper, cut into ¼-inch strips
2 cloves garlic, finely chopped
2 tablespoons paprika
1 tablespoon snipped fresh oregano leaves or 1½ teaspoons dried oregano leaves
¼ teaspoon pepper
3 cups hot cooked noodles

Heat oven to 325°. Trim fat from lamb shoulder; cut lamb into ½-inch cubes. Cook and stir lamb over medium heat in 4-quart nonstick Dutch oven until brown, about 5 minutes. Stir in tomato paste. Mix in reserved tomato liquid and the remaining ingredients except noodles; break up tomatoes. Cover and bake, stirring once, until lamb is tender, 45 to 55 minutes. Serve over noodles.

6 SERVINGS, ABOUT ⅔ CUP LAMB MIXTURE AND ½ CUP NOODLES EACH

Lamb Patties with Fresh Mint Sauce

Weekend Brunch

....

FRESH FRUIT

SCRAMBLED EGGS MÉLANGE (PAGE 134) OR
QUICK CHILI-CHEESE PUFF (PAGE 133)

LEAN HAM

WHEAT MUFFINS (PAGE 199)

EGGS, CHEESE & LEGUMES

Clockwise from top: Wheat Muffins (page 199),
Scrambled Eggs Mélange (page 134) and
Quick Chili-Cheese Puff (page 133)

HEALTHY HINTS

- Although eggs are perfect protein sources, they are high in cholesterol. Because all of the cholesterol in eggs is found in the yolk, the amount of yolks called for in many of these recipes has been reduced. Experts recommend consuming no more than three egg yolks per week.
- When dining out, eat only half of a three- or four-egg omelet; share it with a friend or take the rest home for another meal.
- Cheese is a valuable source of protein and calcium, but it is also high in fat. Use half the amount of shredded cheese in your casseroles to reduce the calories. Substitute Parmesan or Romano cheese for other cheeses; because their flavor is strong, less cheese is needed.
- Herbed Yogurt Cheese (page 24) is a low-fat, low-calorie protein source. It resembles cream cheese in texture, but it has half the calories and no cholesterol or fat.
- Protein-rich legumes are the fruit of any pod bearing a single row of seeds. Lentils, peas and beans are some of the more common varieties that are available in most markets. When legumes are combined with such whole grains as rice, barley or oats, they become complete protein sources. Small amounts of cheese and milk also enhance their protein values.

DELI COUNTERS

There are many low-fat, reduced-calorie cheese and dairy products available in most delicatessen sections. Look for low-fat hard and semisoft cheeses such as Monterey Jack, farmer's cheese or 95 percent fat-free cream cheese. Have portions of cheese thinly sliced so that you will use less. There are also many varieties of low-sodium cheese. Ask for "light" or low-fat dips or spreads. Although they may not currently be available, with frequent requests they may be added to the selection.

Per serving:

Calories	170	Fat	12 g
Protein	12 g	Cholesterol	410 mg
Carbohydrate	3 g	Sodium	480 mg

Mushroom Omelets

Mushroom Filling (below)
6 eggs
2 egg whites
⅓ cup water
½ teaspoon salt
⅛ teaspoon pepper
Vegetable oil

Prepare Mushroom Filling; keep warm. Mix remaining ingredients except vegetable oil just until egg whites and yolks are well blended. Lightly brush 8-inch nonstick omelet pan or skillet with oil; heat over medium-high heat until hot. For each omelet, quickly pour ¼ of the egg mixture (about ½ cup) into pan. As eggs begin to set, run spatula under edge of omelet, lifting cooked portion and allowing uncooked portion to spread to bottom of pan to cook (tilt pan if necessary). When eggs are set but shiny, remove from heat. (Do not overcook—omelet will continue to cook after folding.) Spoon about ¼ cup Mushroom Filling on one side of omelet. Run spatula under unfilled side of omelet; lift over filling. Tilting pan slightly, turn omelet onto plate.

4 SERVINGS

Mushroom Filling

1 tablespoon reduced-calorie margarine
2 cups sliced mushrooms (about 5 ounces)
1 large clove garlic, finely chopped
2 tablespoons chopped green onions (with tops)
2 tablespoons snipped parsley
2 tablespoons grated Parmesan cheese

Heat margarine in 10-inch nonstick skillet over medium-high heat until hot. Stir in mushrooms, garlic and onions; cook and stir until moisture is evaporated, about 2 minutes. Remove from heat; stir in parsley and cheese.

Per serving:

Calories	245	Fat	16 g
Protein	14 g	Cholesterol	550 mg
Carbohydrate	10 g	Sodium	930 mg

Zucchini Frittata

6 eggs
¼ cup water
3 tablespoons snipped parsley
2 tablespoons soft bread crumbs
1 teaspoon salt
1 clove garlic, finely chopped
1 tablespoon olive or vegetable oil
1 cup ¼-inch zucchini slices (about 1 medium)
Flour
1 tablespoon grated Parmesan cheese

Beat eggs, water, parsley, bread crumbs, salt and garlic. Heat oil in 8-inch nonstick ovenproof skillet over medium heat until hot. Coat zucchini lightly with flour; cook until golden, about 2 minutes on each side. Pour egg mixture over zucchini. Cook without stirring until eggs are thickened throughout but still moist, 3 to 5 minutes. Gently lift edge with fork so that uncooked portion can flow to bottom. Sprinkle with cheese.

Set oven control to broil. Broil omelet with top 5 inches from heat until golden brown, 3 to 4 minutes. Loosen edge with spatula; slip cheese side up onto serving plate.

3 SERVINGS

Per serving:

Calories	230	Fat	17 g
Protein	13 g	Cholesterol	550 mg
Carbohydrate	6 g	Sodium	570 mg

Fluffy Omelet with Tomato Sauce

"Fluffy" omelets take a bit more time in preparation, but they are worth the extra effort. The result is a light and tender omelet, dramatically high and very satisfying.

4 eggs, separated
¼ cup water
¼ teaspoon salt
⅛ teaspoon pepper
1 tablespoon reduced-calorie margarine
Tomato Sauce (right)

Heat oven to 325°. Beat egg whites, water and salt on high speed until stiff but not dry. Beat egg yolks and pepper on high speed until very thick and lemon colored, about 3 minutes. Fold into egg whites.

Heat margarine in 10-inch nonstick ovenproof skillet or omelet pan over medium heat just until hot. As margarine melts, tilt skillet to coat bottom completely. Pour egg mixture into skillet. Level surface gently; reduce heat. Cook over low heat until puffy and light brown on bottom, about 5 minutes. (Lift omelet carefully at edge to judge color.) Bake uncovered in oven until knife inserted in center comes out clean, 12 to 15 minutes. Prepare Tomato Sauce.

Tilt skillet; slip pancake turner or spatula under omelet to loosen. Fold omelet in half, being careful not to break it. Slip onto warm plate. Serve with Tomato Sauce.

2 SERVINGS, WITH ABOUT ⅓ CUP SAUCE EACH

Tomato Sauce

1 clove garlic, finely chopped
1 green onion (with top), chopped
1 teaspoon olive or vegetable oil
1 cup chopped tomato (about 1 medium)
1 teaspoon snipped fresh basil leaves or
   ¼ teaspoon dried basil leaves
⅛ teaspoon salt
Dash of sugar
Freshly ground pepper

Cook and stir garlic and onion in oil over medium heat until onion is tender, about 1 minute. Stir in remaining ingredients. Heat uncovered, stirring occasionally, until hot, about 3 minutes.

Per serving:

Calories	115	Fat	7 g
Protein	9 g	Cholesterol	275 mg
Carbohydrate	4 g	Sodium	750 mg

Egg Foo Yong

4 eggs
2 egg whites
1⅓ cups bean sprouts
¼ cup sliced green onions (with tops)
¼ teaspoon salt
Vegetable oil
Brown Sauce (page 131)

Beat eggs and egg whites until thick and lemon colored, about 5 minutes. Stir in bean sprouts, onions and salt. For each patty, lightly brush 10-inch nonstick skillet with oil. Heat over medium heat until hot.

Pour scant ¼ cup egg mixture at a time into skillet. Push cooked egg up over bean sprouts with broad spatula to form a patty. Cook until patty is set; turn. Cook over medium heat until other side is brown. Place on warm platter; keep warm. Prepare Brown Sauce; serve with egg patties.

4 SERVINGS, 2 PATTIES AND ABOUT 2 TABLESPOONS SAUCE EACH

Brown Sauce

½ cup water
2 tablespoons soy sauce
1 teaspoon cornstarch
1 teaspoon sugar
1 teaspoon vinegar

Cook all ingredients until mixture thickens and boils, stirring constantly. Boil and stir 1 minute.

Per serving:			
Calories	210	Fat	12 g
Protein	11 g	Cholesterol	275 mg
Carbohydrate	16 g	Sodium	150 mg

Huevos Rancheros

4 corn tortillas (6-inch)
Salsa (right)
4 Poached Eggs (page 133)
½ cup shredded Monterey Jack cheese
   (2 ounces)

Heat oven to 350°. Make 6 cuts, about 1 inch deep, around edge of tortillas. Carefully fit tortillas into custard cups sprayed with nonstick cooking spray, overlapping cut edges. Place cups in shallow baking pan. Bake until light brown, 15 to 20 minutes. Cool 5 minutes; remove from cups.

Prepare Salsa; keep warm. Prepare Poached Eggs. Place tortilla shells on serving plates. Layer 2 tablespoons sauce, 1 egg, 2 tablespoons sauce and 2 tablespoons cheese in each tortilla shell.

4 SERVINGS

Salsa

¼ cup chopped onion (about 1 small)
2 tablespoons chopped green bell pepper
1 clove garlic, finely chopped
1 teaspoon vegetable oil
1 cup chopped ripe tomato (about 1 large)
1 can (4 ounces) chopped green chilies

Cook and stir onion, bell pepper and garlic in oil in 1-quart nonstick saucepan until bell pepper is tender, about 5 minutes. Stir in tomato and chilies. Heat to boiling; reduce heat. Simmer uncovered until slightly thickened, about 5 minutes longer.

Eggs Benedict

Per serving:			
Calories	215	Fat	13 g
Protein	13 g	Cholesterol	340 mg
Carbohydrate	11 g	Sodium	390 mg

Eggs Benedict

Mock Hollandaise has only 25 calories per tablespoon. Compare that with the traditional version, at 85 calories. This sauce is also delightful on lightly steamed vegetables or fish.

Mock Hollandaise Sauce (below)
2 English muffins
4 thin slices fully cooked Canadian-style
  bacon (about 2 ounces)
4 Poached Eggs (right)

Prepare Mock Hollandaise Sauce; keep warm. Split English muffins; toast. Cook bacon in 10-inch nonstick skillet sprayed with nonstick cooking spray over medium heat until light brown.

Prepare Poached Eggs. Place 1 slice bacon on each muffin half; top with egg. Spoon about 3 tablespoons sauce onto each egg.

4 SERVINGS

Mock Hollandaise Sauce

2 tablespoons reduced-calorie margarine
1 tablespoon all-purpose flour
1/4 teaspoon salt
2/3 cup skim milk
1 egg yolk
1/2 teaspoon grated lemon peel
2 teaspoons lemon juice

Heat margarine in 1-quart nonstick saucepan over low heat until melted. Stir in flour and salt. Cook over low heat until mixture is smooth and bubbly, stirring constantly; remove from heat. Mix milk and egg yolk until smooth; stir into flour mixture. Heat to boiling, stirring constantly. Boil and stir 1 minute. Remove from heat; stir in lemon peel and lemon juice.

POACHED EGGS: Heat water (1 1/2 to 2 inches) to boiling; reduce to simmering. Break each egg into custard cup or saucer; hold cup close to water's surface and slip 1 egg at a time into water. Cook until desired doneness, 3 to 5 minutes. Remove eggs with slotted spoon.

Per serving:			
Calories	200	Fat	12 g
Protein	12 g	Cholesterol	170 mg
Carbohydrate	10 g	Sodium	240 mg

Quick Chili-Cheese Puff

1 cup shredded sharp Cheddar cheese
  (4 ounces)
2 cans (4 ounces each) whole green chilies,
  drained
1/4 cup all-purpose flour
1/2 cup skim milk
1/4 teaspoon pepper
2 eggs

Heat oven to 350°. Layer half of the cheese, the chilies and remaining cheese in 1-quart casserole or four 10-ounce custard cups sprayed with nonstick cooking spray. Beat remaining ingredients with rotary beater until smooth; pour over top. Bake until puffy and golden brown, casserole about 40 minutes, custard cups about 20 minutes.

4 SERVINGS

Per serving:			
Calories	200	Fat	12 g
Protein	13 g	Cholesterol	410 mg
Carbohydrate	10 g	Sodium	840 mg

Per serving:			
Calories	240	Fat	8 g
Protein	19 g	Cholesterol	190 mg
Carbohydrate	22 g	Sodium	1000 mg

Scrambled Eggs Mélange

2 medium green bell peppers, thinly sliced
1 medium onion, thinly sliced
1 clove garlic, chopped
¼ teaspoon salt
1½ teaspoons snipped fresh thyme leaves or
   ½ teaspoon dried thyme leaves
1 tablespoon olive or vegetable oil
2 cups coarsely chopped tomatoes (about
   2 medium)
6 eggs
½ cup skim milk
1 teaspoon salt
¼ teaspoon pepper

Cook and stir bell peppers, onion, garlic, ¼ teaspoon salt and the thyme in the oil in 10-inch nonstick skillet over medium heat until bell peppers are crisp-tender, about 8 minutes. Add tomatoes; heat until hot, about 2 minutes. Drain; place vegetables on platter. Keep warm.

Mix remaining ingredients; pour into skillet. Cook uncovered over medium heat. As mixture begins to set at bottom and side, gently lift cooked portions with spatula so that thin, uncooked portion can flow to bottom. Cook until eggs are thickened throughout but still moist, 3 to 5 minutes. Mound scrambled eggs in center of vegetables. Sprinkle with snipped parsley if desired.

4 SERVINGS

Smoky Beef and Cheese Quiche

1½ cups hot cooked rice
1 tablespoon snipped fresh chives
1 egg white
1 package (2.5 ounces) smoked sliced beef
3 eggs
1 egg yolk
1 can (13 ounces) evaporated skim milk
¼ teaspoon salt
½ cup shredded mozzarella or Monterey Jack
   cheese (2 ounces)
¼ cup finely chopped onion (about 1 small)
8 tomato slices

Heat oven to 350°. Beat rice, chives and egg white with fork. Turn mixture into pie plate, 10 × 1½ inches, sprayed with nonstick cooking spray. Spread evenly with rubber spatula on bottom and halfway up side of pie plate (do not leave any holes). Bake 5 minutes.

Cut meat into small pieces and sprinkle in rice crust. Beat eggs, egg yolk, skim milk and salt; stir in cheese and onion. Carefully pour into rice crust. Bake until knife inserted in center comes out clean, 25 to 30 minutes. Immediately run knife around edge to loosen crust. Let stand 10 minutes before serving. Garnish with tomato slices.

6 SERVINGS

Smoky Beef and Cheese Quiche

Vegetable-filled Soufflé Roll and Wheat Muffins (page 199)

Per serving:			
Calories	305	Fat	20 g
Protein	15 g	Cholesterol	280 mg
Carbohydrate	17 g	Sodium	630 mg

Vegetable-filled Soufflé Roll

A pretty soufflé roll such as this one is lovely for a special breakfast or light luncheon. A quick way to seed tomatoes is to cut them crosswise in half, then squeeze out the seeds. An electric knife makes slicing the soufflé roll especially neat and easy.

¼ cup reduced-calorie margarine
¼ cup all-purpose flour
½ teaspoon salt
Dash of ground red pepper
1½ cups skim milk
4 egg yolks
6 egg whites
½ teaspoon cream of tartar
Basil Vegetables (right)

Spray bottom of jelly roll pan, 15½ × 10½ × 1 inch, with nonstick cooking spray. Line bottom of pan with parchment paper or waxed paper; spray with nonstick cooking spray. Heat margarine in 2-quart saucepan over low heat until melted. Stir in flour, salt and red pepper. Cook, stirring constantly, until smooth and bubbly; remove from heat. Stir in milk. Heat to boiling, stirring constantly. Boil and stir 1 minute; remove from heat. Beat in egg yolks, one at a time.

Heat oven to 350°. Beat egg whites and cream of tartar in large bowl on high speed until stiff but not dry. Stir about ¼ of the egg whites into egg yolk mixture. Fold egg yolk mixture into remaining egg whites. Spread evenly in pan.

Bake until puffed and golden brown, 35 to 40 minutes. Prepare Basil Vegetables. Immediately loosen soufflé from edges of pan; invert on cloth-covered wire rack. Carefully peel off parchment paper. Spread soufflé with Basil Vegetables; roll up from narrow end. Serve immediately.

4 SERVINGS, 2 SLICES ABOUT 1¼ INCHES THICK EACH

Basil Vegetables

¼ cup chopped onion (about 1 small)
2 large cloves garlic, finely chopped
1 tablespoon olive or vegetable oil
2 cups chopped seeded tomatoes (about 2 medium)
1½ cups thinly sliced zucchini (about 1½ small)
¼ cup snipped fresh basil leaves or 1 tablespoon dried basil leaves
¼ cup grated Parmesan cheese

Cook and stir onion and garlic in oil in 10-inch nonstick skillet over medium-high heat until onion is tender, about 2 minutes. Stir in tomatoes, zucchini and basil. Heat to boiling; reduce heat. Simmer uncovered until zucchini is crisp-tender, about 3 minutes longer. Stir in cheese.

Per serving:

Calories	200	Fat	12 g
Protein	12 g	Cholesterol	140 mg
Carbohydrate	11 g	Sodium	320 mg

Mushroom-Cheese Soufflé

Extra egg whites account for the extra large serving size of this delicious soufflé.

3 cups finely chopped mushrooms (about 12 ounces)
2 tablespoons finely chopped onion
1 large clove garlic, finely chopped
3 tablespoons reduced-calorie margarine
2 tablespoons all-purpose flour
⅛ teaspoon ground red pepper
1 cup skim milk
2 egg yolks
⅓ cup grated Parmesan cheese
5 egg whites
½ teaspoon cream of tartar

Heat oven to 350°. Spray 6-cup soufflé dish or 1½-quart casserole with nonstick cooking spray. Make a 4-inch band of triple-thickness aluminum foil 2 inches longer than circumference of dish; spray 1 side with nonstick cooking spray. Secure foil band, sprayed side in, around top edge of dish.

Cook mushrooms, onion and garlic in 1 tablespoon of the margarine in 10-inch nonstick skillet until all the moisture is evaporated, about 5 minutes; drain well.

Heat remaining 2 tablespoons margarine in 1½-quart saucepan over low heat until melted. Stir in flour and red pepper. Cook over low heat, stirring constantly, until smooth and bubbly, about 30 seconds. Remove from heat. Beat milk and egg yolks; stir into flour mixture. Heat to boiling, stirring constantly. Boil and stir 1 minute. Stir in cheese; remove from heat. Stir in mushroom mixture.

Beat egg whites and cream of tartar in medium bowl on high speed until stiff but not dry. Stir about ¼ of the egg white mixture into mushroom mixture. Fold mushroom mixture into remaining egg white mixture.

Carefully pour into soufflé dish. Bake uncovered until golden brown and cracks feel dry when touched lightly, about 45 minutes. Carefully remove foil band and divide soufflé into sections with 2 forks. Serve immediately.

4 SERVINGS

Per serving:

Calories	305	Fat	11 g
Protein	14 g	Cholesterol	410 mg
Carbohydrate	37 g	Sodium	1160 mg

Curried Eggs and Vegetables on Rice

For this dish, you make your own curry; commercial curries vary widely.

8 ounces small whole mushrooms
1 cup finely chopped onion (about 1 large)
1 tablespoon reduced-calorie margarine
1 teaspoon salt
1 teaspoon ground coriander
½ teaspoon ground turmeric
½ teaspoon ground ginger
½ teaspoon ground cumin
3 medium tomatoes, cut into wedges
¼ cup chicken broth
6 hard-cooked eggs
1 teaspoon lemon juice
2 cups hot cooked rice

Cook and stir mushrooms and onion in margarine in 10-inch nonstick skillet until onion is tender, about 5 minutes. Stir in salt, coriander, turmeric, ginger and cumin; cook and stir 1 minute. Stir in tomatoes and chicken broth. Heat to boiling; reduce heat. Simmer uncovered 5 minutes, stirring occasionally.

Cut eggs lengthwise in half. Carefully place eggs yolk side up in skillet; spoon sauce over eggs. Simmer uncovered without stirring until eggs are hot, 3 to 5 minutes. Stir in lemon juice just before serving. Serve over rice.

4 SERVINGS, 3 EGG HALVES AND ½ CUP RICE EACH

Per serving:

Calories	305	Fat	15 g
Protein	18 g	Cholesterol	35 mg
Carbohydrate	24 g	Sodium	580 mg

Vegetable-Cheese Soup with Popcorn

2 tablespoons reduced-calorie margarine
2 tablespoons all-purpose flour
1 cup chicken broth
1 cup coarsely chopped carrots (about 2 medium)
1 cup coarsely chopped celery (about 2 medium stalks)
½ cup chopped onion (about 1 medium)
1 can (15 ounces) evaporated skim milk
½ teaspoon Worcestershire sauce
1 cup shredded sharp Cheddar cheese (4 ounces)
1 cup hot-air-popped popcorn

Heat margarine in 3-quart nonstick saucepan over low heat until melted. Stir in flour. Cook

over low heat until mixture is smooth and bubbly, stirring constantly; remove from heat. Stir in chicken broth, carrots, celery and onion. Heat to boiling; boil and stir 1 minute. Reduce heat; cover and simmer until vegetables are crisp-tender, about 8 minutes. Stir in milk, Worcestershire sauce and cheese. Stir constantly until hot and cheese has melted, 2 to 3 minutes longer. (Do not boil.) Top with popcorn.

4 SERVINGS, ABOUT 1 CUP SOUP AND ¼ CUP POPCORN EACH

Per serving:

Calories	170	Fat	11 g
Protein	5 g	Cholesterol	15 mg
Carbohydrate	13 g	Sodium	190 mg

Toasted Almond-Cheese Sandwich

2 English muffins
2 ounces Neufchâtel cheese, softened
1 tablespoon reduced-calorie margarine, melted
1 tablespoon orange marmalade
¼ cup slivered almonds

Set oven control to broil. Split English muffins; toast. Stir cheese, margarine and marmalade until light and fluffy. Spread about 1 tablespoon cheese mixture on each muffin half; sprinkle with 1 tablespoon almonds. Broil until almonds are light brown and mixture is hot and bubbly, 1 to 2 minutes.

4 SERVINGS, 1 OPEN-FACE SANDWICH EACH

Per serving:			
Calories	130	Fat	6 g
Protein	4 g	Cholesterol	15 mg
Carbohydrate	15 g	Sodium	85 mg

Dilled Cucumber Sandwiches

2 ounces Neufchâtel cheese, softened
1 tablespoon reduced-calorie mayonnaise or
   salad dressing
1 to 2 teaspoons snipped fresh dill weed or
   ½ teaspoon dried dill weed
1 clove garlic, finely chopped
4 thin slices white bread, toasted
2 small cucumbers, thinly sliced
1 teaspoon skim milk
Freshly ground pepper

Mix cheese, mayonnaise, dill and garlic; spread 1 scant tablespoon on each slice toast. Top with cucumber slices. Mix remaining cheese mixture with milk. Place a dollop of cheese mixture on each sandwich; sprinkle with pepper.

4 SERVINGS, 1 OPEN-FACE SANDWICH EACH

Per serving:			
Calories	185	Fat	8 g
Protein	9 g	Cholesterol	15 mg
Carbohydrate	20 g	Sodium	370 mg

Leek and Chèvre Pizza

Look for a slightly dry or crumbly cheese for this pizza. *Fines herbes* can be purchased as a commercially prepared mixture, usually including chervil, parsley, tarragon and often chives.

Pizza Dough (below)
1 teaspoon olive or vegetable oil
1 cup shredded mozzarella cheese (4 ounces)
1 cup thinly sliced leek (with tops)
1 cup well-drained chopped seeded tomato
   (about 1 medium)
1 large clove garlic, finely chopped
10 large pitted ripe olives, cut into fourths
1 ounce chèvre cheese, chopped
½ teaspoon fines herbes

Heat oven to 450°. Prepare Pizza Dough. Brush with oil; sprinkle with remaining ingredients. Bake until cheese is bubbly and crust is golden brown, 15 to 20 minutes.

6 SERVINGS, 1 SLICE EACH

Pizza Dough

1½ teaspoons active dry yeast (about half of
   ¼-ounce package)
⅓ cup warm water (105° to 115°)
½ teaspoon sugar
½ teaspoon salt
2 teaspoons olive or vegetable oil
1 cup whole wheat flour
1 tablespoon yellow or white cornmeal

Dissolve yeast in warm water in medium bowl. Stir in sugar, salt, oil and all of the flour except 2 tablespoons. (If dough is sticky, add remaining flour, 1 to 2 teaspoons at a time, until dough is easy to handle.) Turn onto surface dusted with cornmeal. Knead until smooth and elastic, about 2 minutes. Pat into 10-inch circle on cookie sheet, forming ½-inch rim.

Leek and Chèvre Pizza

Per serving:

Calories	220	Fat	14 g
Protein	12 g	Cholesterol	110 mg
Carbohydrate	13 g	Sodium	220 mg

Gruyère Puff in Mushroom Crust

Mushroom Crust (right)
1 small onion, sliced
2 tablespoons reduced-calorie margarine
2 tablespoons all-purpose flour
¼ teaspoon dry mustard
1 cup skim milk
1 cup shredded Gruyère cheese (4 ounces)
3 egg whites
2 egg yolks
1 tablespoon snipped fresh chives

Prepare Mushroom Crust. Reduce oven temperature to 350°. Cook onion in margarine in 1-quart nonstick saucepan over low heat until onion is tender, about 3 minutes. Stir in flour and mustard until blended. Remove from heat; stir in milk. Heat to boiling over low heat, stirring constantly. Boil and stir 1 minute. Remove from heat; stir in cheese until melted.

Beat egg whites until stiff but not dry. Beat egg yolks until light and lemon colored; stir egg yolks into cheese mixture. Stir about ¼ of the egg white mixture into cheese mixture. Fold cheese mixture into remaining egg whites; stir in chives. Spread in Mushroom Crust. Bake until golden brown and cracks feel dry when touched lightly, about 30 minutes.

6 SERVINGS

Mushroom Crust

3 cups finely chopped mushrooms (about 12 ounces)
1 large clove garlic, finely chopped
2 tablespoons reduced-calorie margarine
¼ cup dry bread crumbs
1 egg white

Heat oven to 375°. Cook mushrooms and garlic in margarine in 10-inch nonstick skillet over medium heat until most of the moisture is evaporated, about 5 minutes. Cool slightly; stir in bread crumbs. Beat egg white until stiff peaks form; stir into mushroom mixture. Spread against bottom and side of pie plate, 9 × 1¼ inches, sprayed with nonstick cooking spray. Bake until edge begins to brown and crust is set, about 10 minutes.

Per serving:

Calories	70	Fat	2 g
Protein	3 g	Cholesterol	2 mg
Carbohydrate	10 g	Sodium	280 mg

Beans and Rice

To serve this as a main dish, increase the serving size to 1 cup (and double the calorie count).

2 cups water
⅔ cup dried kidney beans (about 6 ounces)
1 slice bacon, cut up
1 cup chopped green bell pepper (about 1 medium)
½ cup chopped onion (about 1 medium)
⅔ cup uncooked regular rice
1 teaspoon salt

Heat water and beans to boiling in 3-quart nonstick saucepan. Boil 2 minutes; remove from heat. Cover and let stand 1 hour.

Add enough water to beans to cover if necessary. Heat to boiling; reduce heat. Cover and simmer until tender, 1 to 1½ hours (do not boil or beans will burst).

Drain beans, reserving liquid. Cook bacon in 10-inch skillet until crisp; add bell pepper and onion. Cook and stir until onion is tender. Add enough water to bean liquid to measure 1⅓ cups. Add bean liquid and remaining ingredients to beans in 3-quart saucepan. Heat to boiling, stirring once or twice; reduce heat. Cover and simmer 15 minutes (do not lift cover or stir). Remove from heat. Fluff with fork; cover and let steam 5 to 10 minutes.

8 SERVINGS, ABOUT ½ CUP EACH

Per serving:			
Calories	160	Fat	2 g
Protein	8 g	Cholesterol	0 mg
Carbohydrate	29 g	Sodium	530 mg

Garbanzo Beans with Spinach

1 can (16 ounces) garbanzo beans, drained (reserve liquid)
1 package (10 ounces) frozen chopped spinach
1 clove garlic, finely chopped
¼ teaspoon salt
⅛ to ¼ teaspoon ground nutmeg
⅛ teaspoon pepper

Heat 2 tablespoons reserved liquid and remaining ingredients except beans to boiling in 2-quart nonstick saucepan; reduce heat.

Cover and simmer until spinach is tender, 3 to 5 minutes. Stir in beans and cook uncovered until moisture evaporates and beans are hot, 3 to 5 minutes longer.

4 SERVINGS, ABOUT ¾ CUP EACH

Per serving:			
Calories	165	Fat	4 g
Protein	8 g	Cholesterol	0 mg
Carbohydrate	25 g	Sodium	1200 mg

Red Kidney Bean Soup

1 can (16 ounces) red kidney beans, drained (reserve liquid)
1 cup chopped onion (about 1 large)
1 cup chopped celery (about 2 medium stalks)
2 cloves garlic finely chopped
1 tablespoon reduced-calorie margarine
2 cups chicken broth
1 cup water
½ cup coarsely chopped fully cooked smoked ham
1 teaspoon ground cumin
1 teaspoon chili powder
¼ teaspoon ground thyme
1 tablespoon lemon juice

Place ½ of the beans and reserved liquid in blender container. Cover and blend on high speed until almost smooth, about 1 minute. Cook and stir onion, celery and garlic in margarine in 2-quart saucepan until onion is tender, about 3 minutes. Stir in puréed beans, whole beans and remaining ingredients except lemon juice. Heat to boiling, stirring constantly. Reduce heat and simmer 10 minutes. Stir in lemon juice.

4 SERVINGS, ABOUT 1¼ CUPS EACH

Per serving:			
Calories	220	Fat	14 g
Protein	14 g	Cholesterol	160 mg
Carbohydrate	9 g	Sodium	490 mg

Per serving:			
Calories	100	Fat	1 g
Protein	10 g	Cholesterol	0 mg
Carbohydrate	15 g	Sodium	370 mg

Gouda Strata

Gouda is a distinctive cheese originally from Holland. It is a firm cheese, usually recognizable in a waxy or, today, sometimes plastic casing. The Dutch prefer an aged Gouda; they often keep the cheese until it is dry and hard.

2 tablespoons reduced-calorie margarine
6 slices thin-sliced whole wheat bread
½ cup shredded Monterey Jack cheese
   (2 ounces)
1 cup shredded Gouda cheese (4 ounces)
¼ cup finely chopped onion (about 1 small)
1 large clove garlic, finely chopped
1 teaspoon dry mustard
½ teaspoon salt
3 eggs
1 egg white
1½ cups skim milk
¼ teaspoon red pepper sauce

Heat oven to 325°. Spread margarine on 1 side of each slice of bread. Cut each slice diagonally into 4 triangles. Arrange 16 triangles with margarine sides against sides and bottom of ungreased square baking dish, 8 × 8 × 2 inches. Mix cheeses, onion, garlic, mustard and salt; spread over bread. Arrange remaining 8 triangles, with margarine sides up on cheese mixture. Mix remaining ingredients; pour over bread. Bake uncovered until knife inserted in center comes out clean, about 1 hour. Let stand about 10 minutes before serving.

6 SERVINGS

Skillet Beans and Squash

1½ cups ¼-inch yellow squash slices (about
   1½ medium)
1½ cups ¼-inch zucchini slices (about
   1½ medium)
1 cup cubed pared Hubbard or acorn squash
   (about 4 ounces)
½ cup chopped onion (about 1 medium)
1 cup chicken broth
1 to 2 tablespoons chopped jalapeño chili
   (about 1 small)
1 large clove garlic, finely chopped
2 cans (16 ounces) kidney beans, drained
¼ cup snipped fresh cilantro

Heat all ingredients except cilantro to boiling in 10-inch nonstick skillet; reduce heat. Cover and simmer until vegetables are tender, about 7 minutes. Stir in cilantro.

4 SERVINGS, ABOUT 1½ CUPS EACH

MICROWAVE DIRECTIONS: Decrease chicken broth to ½ cup. Place all ingredients except beans and cilantro in 2-quart microwavable casserole. Cover tightly and microwave on high (100%) 6 minutes; stir in beans. Cover and microwave until vegetables are tender, 4 to 6 minutes longer. Stir in cilantro.

Skillet Beans and Squash

Per serving:			
Calories	170	Fat	5 g
Protein	8 g	Cholesterol	5 mg
Carbohydrate	23 g	Sodium	1140 mg

Per serving:			
Calories	155	Fat	5 g
Protein	7 g	Cholesterol	10 mg
Carbohydrate	20 g	Sodium	1270 mg

Black Bean Soup

½ cup chopped onion (about 1 medium)
1 large clove garlic, finely chopped
1 slice bacon, cut into pieces
3 cups chicken broth
1 cup water
½ cup coarsely chopped carrot (about
    1 medium)
½ cup coarsely chopped celery (about
    1 medium stalk)
½ cup dried black beans (about 4 ounces)
2 tablespoons snipped parsley
1 teaspoon dried oregano leaves
½ small dried hot pepper, seeded and crumbled
4 lemon wedges

Cook and stir onion, garlic and bacon in 3-quart nonstick saucepan over medium heat until onion is tender, about 3 minutes. Stir in remaining ingredients except lemon wedges. Heat to boiling; boil 2 minutes. Reduce heat; cover and simmer until beans are tender, about 2 hours.

Place 1 cup of the soup in blender container or workbowl of food processor fitted with steel blade. Cover and blend on high speed until of uniform consistency, about 30 seconds; stir into remaining soup mixture. Serve with lemon wedges.

4 SERVINGS, ABOUT ¾ CUP EACH

Gorgonzola–White Bean Soup

One of Italy's premier cheeses teams with one of her favorite beans. Gorgonzola tastes to some like a strong Danish blue cheese. It makes a smooth, rich-tasting soup.

½ cup chopped onion (about 1 medium)
½ cup chopped celery (about 1 medium stalk)
½ cup chopped carrot (about 1 medium)
1 tablespoon reduced-calorie margarine
3 cups chicken broth
1 cup ¼-inch leek slices (about 1 medium)
½ cup dried white beans (about 4 ounces)
1 cup skim milk
1 ounce Gorgonzola cheese, crumbled

Cook onion, celery and carrot in margarine in 3-quart nonstick saucepan over medium heat until onion is tender, about 3 minutes. Stir in chicken broth, leek and beans. Heat to boiling; boil 2 minutes. Reduce heat and simmer until beans are tender, about 2 hours. (Add water during cooking if liquid does not cover beans.) Stir in milk.

Place 1 cup of the soup in blender container or workbowl of food processor fitted with steel blade. Cover and blend on high speed until of uniform consistency, about 30 seconds; stir into remaining soup mixture. Stir in cheese until melted.

4 SERVINGS, ABOUT 1 CUP EACH

Gorgonzola-White Bean Soup

Per serving:			
Calories	300	Fat	10 g
Protein	16 g	Cholesterol	25 mg
Carbohydrate	38 g	Sodium	170 mg

Bean and Cheese Tacos

These flour tortillas are filled with tender beans and creamy ricotta. The spark of fresh cilantro is not to be missed here. Cilantro, sometimes known as fresh coriander, Mexican parsley or Chinese parsley, can be found in most markets.

Red Salsa (right)
1 can (8 ounces) kidney beans, drained (reserve liquid)
1 clove garlic, finely chopped
4 8-inch flour tortillas
1 cup part skim ricotta cheese (8 ounces)
¼ cup grated Parmesan cheese
¼ cup chopped green onions (with tops)
1 tablespoon snipped fresh cilantro or 1 teaspoon dried cilantro leaves

Prepare Red Salsa. Heat oven to 350°. Mash beans and garlic. (Add 1 to 2 tablespoons reserved bean liquid if beans are dry.) Place tortillas on ungreased cookie sheet. Spread about ¼ cup of the bean mixture on half of each tortilla to within ½ inch of edge. Mix cheeses, onions and cilantro; spread over beans. Fold tortillas over filling. Bake until tortillas begin to brown and filling is hot, about 10 minutes. Serve with Red Salsa.

4 SERVINGS, 1 TACO WITH ABOUT ¼ CUP SALSA EACH

Red Salsa

1 large clove garlic, finely chopped
1 cup chopped tomato (about 1 medium)
¼ cup chopped green onions (with tops)
2 to 3 teaspoons chopped jalapeño chili (about ½ small)
1½ teaspoons finely snipped fresh cilantro, if desired
1½ teaspoon lemon juice
1 teaspoon snipped fresh oregano leaves or ½ teaspoon dried oregano leaves

Mix all ingredients; cover and refrigerate at least 1 hour.

MICROWAVE DIRECTIONS: Prepare Red Salsa and tortillas as directed. Place double layer of microwavable paper towels in rectangular microwavable dish, 12 × 7½ × 2 inches. Place tortillas, folds to outside edges, in dish. Cover with waxed paper and microwave on high (100%) 2 minutes; rotate ½ turn. Microwave until hot, 2 to 5 minutes longer.

Per serving:			
Calories	110	Fat	0 g
Protein	7 g	Cholesterol	0 mg
Carbohydrate	21 g	Sodium	480 mg

Middle Eastern Stew

Lentils are loved all over the world, but nowhere more so than in the Middle East. The dusky flavor of cumin is often added to lentil dishes.

3 cups water
1¼ cups dried lentils (about 8 ounces)
2 cups 1-inch potato cubes (about 2 medium)
½ cup chopped onion (about 1 medium)
½ cup chopped celery (about 1 stalk)
2 cloves garlic, finely chopped
1 tablespoon finely snipped parsley
1 tablespoon instant beef bouillon
1 teaspoon salt
1 teaspoon ground cumin
2 cups ½-inch zucchini slices (about 2 medium)
Lemon wedges

Heat water and lentils to boiling in 4-quart nonstick Dutch oven; reduce heat. Cover and cook until lentils are almost tender, about 30 minutes. Stir in potatoes, onion, celery, garlic, parsley, bouillon (dry), salt and cumin. Cover and cook until potatoes are tender, about 20 minutes.

Stir in zucchini; cover and cook until zucchini is tender, 10 to 15 minutes. Serve with lemon wedges.

6 SERVINGS, ABOUT 1 CUP EACH

Per serving:			
Calories	75	Fat	1 g
Protein	5 g	Cholesterol	0 mg
Carbohydrate	11 g	Sodium	610 mg

Herbed Vegetables and Lentils

1½ cups chicken broth
¾ cup dried lentils (about 4 ounces)
1 cup sliced zucchini (about 1 small)
1 cup sliced yellow squash (about 1 small)
½ cup sliced green onions (with tops)
1½ teaspoons snipped fresh oregano leaves
   or ½ teaspoon dried oregano leaves
¼ teaspoon ground thyme
2 large cloves garlic, finely chopped
1 jar (2 ounces) diced pimientos, drained
2 tablespoons grated Parmesan cheese

Heat chicken broth and lentils to boiling in 2-quart nonstick saucepan, stirring occasionally. Cover and simmer 20 minutes. Stir in zucchini, squash, onions, oregano, thyme and garlic. Heat to boiling; reduce heat and simmer 5 minutes. Stir in pimientos. Cook uncovered until vegetables are crisp-tender and mixture is of desired consistency, 2 to 3 minutes longer. Sprinkle with cheese.

4 SERVINGS, ABOUT ¾ CUP EACH

MICROWAVE DIRECTIONS: Increase chicken broth to 2 cups. Place broth and lentils in 2-quart microwavable casserole. Cover tightly and microwave on high (100%) 20 minutes. Stir in zucchini, squash, onions, oregano, thyme and garlic. Cover and microwave on medium (50%) 5 minutes; stir in pimientos. Microwave uncovered until vegetables are crisp-tender and mixture is of desired consistency, 2 to 4 minutes longer. Sprinkle with cheese.

Bean and Cheese Tacos (page 148) and Herbed Vegetables and
Lentils (page 149)

Octoberfest

....

PRETZEL PORK WITH SAUERKRAUT

RELISH (PAGE 114)

VEGETABLE-STUFFED POTATOES (PAGE 169)

CABBAGE-APPLE MEDLEY (PAGE 160)

WHOLE GREEN BEANS

GINGERBREAD WITH ORANGE SAUCE (PAGE 221)

VEGETABLES

Clockwise from top: Vegetable-stuffed Potatoes (page 169),
Pretzel Pork with Sauerkraut Relish (page 114) and
Cabbage-Apple Medley (page 160)

Healthy Hints

- Season fresh, cooked vegetables with lemon juice, broth or herbs and spices instead of calorie-laden butter or cream.
- Vegetables that are sliced diagonally are attractive and cook slightly faster than regularly sliced vegetables because more surface area is exposed to the heat.
- Cutting vegetables into julienne strips or slices creates an effective illusion that there are more vegetables. A food processor can be a real time-saver here.
- Most vegetables need a gentle scrubbing before they are cooked. Leaving the skin intact saves not only preparation time, but nutrients as well.
- Buy frozen vegetables in loose-pack bags so that you can mix and match variety and quantity. Avoid frozen vegetables in heavy cream sauces because they contain large amounts of fat. Be sure to check the labels carefully.

Deli Counters

To save time at home, buy prepared fresh vegetables from the salad bar for stir-fries, soups, salads and snacks. For a change of pace, serve marinated vegetable dishes hot, but drain the marinade before serving to reduce the fat content. Avoid creamed vegetables.

Calories	40	Fat	0 g
Protein	2 g	Cholesterol	0 mg
Carbohydrate	9 g	Sodium	145 mg

Calories	45	Fat	0 g
Protein	2 g	Cholesterol	0 mg
Carbohydrate	10 g	Sodium	115 mg

Creole Artichoke Hearts

Stewed tomatoes and Creole seasoning give this dish a Southern slant. You can slice the celery and green onions on the diagonal for a festive look.

1 package (9 ounces) frozen artichoke hearts*
1 can (14½ ounces) stewed tomatoes, drained
⅓ cup thinly sliced celery
¼ to ½ teaspoon Creole or Cajun seasoning
⅛ teaspoon pepper
½ cup 1-inch pieces green onions with tops (about 3)

Heat all ingredients except onions to boiling; reduce heat. Cover and simmer 5 minutes, stirring occasionally. Stir in onions. Cook until celery is crisp-tender, 2 to 3 minutes longer.

4 SERVINGS, ABOUT ⅔ CUP EACH

MICROWAVE DIRECTIONS: Place all ingredients except onions in 1½-quart microwavable casserole. Cover tightly and microwave on high (100%) 4 minutes; stir in onions. Cover and microwave until celery is crisp-tender, 2 to 3 minutes longer.

*1 can (14 ounces) artichoke hearts, drained and quartered, can be substituted for the frozen artichoke hearts.

Italian Green Beans and Tomatoes

1 package (10 ounces) frozen Italian green beans
1 can (14½ ounces) Italian tomatoes, drained and cut into pieces
¼ cup chopped onion (about 1 small)
1 clove garlic, finely chopped
1 teaspoon snipped fresh oregano leaves or ½ teaspoon dried oregano leaves
1 teaspoon snipped fresh basil leaves or ½ teaspoon dried basil leaves
⅛ teaspoon pepper

Heat all ingredients to boiling; reduce heat. Cover and simmer until beans are crisp-tender, 7 to 10 minutes.

4 SERVINGS, ABOUT ⅔ CUP EACH

MICROWAVE DIRECTIONS: Place all ingredients in 1½-quart microwavable casserole. Cover tightly and microwave on high (100%) 5 minutes; stir. Cover and microwave until beans are crisp-tender, 3 to 5 minutes longer.

Sole Gratin (page 58),
Asparagus with Toasted Cashews and Sweet and Sour Beets

Calories	40	Fat	2 g
Protein	2 g	Cholesterol	0 mg
Carbohydrate	3 g	Sodium	30 mg

Calories	55	Fat	0 g
Protein	1 g	Cholesterol	0 mg
Carbohydrate	13 g	Sodium	330 mg

Asparagus with Toasted Cashews

This may be the easiest way ever invented to cook asparagus. If the stalks are very tender, reduce the baking time.

3 tablespoons chopped dry roasted cashews
1½ pounds fresh asparagus*

Heat oven to 400°. Place cashews in ungreased shallow pan. Bake until light brown, 3 to 5 minutes.

Arrange asparagus in ungreased rectangular baking dish, 13 × 9 × 2 inches. Cover and bake until tender, 20 to 30 minutes. Sprinkle with cashews.

6 SERVINGS, ABOUT 8 MEDIUM SPEARS EACH

*2 packages (10 ounces each) frozen asparagus spears can be substituted for the fresh asparagus. Bake as directed except—separate spears after 10 minutes.

Sweet and Sour Beets

1 can (16 ounces) sliced beets, drained (reserve liquid)
1 tablespoon cornstarch
1 tablespoon sugar
½ teaspoon salt
Dash of pepper
¼ cup vinegar

Add enough water to reserved beet liquid to measure ⅔ cup. Mix cornstarch, sugar, salt and pepper in 1½-quart saucepan. Gradually stir in reserved beet liquid and vinegar. Cook until mixture thickens and boils, stirring constantly. Boil and stir 1 minute. Stir in beets; heat through.

4 SERVINGS, ABOUT ½ CUP EACH

Per serving:			
Calories	60	Fat	2 g
Protein	4 g	Cholesterol	0 mg
Carbohydrate	7 g	Sodium	115 mg

Per serving:			
Calories	65	Fat	0 g
Protein	3 g	Cholesterol	0 mg
Carbohydrate	14 g	Sodium	95 mg

Broccoli with Mushrooms and Thyme

1 pound broccoli, cut lengthwise into thin spears*
1½ cups mushrooms, sliced (about 4 ounces)
½ teaspoon instant beef bouillon
¾ teaspoon snipped fresh thyme leaves or
  ¼ teaspoon dried thyme leaves
2 teaspoons reduced-calorie margarine

Place steamer basket in ½ inch water (water should not touch bottom of basket). Place broccoli in basket. Cover tightly and heat to boiling; reduce heat. Steam until tender, about 15 minutes. Cook and stir mushrooms, bouillon (dry) and thyme in margarine until mushrooms are hot, about 3 minutes. Toss with broccoli.

4 SERVINGS, ABOUT 3 SPEARS EACH

MICROWAVE DIRECTIONS: Place ¼ cup water and ½ teaspoon salt in 2-quart microwavable casserole. Arrange fresh broccoli spears with flowery ends in center of casserole. Cover tightly and microwave on high (100%) 3 minutes; rotate casserole ½ turn. Microwave until tender, 2 to 4 minutes longer; drain. Mix remaining ingredients in 1-quart microwavable casserole. Cover and microwave until mushrooms are hot, 1 to 2 minutes. Toss with broccoli.

*1 package (10 ounces) frozen broccoli spears can be substituted for fresh broccoli. Cook as directed on package; drain.

Festive Broccoli and Corn

1 package (10 ounces) frozen broccoli cuts
  or broccoli flowerets
1 cup frozen whole kernel corn
½ cup chopped onion (about 1 medium)
½ cup water
2 teaspoons snipped fresh basil leaves or
  ½ teaspoon dried basil leaves
½ teaspoon instant vegetable bouillon (dry)
1 clove garlic, finely chopped
1 jar (2 ounces) diced pimientos, drained

Heat all ingredients to boiling; reduce heat. Cover and simmer until broccoli is crisp-tender, 4 to 5 minutes.

4 SERVINGS, ABOUT ⅔ CUP EACH

MICROWAVE DIRECTIONS: Omit water. Place all ingredients in 1½-quart microwavable casserole. Cover tightly and microwave on high (100%) 5 minutes; stir, separating flowerets if necessary. Cover and microwave until broccoli is crisp-tender, 2 to 4 minutes longer.

Per serving:			
Calories	60	Fat	4 g
Protein	2 g	Cholesterol	0 mg
Carbohydrate	4 g	Sodium	430 mg

Per serving:			
Calories	65	Fat	2 g
Protein	3 g	Cholesterol	0 mg
Carbohydrate	10 g	Sodium	90 mg

Bok Choy Stir-Fry

The pale, Oriental bok choy has become nearly a staple in American markets. Bok choy leaves cook more rapidly than the stems, so they are added for only a brief toss in the skillet.

1½ pounds bok choy
1 tablespoon cornstarch
2 tablespoons soy sauce
1 tablespoon vegetable oil
1 tablespoon reduced-calorie margarine
2 teaspoons finely chopped gingerroot
1 clove garlic, finely chopped
2 tablespoons water

Separate bok choy leaves from stems. Cut leaves into ½-inch strips; cut stems into ¼-inch slices. Mix cornstarch and soy sauce. Heat oil and margarine in 12-inch skillet over medium-high heat until margarine is melted. Add gingerroot and garlic; stir-fry until garlic is light brown. Add bok choy stems; stir-fry 2 minutes. Add water; cover and cook until stems are crisp-tender, about 2 minutes. Stir in cornstarch mixture and bok choy leaves; stir-fry until leaves are wilted, 1 to 2 minutes.

6 SERVINGS, ABOUT ½ CUP EACH

Savory Brussels Sprouts

Fresh Brussels sprouts cook more quickly and evenly if they are halved first. These cabbages-in-miniature are sauced with a rich-tasting mustard cream, flavored with celery seed.

¾ pound Brussels sprouts
Dijon Mustard Sauce (below)

Cut each Brussels sprout into halves. Place steamer basket in ½ inch water (water should not touch bottom of basket). Place Brussels sprouts in basket. Cover tightly and heat to boiling; reduce heat. Steam until tender, 15 to 20 minutes. Serve with Dijon Mustard Sauce.

4 SERVINGS, ABOUT ½ CUP VEGETABLES AND 2 TABLESPOONS SAUCE EACH

Dijon Mustard Sauce

½ cup nonfat plain yogurt
1 tablespoon reduced-calorie mayonnaise or salad dressing
1½ teaspoons Dijon-style mustard
1 teaspoon celery seed

Heat all ingredients, stirring occasionally, just until hot (do not boil).

Per serving:

Calories	80	Fat	2 g
Protein	2 g	Cholesterol	2 mg
Carbohydrate	15 g	Sodium	35 mg

Per serving:

Calories	30	Fat	0 g
Protein	1 g	Cholesterol	0 mg
Carbohydrate	8 g	Sodium	20 mg

Cabbage-Apple Medley

Even though raisins are calorie-concentrated, they're not forbidden. Chop them up and sprinkle them around; they go further that way.

2 cups shredded red cabbage
1 cup chopped pared or unpared tart apple (about 1 medium)
1 cup chopped turnip (about 1 medium)
½ cup sugar-free lemon or apple-flavored carbonated beverage or apple juice
2 tablespoons chopped raisins
1 tablespoon finely chopped onion
2 teaspoons apple cider vinegar
1 tablespoon finely chopped toasted almonds
4 teaspoons reduced-calorie sour cream

Heat all ingredients except almonds and sour cream to boiling; reduce heat. Cover and simmer until cabbage is tender, 5 to 8 minutes; drain. Sprinkle with almonds and top with sour cream.

4 SERVINGS, ABOUT ⅔ CUP EACH

MICROWAVE DIRECTIONS: Decrease carbonated beverage to ¼ cup. Mix all ingredients except almonds and sour cream in 1½-quart microwavable casserole. Cover tightly and microwave on high (100%) 4 minutes; stir. Cover and microwave until vegetables are crisp-tender, 3 to 5 minutes longer. Let stand covered 1 minute. Sprinkle with almonds and top with sour cream.

Honey-Mint Carrots

3 cups ¼-inch diagonal carrot slices* (about 6 medium)
1 tablespoon honey
1 tablespoon snipped fresh mint leaves or 1 teaspoon dried mint leaves

Heat 1 inch water to boiling. Add carrots. Heat to boiling; reduce heat. Cover and cook until crisp-tender, about 10 minutes; drain. Toss with honey and mint leaves.

6 SERVINGS, ABOUT ½ CUP EACH

*1 bag (16 ounces) frozen sliced carrots, cooked and drained, can be substituted for the fresh carrots.

Honey-Mint Carrots and Savory Brussels Sprouts (page 159)

Cauliflower Wedges with Salsa

1 medium head cauliflower (about 2 pounds)
2½ cups chopped seeded tomatoes (about 3 medium)
½ cup chopped onion (about 1 medium)
1 can (4 ounces) chopped green chilies, drained
½ teaspoon salt
¼ teaspoon ground cinnamon
2 tablespoons chopped ripe olives

Heat 1 inch water to boiling. Add cauliflower. Cover and heat to boiling; reduce heat. Simmer until tender, 20 to 25 minutes; drain. Cook and stir remaining ingredients except olives in 10-inch nonstick skillet over medium heat until hot. Place cauliflower on serving plate. Cut into 8 wedges; separate wedges slightly. Spoon tomato mixture over and around cauliflower wedges. Sprinkle with olives.

8 SERVINGS, ⅛ CAULIFLOWER AND ABOUT ⅓ CUP SAUCE EACH

MICROWAVE DIRECTIONS: Cut cone-shaped center from core of cauliflower. Place cauliflower and ¼ cup water in microwavable pie plate, 9 × 1¼ inches. Cover tightly and microwave on high (100%) 4 minutes; rotate pie plate ½ turn. Microwave until tender, 3 to 4 minutes longer; drain. Mix remaining ingredients except olives in microwavable 1½-quart casserole. Microwave uncovered until hot, 4 to 7 minutes. Continue as directed.

NOTE: Tomatoes vary in moisture. If necessary, spoon off extra liquid before topping cauliflower.

Cauliflower with Cheeses

4 cups small cauliflowerets (about 1½ pounds)
1 cup small curd low-fat cottage cheese, well drained
½ cup shredded sharp Cheddar cheese (2 ounces)
1 jar (2 ounces) diced pimientos, drained
1 tablespoon snipped fresh dill weed or ½ teaspoon dried dill weed

Heat 1 inch water to boiling. Add cauliflower. Cover and heat to boiling; reduce heat. Simmer until crisp-tender, 8 to 10 minutes; drain. Stir in cheeses and pimientos; sprinkle with dill weed.

6 SERVINGS, ABOUT ⅔ CUP EACH

MICROWAVE DIRECTIONS: Place cauliflower and ¼ cup water in 2-quart microwavable casserole. Cover tightly and microwave on high (100%) 4 minutes; stir. Cover and microwave until crisp-tender, 4 to 7 minutes longer; drain. Continue as directed.

Per serving:			
Calories	55	Fat	0 g
Protein	5 g	Cholesterol	0 mg
Carbohydrate	9 g	Sodium	330 mg

Cold Cucumber-Yogurt Soup

2 medium cucumbers
1½ cups nonfat plain yogurt
½ teaspoon salt
1 teaspoon snipped fresh mint leaves or
    ¼ teaspoon dried mint leaves
⅛ teaspoon white pepper

Cut 4 thin slices from cucumber; reserve. Cut remaining cucumber into ¾-inch chunks. Place half the cucumber chunks and ¼ cup of the yogurt in blender container or workbowl of food processor fitted with steel blade. Cover and blend on high speed until smooth.

Add remaining cucumber chunks, the salt, mint and white pepper. Cover and blend until smooth. Add remaining yogurt; cover and blend on low speed until smooth. Cover and refrigerate at least 1 hour. Garnish with reserved cucumber slices and fresh mint leaves if desired.

4 SERVINGS, ABOUT ¾ CUP EACH

Per serving:			
Calories	70	Fat	2 g
Protein	4 g	Cholesterol	70 mg
Carbohydrate	10 g	Sodium	210 mg

Fluffy Corn Pudding

This version of the Southern classic has a sweet flavor and puffs up high.

1 can (8 ounces) cream-style corn
1 egg yolk
⅛ teaspoon ground nutmeg
3 egg whites
¼ teaspoon cream of tartar

Heat oven to 350°. Spray 4-cup soufflé dish or 1-quart casserole with nonstick cooking spray. Mix corn, egg yolk and nutmeg in 1-quart saucepan. Cook over low heat until mixture is slightly thickened, stirring constantly; remove from heat.

Beat egg whites and cream of tartar in medium bowl until stiff. Stir about one-fourth of the egg whites into sauce mixture; fold into remaining egg whites.

Carefully pour into soufflé dish. Set soufflé dish in pan of hot water (1 inch deep). Bake until puffed and golden and knife inserted halfway between center and edge comes out clean, 40 to 45 minutes. Serve immediately.

4 SERVINGS, ABOUT 1 CUP EACH

Per serving:

Calories	105	Fat	4 g
Protein	3 g	Cholesterol	0 mg
Carbohydrate	14 g	Sodium	140 mg

Per serving:

Calories	80	Fat	1 g
Protein	5 g	Cholesterol	2 mg
Carbohydrate	14 g	Sodium	90 mg

Baked Eggplant with Curry Sauce

Yogurt will curdle when heated, unless it is warmed over low heat. The addition of a small quantity of reduced-calorie mayonnaise helps prevent curdling.

1 small eggplant (about 1 pound)
1 tablespoon plus 1 teaspoon reduced-calorie margarine, melted
1 teaspoon lemon juice
½ cup herb-seasoned stuffing mix
Curry Sauce (below)

Heat oven to 400°. Cut eggplant into 8 slices; place in jelly roll pan, 15½ × 10½ × 1 inch, sprayed with nonstick cooking spray. Mix margarine and lemon juice; brush over eggplant. Sprinkle 1 tablespoon stuffing mix on each slice. Bake uncovered until eggplant is tender and crumbs are golden brown, 20 to 25 minutes. Serve hot with Curry Sauce.

4 SERVINGS, WITH ABOUT 2 TABLESPOONS SAUCE EACH

Curry Sauce

½ cup nonfat plain yogurt
1 tablespoon reduced-calorie mayonnaise or salad dressing
½ teaspoon curry powder

Heat all ingredients, stirring occasionally, just until hot (do not boil).

Peas in Tomato Shells

Serve these melting tomatoes in individual dishes to enjoy every juicy bit.

5 medium tomatoes (about 1½ pounds)
1 package (10 ounces) frozen green peas
2 tablespoons finely chopped green onions (with tops)
1 tablespoon snipped fresh dill weed or 1 teaspoon dried dill weed
⅛ teaspoon pepper
2 tablespoons reduced-calorie sour cream

Remove stem ends from tomatoes; remove pulp to wall of each tomato, leaving bottom ½ inch thick. Cut thin slice from bottom of each tomato to prevent tipping, if necessary.

Heat oven to 350°. Separate peas under running cold water; drain well. Mix peas, onion, dill weed and pepper. Place tomatoes in ungreased pie plate, 9 × 1¼ inches. Fill tomatoes with pea mixture. Bake uncovered until tomatoes are heated through, 20 to 25 minutes. Place in individual serving dishes. Top with sour cream.

5 SERVINGS

Per serving:			
Calories	35	Fat	1 g
Protein	2 g	Cholesterol	0 mg
Carbohydrate	5 g	Sodium	10 mg

Per serving:			
Calories	40	Fat	1 g
Protein	1 g	Cholesterol	0 mg
Carbohydrate	7 g	Sodium	200 mg

Lemon-Pepper Vegetables

1 cup ¼-inch yellow squash slices (about
   1 medium)
1 small red bell pepper, cut into ¼-inch strips
⅓ cup diagonally cut celery slices (about
   1 small stalk)
⅓ cup 1-inch green onion pieces with tops
   (about 3)
1 teaspoon vegetable oil
1 tablespoon lemon juice
¼ teaspoon lemon pepper
4 ounces Chinese pea pods*

Cook and stir squash, bell pepper, celery and
onions in oil in 10-inch nonstick skillet over
medium-high heat until pepper is crisp-tender,
about 2 minutes. Stir in remaining ingredients; cook and stir until pea pods are hot,
about 1 minute longer.

6 SERVINGS, ABOUT ½ CUP EACH

MICROWAVE DIRECTIONS: Mix all ingredients except pea pods in 1½-quart microwavable casserole. Cover tightly and microwave on high
(100%) 3 minutes. Stir in pea pods. Cover
and microwave until pea pods are hot, 1 to 3
minutes longer.

*1 package (6 ounces) frozen pea pods,
thawed, can be substituted for pea pods.

Colorful Pepper Skillet

This dish is simply beautiful. Four brightly colored peppers, shiny with a touch of oil, are
seasoned with cumin seed and the fresh flavor
of cilantro.

1 teaspoon olive or vegetable oil
4 small bell peppers (green, purple, red and
   yellow), cut into strips
1 medium onion, thinly sliced
2 cloves garlic, finely chopped
1 tablespoon snipped fresh cilantro or
   1 teaspoon dried cilantro leaves
1 teaspoon cumin seed

Heat oil in 10-inch nonstick skillet over medium-high heat until hot. Stir in remaining ingredients. Cook, stirring occasionally, until
peppers are crisp-tender, 4 to 5 minutes.

6 SERVINGS, ABOUT ⅔ CUP EACH

Onion and Pepper Tart

Per serving:			
Calories	120	Fat	4 g
Protein	5 g	Cholesterol	45 mg
Carbohydrate	17 g	Sodium	150 mg

Onion and Pepper Tart

Crust (right)
2 cups chopped onion (about 2 large)
1 medium red or green bell pepper, cut into
   thin slices
2 cloves garlic, finely chopped
¼ teaspoon pepper
1 tablespoon snipped fresh thyme leaves or
   1 teaspoon dried thyme leaves
1 egg
1 egg white
¼ cup skim milk
1 tablespoon grated Parmesan cheese

Heat oven to 400°. Prepare Crust. Roll into
9-inch circle; fit into bottom and up side of
quiche dish or round pan, 8 × 1½ inches. Prick
bottom of crust with fork 6 to 8 times. Bake
until crust begins to brown, 8 to 10 minutes.

Cook and stir onions, bell pepper, garlic and
pepper in nonstick skillet until onion is tender. Spoon into crust; sprinkle with thyme.
Beat egg, egg white and milk; pour over onion mixture. Sprinkle with cheese. Bake until
edge is golden brown and center is set, 20 to
25 minutes. Let stand 5 minutes.

6 SERVINGS

Crust

⅔ cup all-purpose flour
¼ teaspoon baking powder
¼ teaspoon salt
2 tablespoons nonfat plain yogurt
1 tablespoon vegetable oil
1 tablespoon cold water

Mix flour, baking powder and salt in small
bowl. Beat yogurt, oil and water until blended;
stir into flour mixture until dough forms. If
dough is dry, add 1 to 2 teaspoons water.
Gather dough into a ball; knead until smooth,
about 20 times. Cover; let stand 3 to 5 minutes.

Per serving:			
Calories	40	Fat	1 g
Protein	3 g	Cholesterol	0 mg
Carbohydrate	6 g	Sodium	770 mg

Easy Spinach Soup

2½ cups water
1 tablespoon instant beef or chicken bouillon
1 package (10 ounces) frozen chopped spinach
1 can (4 ounces) mushroom stems and pieces,
   undrained
1 jar (2 ounces) sliced pimientos, drained
½ teaspoon garlic salt
Dash of dried rosemary leaves
4 tablespoons nonfat plain yogurt

Heat water, bouillon (dry) and spinach to boiling; break up spinach with fork. Cover and
cook until tender, about 3 minutes. Stir in
mushrooms, pimientos, garlic salt and rosemary; heat until hot. Garnish with yogurt.

4 SERVINGS, ABOUT 1 CUP EACH

Per serving:

Calories	75	Fat	0 g
Protein	3 g	Cholesterol	0 mg
Carbohydrate	16 g	Sodium	55 mg

Per serving:

Calories	80	Fat	3 g
Protein	2 g	Cholesterol	0 mg
Carbohydrate	11 g	Sodium	130 mg

Spinach Mélange

1 package (10 ounces) frozen chopped spinach
1 jar (4 ounces) mushroom stems and pieces, drained
1 can (8 ounces) sliced water chestnuts, drained
1 medium tomato, seeded and chopped
1 tablespoon finely chopped onion
1 medium clove garlic, finely chopped
2 tablespoons nonfat plain yogurt

Cook spinach as directed on package; drain. Stir in remaining ingredients except yogurt. Heat over low heat just until heated through, stirring occasionally; drain. Top with yogurt.

4 SERVINGS, ABOUT ⅔ CUP EACH

MICROWAVE DIRECTIONS: Place spinach in 1½-quart microwavable casserole. Cover tightly and microwave on high (100%) 5 minutes; break up and stir. Cover tightly and microwave until tender, 2 to 3 minutes longer; drain. Stir in remaining ingredients except yogurt. Cover tightly and microwave until hot, 1 to 3 minutes. Top with yogurt.

Gingered Spinach

Wash fresh spinach very thoroughly in cold water to rid it completely of sand.

2 teaspoons finely chopped gingerroot
2 teaspoons peanut or vegetable oil
¼ teaspoon sesame oil
1 teaspoon soy sauce
½ pound fresh spinach
1 cup julienne strips jícama (about 4 ounces)
2 teaspoons toasted sesame seed

Cook and stir gingerroot in peanut and sesame oils in 10-inch nonstick skillet over medium-high heat. Stir in soy sauce and half of the spinach. Cook and stir until spinach begins to wilt. Stir in remaining spinach and the jícama. Cook and stir until spinach is wilted and jícama is hot, about 2 minutes longer. Sprinkle with sesame seed.

4 SERVINGS, ABOUT ½ CUP EACH

Per serving:

Calories	95	Fat	0 g
Protein	5 g	Cholesterol	0 mg
Carbohydrate	19 g	Sodium	180 mg

Vegetable-stuffed Potatoes

2 medium baking potatoes (about
  6 ounces each)
½ cup nonfat plain yogurt
2 tablespoons chopped onion
¼ teaspoon salt
⅛ teaspoon pepper
1 cup hot cooked chopped broccoli
1 tablespoon chopped pimientos

Heat oven to 375°. Prick potatoes with fork.
Bake until tender, about 1 hour. Cool slightly;
cut potatoes lengthwise into halves. Scoop
out inside, leaving thin shell. Mash potatoes
until no lumps remain. Beat in yogurt, onion,
salt and pepper until light and fluffy. Stir in
broccoli and pimientos.

Heat oven to 450°. Fill shells with potato
mixture. Place on ungreased cooking sheet.
Bake uncovered until hot, about 10 minutes.

4 SERVINGS

MICROWAVE DIRECTIONS: Prick potatoes with
fork. Place in microwave oven. Microwave
uncovered on high (100%) 4 minutes; turn
potatoes over. Microwave until tender, 3 to 5
minutes longer. Let stand 5 minutes. Continue
as directed. Arrange stuffed potatoes in circle on 10-inch microwavable plate. Cover with
waxed paper and microwave until hot, 2 to 3
minutes.

Per serving:

Calories	45	Fat	3 g
Protein	2 g	Cholesterol	0 mg
Carbohydrate	4 g	Sodium	110 mg

Triple Mushroom Stir-Fry

Dried black mushrooms are also known as
Chinese dried mushrooms or winter mushrooms. They're more dark brown than actually black. Enoki mushrooms are delicate
newcomers from Japan, fragile-looking and
long-stemmed, sometimes mistaken for bean
sprouts.

8 medium dried black mushrooms
2 teaspoons vegetable oil
3 cups ¼-inch mushroom slices (about
  8 ounces)
1 jar (7 ounces) enoki mushrooms, drained
1 clove garlic, finely chopped
½ cup 1-inch green onion pieces, with tops
  (about 3)

Soak black mushrooms in warm water to cover
until soft, about 30 minutes; drain. Remove
and discard stems; slice caps.

Heat oil in wok or 10-inch nonstick skillet
over medium-high heat until hot. Add mushrooms and garlic; stir-fry 1 minute. Add onions; stir-fry 1 minute longer.

4 SERVINGS, ABOUT ⅔ CUP EACH

Per serving:

Calories	55	Fat	0 g
Protein	4 g	Cholesterol	0 mg
Carbohydrate	10 g	Sodium	125 mg

Steamed Vegetables with Herb Sauce

Herb Sauce (below)
3 cups caulifloweretts (about 1 pound)
2 medium zucchini, cut into 1-inch slices
1 medium red or green bell pepper, cut into
  ¼-inch strips
1 lemon half

Prepare Herb Sauce. Place steamer basket in ½ inch water (water should not touch bottom of basket). Place cauliflower, zucchini and bell pepper in basket. Cover tightly and heat to boiling; reduce heat. Steam until vegetables are crisp-tender, about 6 minutes. Arrange vegetables on plate; squeeze lemon over vegetables. Serve with Herb Sauce.

6 SERVINGS, ABOUT 1 CUP VEGETABLES AND 2 TABLESPOONS SAUCE EACH

Herb Sauce

¾ cup nonfat plain yogurt
1 teaspoon honey
¼ teaspoon salt
¾ teaspoon snipped fresh basil leaves or
  ¼ teaspoon dried basil leaves
¾ teaspoon snipped fresh tarragon leaves or
  ¼ teaspoon dried tarragon leaves
1 clove garlic, crushed
Pinch of dried dill weed

Mix all ingredients. Cover and refrigerate at least 2 hours but no longer than 24 hours.

MICROWAVE DIRECTIONS: Prepare Herb Sauce. Place cauliflower, zucchini, bell pepper, ¼ cup water and ¼ teaspoon salt in 2-quart microwavable casserole. Cover tightly and microwave on high (100%) 4 minutes; stir. Cover and microwave until crisp-tender, 3 to 5 minutes longer; drain. Continue as directed.

Per serving:

Calories	80	Fat	1 g
Protein	2 g	Cholesterol	0 mg
Carbohydrate	18 g	Sodium	10 mg

Poppy Seed Squash

1 medium zucchini, cut into julienne strips
1 small yellow squash, cut into julienne strips
1½ cups julienne strips jícama (about 6 ounces)
1 tablespoon apple cider vinegar
1 tablespoon honey
1 teaspoon poppy seed
2 drops red pepper sauce

Place steamer basket in ½ inch water (water should not touch bottom of basket). Place zucchini, yellow squash and jícama in basket. Cover tightly and heat to boiling; reduce heat. Steam until squash is crisp-tender, 3 to 5 minutes; drain. Mix remaining ingredients; stir into vegetables.

4 SERVINGS, ABOUT ⅔ CUP EACH

Poppy Seed Squash and Sherried Orange Chicken (page 84)

Ratatouille

Per serving:			
Calories	25	Fat	0 g
Protein	1 g	Cholesterol	0 mg
Carbohydrate	5 g	Sodium	140 mg

Per serving:			
Calories	50	Fat	0 g
Protein	2 g	Cholesterol	0 mg
Carbohydrate	7 g	Sodium	5 mg

Ratatouille

3 cups ½-inch cubes eggplant (about
   ½ pound)
1 cup ¼-inch zucchini slices (1 small)
2 cloves garlic, chopped
1 small onion, sliced
½ medium green bell pepper, cut into strips
2 tablespoons snipped parsley
1 tablespoon snipped fresh basil leaves or
   ½ teaspoon dried basil leaves
2 tablespoons water
½ teaspoon salt
¼ teaspoon pepper
2 medium tomatoes, cut into eighths

Heat all ingredients except tomatoes in 10-inch skillet over medium heat until vegetables are tender, about 10 minutes. Remove from heat; stir in tomatoes. Cover and let stand 2 to 3 minutes.

8 SERVINGS, ABOUT ½ CUP EACH

MICROWAVE DIRECTIONS: Omit water. Mix all ingredients in 2-quart microwavable casserole. Cover tightly and microwave on high (100%) 5 minutes; stir. Cover and microwave until vegetables are tender, 2 to 5 minutes longer.

Zucchini in Wine

⅓ cup dry white wine
4 cups ½-inch zucchini slices (about 1 pound)
2 cloves garlic, finely chopped
2 tablespoons snipped fresh basil leaves or
   2 teaspoons dried basil leaves
1 small onion, sliced and separated into rings

Heat wine to boiling in 10-inch skillet. Stir in zucchini, garlic and basil. Cover and heat to boiling; reduce heat. Simmer 5 minutes, stirring occasionally. Stir in onion. Cook uncovered until zucchini is crisp-tender and liquid is reduced, 3 to 5 minutes longer.

4 SERVINGS, ABOUT ⅔ CUP EACH

MICROWAVE DIRECTIONS: Decrease wine to 2 tablespoons. Mix wine, zucchini, garlic and basil in 1½-quart microwavable casserole. Cover tightly and microwave on high (100%) 4 minutes; stir in onion. Cover tightly and microwave until zucchini is crisp-tender, 2 to 5 minutes longer.

Picnic in the Park

....

Roast Beef Pocket Sandwiches (page 109)

Garden Potato Salad (page 187)

Creamy Cucumbers (page 187)

Celery and Carrot Sticks

Brownies (page 226)

SALADS

Clockwise from top: Creamy Cucumbers (page 187),
Garden Potato Salad (page 187) and
Roast Beef Pocket Sandwiches (page 109)

Healthy Hints

- Many recipes for salad dressings accompany our salad recipes. They work as versatile accompaniments for other salad combinations as well.
- Salads and vegetables can be conveniently marinated in plastic bags. This allows for easy turning and uses less space in the refrigerator.
- Top salads with only small amounts of such high-calorie condiments as raisins, nuts, olives or bacon. Finely chopping these toppings not only means less of the topping is needed, but spreads the flavor throughout the dish as well.
- When making salad dressings from scratch, use nonfat plain yogurt alone or with reduced-calorie mayonnaise, salad dressing or sour cream to add creamy richness without excess calories.

Deli Counters

An assortment of fresh vegetables makes for healthy and nutritious salads, but adding dressings and toppings adds unwanted calories. When purchasing deli salads, select vinaigrette-based rather than cream- or mayonnaise-based salad dressings, or use fresh lemon or small amounts of wine vinegar to enhance the flavor. Limit yourself to a few toppings and add the following sparingly: shredded cheese, chopped eggs, olives, nuts, croutons, dried fruits and bacon. Ask to sample marinated salads before you order them, to ensure that large amounts of oil, sugar or salt have not been added. When choosing main dish salads, chicken, turkey, beef and seafood are preferable to ham, sausage and pepperoni.

Per serving:			
Calories	250	Fat	11 g
Protein	26 g	Cholesterol	60 mg
Carbohydrate	12 g	Sodium	130 mg

Raspberry Chicken Salad

Use any raspberries you like, so long as they are unsweetened. Fresh black and golden are the more unusual alternatives to red.

4 cups bite-size pieces mixed salad greens
   (iceberg, Bibb, romaine or spinach)
2 cups cut-up cooked chicken
1 cup raspberries*
⅓ cup thinly sliced celery
¼ cup toasted sliced almonds
Raspberry Dressing (below)
Freshly ground pepper

Toss salad greens, chicken, raspberries and celery; sprinkle with sliced almonds. Serve with Raspberry Dressing and pepper.

4 SERVINGS, ABOUT 1¾ CUPS SALAD AND ⅓ CUP DRESSING EACH

Raspberry Dressing

1 cup nonfat plain yogurt
½ cup raspberries*
1 tablespoon raspberry or red wine vinegar
2 teaspoons sugar

Place all ingredients in blender container. Cover and blend on high speed until smooth, about 15 seconds.

*Frozen unsweetened loose-pack raspberries can be substituted for the fresh raspberries.

Per serving:			
Calories	195	Fat	4 g
Protein	14 g	Cholesterol	65 mg
Carbohydrate	26 g	Sodium	160 mg

Tangy Shrimp Noodle Salad

2 cups uncooked noodles (about 4 ounces)
2 cups coarsely chopped zucchini (about
   2 medium)
½ cup sliced celery (1 medium stalk)
¼ cup sliced ripe olives
1 can (4¼ ounces) tiny shrimp, rinsed and
   drained
Horseradish Dressing (below)
Salad greens

Cook noodles as directed on package; drain. Mix all ingredients except salad greens. Refrigerate at least 2 hours but no longer than 24 hours. Spoon onto salad greens.

4 SERVINGS, ABOUT 1½ CUPS EACH

Horseradish Dressing

1 cup plain nonfat yogurt
⅓ cup reduced-calorie sour cream
2 tablespoons prepared horseradish
1 tablespoon finely chopped onion

Mix all ingredients.

Salmon-Rice Salad with Dilled Cucumber Dressing

Per serving:				
Calories	350	Fat	12 g
Protein	26 g	Cholesterol	60 mg
Carbohydrate	36 g	Sodium	510 mg

Salmon-Rice Salad with Dilled Cucumber Dressing

Winter cucumbers sometimes grow a thick, almost bitter skin. If that is the case, run the tines of a fork down the length of a pared cucumber, scoring deeply into the pale flesh. You'll still be able to enjoy the pale green color (and fiber, too).

Dilled Cucumber Dressing (right)
2 medium cucumbers, thinly sliced
1 pound salmon steaks*, poached, chilled and flaked
1 cup cold cooked wild rice
½ cup cold cooked white rice
¼ cup sliced green onions (with tops)
12 cherry tomatoes, cut into halves

Prepare Dilled Cucumber Dressing. Arrange cucumber slices, overlapping edges, in circle on each of 4 plates. Toss remaining ingredients; spoon into center of cucumbers. Spoon Dilled Cucumber Dressing over salads.

4 SERVINGS, ABOUT 1 CUP SALMON MIXTURE AND ⅓ CUP DRESSING EACH

*1 can (15½ ounces) salmon, drained and flaked, can be substituted for the salmon steaks.

Dilled Cucumber Dressing

1 cup nonfat plain yogurt
½ cup chopped seeded cucumber
2 tablespoons reduced-calorie mayonnaise or salad dressing
1 tablespoon snipped fresh dill weed or 1 teaspoon dried dill weed
½ teaspoon celery salt
½ teaspoon onion powder

Place all ingredients in blender container. Cover and blend on high speed until smooth, about 15 seconds. Cover and refrigerate until chilled, at least 2 hours.

Per serving:

Calories	345	Fat	13 g
Protein	27 g	Cholesterol	50 mg
Carbohydrate	30 g	Sodium	580 mg

Turkey Taco Salad

Ordinary taco salads run about 200 calories higher per serving than this one. Although an 8-inch flour tortilla has 130 calories, take a hint from the tortilla strips below and stretch them.

3 flour tortillas (8-inch)
½ pound ground turkey
⅓ cup water
1 to 2 teaspoons chili powder
½ teaspoon salt
¼ teaspoon garlic powder
¼ teaspoon ground red pepper
1 can (8 ounces) kidney beans, drained
5 cups shredded lettuce
1 cup chopped tomato (about 1 medium)
½ cup shredded Monterey Jack cheese (2 ounces)
¼ cup chopped onion (about 1 small)
¼ cup reduced-calorie Thousand Island dressing
¼ cup reduced-calorie sour cream
4 pitted ripe olives, sliced

Heat oven to 400°. Cut tortillas into 12 wedges, or strips about 3 × ¼ inch. Place in ungreased jelly roll pan, 15½ × 10½ × 1 inch. Bake, stirring at least once, until golden brown and crisp, 6 to 8 minutes; cool.

Cook and stir ground turkey in 10-inch nonstick skillet over medium heat until brown. Stir in water, chili powder, salt, garlic powder, red pepper and kidney beans. Heat to boiling; reduce heat. Simmer uncovered, stirring oc-

casionally, until liquid is absorbed, 2 to 3 minutes; cool 10 minutes.

Mix lettuce, tomato, cheese and onion in large bowl; toss with Thousand Island dressing. Divide among 4 serving plates; top each salad with about ½ cup turkey mixture. Arrange tortilla wedges around salad. Garnish with sour cream and ripe olives.

4 SERVINGS, ABOUT 1¾ CUP EACH

Per serving:

Calories	275	Fat	16 g
Protein	17 g	Cholesterol	35 mg
Carbohydrate	18 g	Sodium	1010 mg

Crunchy Ham Salad

1 package (9 ounces) frozen French-style green beans, cooked and drained
1 cup sliced celery (about 2 medium stalks)
½ cup chopped onion (about 1 medium)
Parsley Dressing (page 181)
¼ cup water
2 tablespoons Dijon-style mustard
2 tablespoons corn syrup
¼ teaspoon red pepper sauce
3 cups cut-up fully cooked smoked ham
¼ cup broken walnut pieces
6 cups bite-size pieces iceberg lettuce (about 1 small head)
1 tart unpared apple, cut into thin wedges

Toss green beans, celery and onion with Parsley Dressing in glass or plastic bowl. Cover and refrigerate at least 3 hours.

Heat water, mustard, corn syrup and pepper sauce to boiling in 10-inch skillet, stirring constantly. Boil and stir 1 minute. Stir in ham and walnuts until lightly glazed, about 3 minutes; cool. Arrange ham mixture and vegetables on lettuce. Garnish with apple wedges.

6 SERVINGS, ABOUT 1½ CUPS EACH

Parsley Dressing

¼ cup vegetable oil
2 tablespoons snipped parsley
1 tablespoon lemon juice
2 teaspoons Dijon-style mustard
¼ teaspoon salt
⅛ teaspoon pepper

Shake all ingredients in tightly covered container.

Per serving:			
Calories	170	Fat	6 g
Protein	21 g	Cholesterol	55 mg
Carbohydrate	9 g	Sodium	560 mg

Spicy Beef Salad

The Oriental influence in this salad is unmistakable: rice wine vinegar, soy sauce, gingerroot and sesame oil.

1 pound beef flank steak or boneless sirloin steak
2 tablespoons sherry
1 tablespoon soy sauce
2 teaspoons sugar
½ cup thinly sliced green onions (with tops)
2 medium tomatoes, cut into chunks
4 cups sliced mushrooms (about 10 ounces)
6 cups shredded lettuce (about 1 small head) or radicchio (about 2 small heads)
Spicy Dressing (right)

Trim fat from beef steak; cut beef with grain into 2-inch strips. Cut strips across grain into ⅛-inch slices. (For ease in cutting, partially freeze beef, about 1½ hours.) Toss beef, sherry, soy sauce and sugar in glass or plastic bowl or in heavy plastic bag. Cover and refrigerate 30 minutes.

Heat 10-inch nonstick skillet over medium-high heat until 1 or 2 drops of water bubble and skitter when sprinkled on surface. Add half of the beef; stir-fry until beef is no longer pink, about 3 minutes. Remove beef from skillet; drain. Repeat with remaining beef; toss beef with green onions in large bowl.

Layer tomatoes, mushrooms and lettuce over beef. Cover and refrigerate at least 1 hour but no longer than 10 hours.

Pour Spicy Dressing over salad; toss until well coated.

6 SERVINGS, ABOUT 1½ CUPS EACH

Spicy Dressing

¼ cup rice wine or white wine vinegar
2 tablespoons soy sauce
1 teaspoon finely chopped gingerroot
1 teaspoon sesame oil
⅛ teaspoon ground red pepper
1 clove garlic, finely chopped

Shake all ingredients in tightly covered container.

Turkey Taco Salad (page 180) and Spicy Beef Salad (page 181)

Spinach with Sprouts

8 ounces fresh spinach or curly endive
Sesame Dressing (below)
1 can (16 ounces) bean sprouts*, rinsed and
    drained
1 can (8½ ounces) water chestnuts, drained
    and sliced
1 cup croutons

Tear spinach into bite-size pieces. Prepare Sesame Dressing. Add bean sprouts, water chestnuts and dressing; toss. Sprinkle with croutons.

8 SERVINGS, ABOUT ¾ CUP EACH

*2 cups fresh sprouts can be substituted for the canned bean sprouts.

Sesame Dressing

¼ cup soy sauce
2 tablespoons toasted sesame seed
2 tablespoons lemon juice
1 tablespoon finely chopped onion
½ teaspoon sugar
¼ teaspoon pepper

Shake all ingredients in tightly covered container.

Lemon Greek Salad

There is only 1 tablespoon of olive oil in this salad, so you may want to use one with a good olive flavor. As a rule of thumb, the darker the color of the oil, the stronger the olive flavor. Oils that are quite green in appearance usually have rich flavor.

1 medium unpared cucumber
2 cups bite-size pieces spinach
2 cups bite-size pieces Boston lettuce
¼ cup crumbled feta cheese
2 tablespoons sliced green onions (with tops)
10 pitted ripe olives, sliced
1 medium tomato, cut into thin wedges
Lemon and Mustard Dressing (below)

Score cucumber by running tines of fork lengthwise down sides; slice. Toss cucumber slices and remaining ingredients with Lemon and Mustard Dressing.

4 SERVINGS, ABOUT 1⅓ CUPS EACH

Lemon and Mustard Dressing

2 tablespoons lemon juice
1 tablespoon olive or vegetable oil
1 teaspoon sugar
1 teaspoon Dijon-style mustard
⅛ teaspoon pepper

Shake all ingredients in tightly covered container.

Lemon Greek Salad

Per serving:

Calories	80	Fat	1 g
Protein	3 g	Cholesterol	0 mg
Carbohydrate	16 g	Sodium	20 mg

Pimiento Pasta Salad

2 cups cooked rotini or spiral macaroni
2 cups thinly sliced zucchini (about 1 medium)
1 tablespoon snipped fresh basil leaves or
   1 teaspoon dried basil leaves
1 tablespoon white wine vinegar
1 teaspoon lemon juice
¼ teaspoon coarsely cracked pepper
1 clove garlic, finely chopped
1 jar (4 ounces) pimiento strips, undrained
1 tablespoon grated Parmesan cheese

Mix all ingredients except cheese. Cover and refrigerate at least 2 hours. Sprinkle with Parmesan cheese.

6 SERVINGS, ABOUT ⅔ CUP EACH

Per serving:

Calories	45	Fat	1 g
Protein	1 g	Cholesterol	0 mg
Carbohydrate	8 g	Sodium	280 mg

Marinated Cauliflower Salad

4 cups thinly sliced cauliflowerets
1 small onion, thinly sliced and separated
   into rings
12 small pimiento-stuffed olives, sliced
⅓ cup reduced-calorie Russian dressing
⅛ teaspoon pepper

Mix all ingredients in medium glass or plastic bowl or in heavy plastic bag. Cover and refrigerate at least 1 hour but no longer than 36 hours, stirring occasionally.

6 SERVINGS, ABOUT ⅔ CUP EACH

Per serving:

Calories	50	Fat	2 g
Protein	2 g	Cholesterol	0 mg
Carbohydrate	7 g	Sodium	155 mg

Creamy Coleslaw

It is hard to believe that coleslaw can be part of a lower-calorie menu. This one is as crunchy and creamy as delicatessen coleslaw.

⅓ cup nonfat plain yogurt
2 tablespoons Dijon-style mustard
1 tablespoon reduced-calorie mayonnaise or
   salad dressing
2 teaspoons sugar
Freshly ground pepper
3 cups finely shredded red or green cabbage
½ cup shredded carrot (about 1 small)
3 tablespoons chopped red onion

Mix yogurt, mustard, mayonnaise, sugar and pepper in medium glass or plastic bowl or in heavy plastic bag. Stir in remaining ingredients until evenly coated. Cover and refrigerate at least 1 hour.

4 SERVINGS, ABOUT ⅔ CUP EACH

Per serving:

Calories	20	Fat	0 g
Protein	1 g	Cholesterol	0 mg
Carbohydrate	4 g	Sodium	200 mg

Creamy Cucumbers

½ cup nonfat plain yogurt
½ teaspoon salt
½ teaspoon snipped fresh dill weed or
   ¼ teaspoon dried dill weed
⅛ teaspoon pepper
2 cups thinly sliced cucumbers (about 2 medium)
1 small onion, thinly sliced and separated
   into rings

Mix all ingredients; cover and refrigerate at least 4 hours.

6 SERVINGS, ABOUT ½ CUP EACH

Per serving:

Calories	20	Fat	0 g
Protein	1 g	Cholesterol	0 mg
Carbohydrate	4 g	Sodium	190 mg

Spicy Mushrooms

There are numerous brands of reduced-calorie dressings available. They vary in texture and flavor; try several to find a favorite.

⅓ cup reduced-calorie Italian dressing
1 to 2 tablespoons snipped fresh basil leaves
   or 1 to 2 teaspoons dried basil leaves
4 cups sliced mushrooms (about 10 ounces)

Mix Italian dressing and basil in medium glass or plastic bowl or in heavy plastic bag. Stir in mushrooms until coated. Cover and refrigerate at least 4 hours, stirring occasionally.

6 SERVINGS, ABOUT ½ CUP EACH

Per serving:

Calories	60	Fat	1 g
Protein	3 g	Cholesterol	45 mg
Carbohydrate	9 g	Sodium	150 mg

Garden Potato Salad

Ordinary potato salad weighs in at about three times the calories of this version, crunchy with added vegetables.

1 cup nonfat plain yogurt
1 tablespoon reduced-calorie French dressing
2 teaspoons prepared mustard
½ teaspoon celery seed
½ teaspoon salt
¼ teaspoon pepper
2 cups diced cooked potatoes
1 cup sliced radishes
1 cup diced zucchini (about 1 medium)
1 cup thinly sliced celery (about 2 medium
   stalks)
½ cup shredded carrots (about 2 medium)
½ cup sliced green onions (with tops)
2 hard-cooked eggs, chopped

Mix yogurt, French dressing, mustard, celery seed, salt and pepper in medium glass or plastic bowl or in heavy plastic bag. Add remaining ingredients; toss until vegetables are evenly coated. Cover and refrigerate at least 3 hours.

12 SERVINGS, ABOUT ½ CUP EACH

Tarragon Tomato Slices and Hot German Vegetable Salad

Per serving:

Calories	110	Fat	5 g
Protein	2 g	Cholesterol	5 mg
Carbohydrate	14 g	Sodium	230 mg

Per serving:

Calories	35	Fat	2 g
Protein	1 g	Cholesterol	0 mg
Carbohydrate	4 g	Sodium	5 mg

Hot German Vegetable Salad

½ pound new potatoes (3 or 4), cut into fourths
½ pound turnips (2 or 3 small), pared and cut into fourths
2 slices bacon
½ cup chopped onion (about 1 medium)
1 tablespoon all-purpose flour
2 teaspoons sugar
½ teaspoon salt
¼ teaspoon celery seed
Dash of pepper
½ cup water
¼ cup vinegar
1 cup coarsely shredded cabbage

Heat 1 inch water to boiling. Add potatoes and turnips. Heat to boiling; reduce heat. Cover and cook until tender, 15 to 20 minutes; drain. Cool slightly; cut into ½-inch pieces.

Cook bacon in 10-inch skillet until crisp; remove bacon and drain. Cook and stir onion in bacon fat until tender. Stir in flour, sugar, salt, celery seed and pepper. Cook over low heat until onion is evenly coated, stirring constantly; remove form heat. Stir in water and vinegar. Heat to boiling, stirring constantly. Boil and stir 1 minute; remove from heat. Stir in shredded cabbage. Crumble bacon; stir bacon, potatoes and turnips into cabbage mixture. Cook until hot and bubbly, stirring gently to coat vegetables.

6 SERVINGS, ABOUT ½ CUP EACH

Tarragon Tomato Slices

To remove fresh tarragon leaves easily from the stem, hold the tip of the stem in one hand and run the thumb and index finger of your other hand down the stem.

3 medium tomatoes, cut into four ¼-inch slices each
¼ cup tarragon wine vinegar
1 tablespoon vegetable oil
1 tablespoon snipped fresh tarragon leaves or 1 teaspoon dried tarragon leaves
Freshly ground pepper
Lettuce leaves

Place tomatoes in glass or plastic dish. Shake vinegar, oil and tarragon in tightly covered container; pour over tomatoes. Sprinkle with pepper. Cover and refrigerate at least 2 hours. Serve over lettuce leaves.

6 SERVINGS, 2 SLICES EACH

Per serving:

Calories	40	Fat	0 g
Protein	3 g	Cholesterol	0 mg
Carbohydrate	7 g	Sodium	360 mg

Gazpacho Mold

This recipe uses tomato-vegetable juice at two temperatures: cold, to soften gelatin, and hot, to dissolve it thoroughly.

1 can (16 ounces) whole tomatoes, undrained
1 cup chopped green bell pepper (about
    1 medium)
1 cup chopped seeded cucumber (about
    1 medium)
½ cup chopped onion (about 1 medium)
2 large cloves garlic, chopped
2 tablespoons lemon juice
1 teaspoon ground cumin
½ teaspoon salt
2 or 3 drops red pepper sauce
2 envelopes unflavored gelatin
¼ cup chilled tomato-vegetable juice
1 cup hot tomato-vegetable juice
Salad greens

Place tomatoes, ¼ cup of the bell pepper, ¼ cup of the cucumber, ¼ cup of the onion, the garlic, lemon juice, cumin, salt and pepper sauce in food processor workbowl fitted with steel blade or blender container. Cover and process until smooth, about 10 seconds. Pour into medium bowl. Sprinkle gelatin on ¼ cup chilled tomato-vegetable juice to soften; stir in 1 cup hot tomato-vegetable juice until gelatin is dissolved. Stir gelatin mixture into vegetable mixture.

Refrigerate until slightly thickened but not set. Stir in remaining bell pepper, cucumber and onion. Pour into 4-cup mold. Refrigerate until firm, at least 4 hours. Unmold on salad greens.

8 SERVINGS, ABOUT ½ CUP EACH

Per serving:

Calories	55	Fat	0 g
Protein	0 g	Cholesterol	0 mg
Carbohydrate	14 g	Sodium	75 mg

Spiced Apples and Pears

With so many varieties of both apples and pears to choose from year-round, this salad is never lacking delicious variations.

2 medium apples, sliced
2 medium pears, sliced
½ cup diagonally cut celery slices (about
    1 medium stalk)
2 tablespoons lemon juice
1 tablespoon honey
¼ teaspoon salt
¼ teaspoon pumpkin pie spice
Lettuce leaves

Mix apples, pears and celery. Shake lemon juice, honey, salt and pumpkin pie spice in tightly covered container; pour over apple mixture. Toss until evenly coated. Cover and refrigerate at least 1 hour. Serve over lettuce leaves.

8 SERVINGS, ABOUT ⅔ CUP EACH

Per serving:				
Calories	45	Fat	0 g	
Protein	1 g	Cholesterol	0 mg	
Carbohydrate	11 g	Sodium	50 mg	

Per serving:				
Calories	75	Fat	1 g	
Protein	1 g	Cholesterol	0 mg	
Carbohydrate	14 g	Sodium	40 mg	

Citrus Salad

6 medium radishes, thinly sliced
2 grapefruit, pared, sectioned and cut into halves
2 medium oranges, pared and sectioned
1 small onion, thinly sliced and separated into rings
Lemon Dressing (below)
Lettuce leaves

Mix radishes, grapefruit, oranges and onion. Pour Lemon Dressing over fruit mixture. Cover and refrigerate at least 1 hour, stirring occasionally. Remove fruit with slotted spoon. Serve over lettuce leaves.

6 SERVINGS, ABOUT ½ CUP EACH

Lemon Dressing

¼ cup water
2 tablespoons sugar
1 tablespoon lemon juice
⅛ teaspoon salt
⅛ teaspoon paprika

Shake all ingredients in tightly covered container.

Melon Salad with Tea-flavored Cream

Tea adds a gently mysterious flavor to the topping. Most people wouldn't be able to identify it as tea—they just like it.

1 cup boiling water
1 package (0.3 ounce) sugar-free orange-flavored gelatin
¾ cup unsweetened orange juice
¼ teaspoon ground ginger
2 cups small cantaloupe or honeydew balls
Tea-flavored Cream (below)

Pour boiling water on gelatin in medium bowl; stir until gelatin is dissolved. Stir in orange juice and ginger. Refrigerate until slightly thickened but not set.

Stir in melon balls. Pour into a 4-cup mold or 6 individual molds. Refrigerate until firm, at least 4 hours; unmold. Spoon about 1 tablespoon Tea-flavored Cream onto each serving.

6 SERVINGS, ABOUT ⅔ CUP WITH 1 TABLESPOON TOPPING EACH

Tea-flavored Cream

½ cup frozen (thawed) whipped topping
1 teaspoon instant unsweetened tea (dry)

Mix ingredients.

Per serving:

Calories	100	Fat	4 g
Protein	2 g	Cholesterol	2 mg
Carbohydrate	14 g	Sodium	90 mg

Per serving:

Calories	40	Fat	0 g
Protein	3 g	Cholesterol	0 mg
Carbohydrate	7 g	Sodium	60 mg

Blue Cheese Waldorf Salad

Blue Cheese Dressing (below)
2 medium unpared red eating apples, cut into
   ¼-inch slices
Lemon juice
Spinach leaves
½ cup thinly sliced celery (about 1 medium
   stalk)
2 tablespoons chopped toasted walnuts

Prepare Blue Cheese Dressing. Sprinkle apple slices with lemon juice. Arrange apple slices on spinach leaves. Spoon Blue Cheese Dressing over salad and sprinkle with celery and walnuts.

4 SERVINGS

Blue Cheese Dressing

⅓ cup nonfat plain yogurt
1 tablespoon reduced-calorie mayonnaise or
   salad dressing
1 tablespoon finely crumbled blue cheese

Mix all ingredients; cover and refrigerate at least 1 hour.

Orange Yogurt Salad

¾ cup boiling water
1 package (0.3 ounce) sugar-free orange-
   flavored gelatin
1½ cups nonfat plain yogurt
1 can (11 ounces) mandarin orange segments,
   undrained

Pour boiling water on gelatin; stir until dissolved. Stir in yogurt and orange segments; pour into 4-cup mold. Refrigerate until firm, at least 4 hours; unmold.

8 SERVINGS, ABOUT ½ CUP EACH

Per tablespoon:

Calories	14	Fat	0 g
Protein	0 g	Cholesterol	0 mg
Carbohydrate	3 g	Sodium	110 mg

Honey-Mustard Dressing

⅓ cup water
¼ cup lemon juice
2 tablespoons honey
1 tablespoon prepared mustard
½ teaspoon salt
¼ teaspoon paprika
1 clove garlic, crushed

Shake all ingredients in tightly covered container. Refrigerate at least 1 hour.

ABOUT ¾ CUP DRESSING

Blue Cheese Waldorf Salad

Per tablespoon:

Calories	8	Fat	0 g
Protein	1 g	Cholesterol	0 mg
Carbohydrate	1 g	Sodium	75 mg

Cucumber Dressing

⅔ cup nonfat plain yogurt
½ cup finely chopped seeded cucumber
1½ teaspoons instant minced onion
1½ teaspoons sugar
1 teaspoon prepared horseradish
½ teaspoon salt

Mix all ingredients. Cover and refrigerate, at least 2 hours.

ABOUT 1 CUP DRESSING

Per tablespoon:

Calories	18	Fat	1 g
Protein	1 g	Cholesterol	0 mg
Carbohydrate	1 g	Sodium	80 mg

Creamy Garlic Dressing

½ cup skim milk
2 tablespoons lemon juice
1 tablespoon olive or vegetable oil
1½ cups low-fat cottage cheese (12 ounces)
¼ cup chopped onion (about 1 small)
2 cloves garlic, crushed
½ teaspoon salt
¼ teaspoon pepper
¼ teaspoon paprika

Place all ingredients in blender container in order listed. Cover and blend on medium speed until smooth, about 1 minute. Cover and refrigerate at least 2 hours.

ABOUT 2 CUPS DRESSING

Per tablespoon:

Calories	25	Fat	2 g
Protein	0 g	Cholesterol	0 mg
Carbohydrate	1 g	Sodium	50 mg

Mexican-style Salad Dressing

¼ cup vegetable oil
⅔ cup nonfat plain yogurt
1 clove garlic, crushed
1 green chili, roasted, peeled, seeded and chopped
¼ cup snipped fresh cilantro or 1 tablespoon dried cilantro leaves
1 tablespoon snipped fresh oregano leaves or ¼ teaspoon dried oregano leaves
1 tablespoon vinegar
½ teaspoon salt
Dash of pepper

Gradually stir oil into yogurt in small bowl. Stir in remaining ingredients thoroughly. Cover and refrigerate until chilled, at least 2 hours.

ABOUT 1½ CUPS DRESSING

Per tablespoon:

Calories	18	Fat	0 g
Protein	1 g	Cholesterol	0 mg
Carbohydrate	4 g	Sodium	10 mg

Per tablespoon:

Calories	18	Fat	1 g
Protein	1 g	Cholesterol	0 mg
Carbohydrate	1 g	Sodium	65 mg

Creamy Fruit Dressing

1 cup nonfat plain yogurt
3 tablespoons raspberry or strawberry jam or
   orange marmalade

Beat ingredients with hand beater until blended.
Cover and refrigerate.

ABOUT 1 CUP

Per tablespoon:

Calories	7	Fat	0 g
Protein	0 g	Cholesterol	0 mg
Carbohydrate	1 g	Sodium	35 mg

Curry Dressing

1 cup nonfat plain yogurt
¼ cup reduced-calorie mayonnaise or
   salad dressing
¼ teaspoon salt
¼ teaspoon curry powder
⅛ teaspoon garlic powder
½ teaspoon instant beef bouillon (dry)
2 tablespoons capers, drained

Place all ingredients in blender container.
Cover and blend on medium speed 10 sec-
onds. Scrape sides; blend 10 seconds longer.
Cover and refrigerate at least 2 hours.

ABOUT 1½ CUPS DRESSING

Rich Mock Mayonnaise

1 cup nonfat plain yogurt
¼ cup reduced-calorie mayonnaise or
   salad dressing
¼ teaspoon salt
Dash of paprika
1 drop yellow food color, if desired

Beat all ingredients with hand beater until
smooth. Cover and refrigerate at least 2 hours.

ABOUT 1 CUP DRESSING

Per tablespoon:

Calories	15	Fat	1 g
Protein	1 g	Cholesterol	2 mg
Carbohydrate	1 g	Sodium	105 mg

Garlic Blue Cheese Dressing

⅔ cup nonfat plain yogurt
¼ cup crumbled blue cheese
1 tablespoon finely chopped green onion
   (with top)
½ teaspoon salt
⅛ teaspoon garlic powder

Mix all ingredients; cover and refrigerate at
least 2 hours.

ABOUT 1 CUP DRESSING

Sunday Supper

....

Macaroni with Marinated

Tomatoes (page 209)

Wedge of Cheese

Sliced Apples or Pears

Easy Herb Rolls (page 199)

Brownies (page 226)

BREADS, GRAINS & PASTA

Macaroni with Marinated Tomatoes (page 209) and
Easy Herb Rolls (page 199)

HEALTHY HINTS

- Bread, without added butters and spreads, is a vital component of any healthy diet. Enriched with vitamins, fiber and carbohydrates, it is the staple of our daily regimen. The majority of the breads in this chapter are quick breads.
- Large rolls, bagels, English muffins and hamburger and frankfurter buns have more calories than the standard one-slice-of-bread serving. We recommend eating only half of each of these at a time.
- Muffins are wonderful highlights to meals and delicious, filling snacks. An average medium blueberry muffin (about 2½ inches), without butter, has about 190 cal-

ories. Try our recipes for Wheat Muffins (page 199) and Cranberry Muffins (page 201) to significantly trim the calories.
- When preparing quick breads and muffins from your favorite recipes, experiment with reducing high-calorie ingredients such as fat and sugar. Reduce these ingredients by ¼, to start, and make further adjustments as needed.
- Fortify grain and pasta dishes with other nutritious ingredients—vegtables, water chestnuts, fruit or grated cheese. Mix and match the many colorful pastas available, so long as the sizes are similar.

DELI COUNTERS

Try a variety of the whole grain breads, pocket breads, bagels and muffins that are prevalent in delicatessen sections. These breads have fewer calories than specialty breads, such as croissants, and are lower in fat, too. Note that larger, jumbo muffins may contain as many as 1000 calories. Deli pasta salads and casseroles should be eaten only occasionally, as they are often enriched with high-fat ingredients.

Easy Herb Rolls

2¼ cups all-purpose flour
2 tablespoons sugar
1 teaspoon salt
1 teaspoon caraway seed
1 tablespoon snipped fresh sage leaves or
    ½ teaspoon dried sage leaves, crumbled
¼ teaspoon ground nutmeg
1 package active dry yeast
1 cup very warm water (120° to 130°)
2 tablespoons shortening
1 egg

Mix 1¼ cups of the flour, the sugar, salt, caraway seed, sage, nutmeg and yeast in large bowl. Add water, shortening and egg; beat until smooth. Stir in remaining flour until smooth. Scrape batter from side of bowl. Cover and let rise in warm place until double, about 30 minutes.

Spray 12 medium muffin cups, 2½ × 1¼ inches, with nonstick cooking spray. Stir down batter, beating about 25 strokes. Spoon into muffin cups. Let rise until batter rounds over tops of cups, 20 to 30 minutes.

Heat oven to 400°. Bake until golden brown, 15 to 20 minutes.

12 ROLLS

Wheat Muffins

1 cup buttermilk
2 cups whole wheat flake cereal
1 cup whole wheat flour
½ cup finely chopped pared apple (about
    ½ medium)
¼ cup unsweetened apple juice
¼ cup molasses
1 egg
¾ teaspoon baking soda
¼ teaspoon salt
¼ teaspoon ground cinnamon

Heat oven to 400°. Line 12 medium muffin cups, 2½ × 1¼ inches, with paper baking cups; spray with nonstick cooking spray. Pour buttermilk over cereal in medium bowl. Let stand until cereal is soft, about 5 minutes. Stir in remaining ingredients, all at once, just until flour is moistened. Fill cups about ¾ full. Bake until wooden pick inserted in center comes out almost clean, about 20 minutes. Immediately remove from pan.

12 MUFFINS

MICROWAVE DIRECTIONS: Prepare microwavable muffin ring and batter as directed. Microwave 6 muffins at a time uncovered on high (100%) 1 minute; rotate ring ½ turn. Microwave until wooden pick inserted in center comes out almost clean, 1 to 3 minutes longer. Let stand 1 minute; remove to rack. (Parts of muffins will appear moist but will continue to cook while standing.)

Cranberry Muffins and Turkey-Vegetable Chili (page 92)

Per muffin:

Calories	110	Fat	3 g
Protein	3 g	Cholesterol	25 mg
Carbohydrate	17 g	Sodium	170 mg

Cranberry Muffins

Sugar sprinkled over the tops of these moist, tart muffins gives them a crunchy crust.

1 cup nonfat plain yogurt
3 tablespoons reduced-calorie margarine, melted
1 teaspoon grated lemon peel
2 teaspoons lemon juice
1 egg
1½ cups all-purpose flour
3 tablespoons sugar
1 teaspoon baking powder
1 teaspoon baking soda
⅔ cup coarsely chopped fresh or frozen cranberries
1 tablespoon sugar
Ground nutmeg, if desired

Heat oven to 400°. Spray 12 medium muffin cups, 2½ × 1¼ inches, with nonstick cooking spray or line with paper baking cups. Beat yogurt, margarine, lemon peel, lemon juice and egg until smooth. Stir in flour, 3 tablespoons sugar, the baking powder and baking soda all at once, just until flour is moistened (batter will be lumpy). Fold in cranberries. Fill cups about ¾ full; sprinkle with 1 tablespoon sugar and the nutmeg. Bake until golden brown, 18 to 20 minutes. Immediately remove from pan.

12 MUFFINS

MICROWAVE DIRECTIONS: Prepare microwavable muffin ring and batter as directed. Microwave 6 muffins at a time uncovered on high (100%) 1 minute; rotate ring ½ turn. Microwave until tops are almost dry, 1 to 2 minutes longer. Let stand 1 minute; remove to rack.

Per popover:

Calories	100	Fat	1 g
Protein	5 g	Cholesterol	45 mg
Carbohydrate	17 g	Sodium	145 mg

Popovers

Because this recipe calls for skim milk, it is important to use a blender in order to blend the flour thoroughly into the batter.

1 egg
2 egg whites
1 cup all-purpose flour
1 cup skim milk
¼ teaspoon salt

Heat oven to 450°. Spray six 6-ounce custard cups with nonstick cooking spray. Place all ingredients in blender container. Cover and blend on medium speed just until smooth, about 15 seconds, stopping blender to scrape sides if necessary.

Fill custard cups about ½ full. Bake 20 minutes. Decrease oven temperature to 350°. Bake until deep golden brown, 15 to 20 minutes longer. Immediately remove from cups; serve hot.

6 POPOVERS

Per serving:			
Calories	90	Fat	3 g
Protein	3 g	Cholesterol	35 mg
Carbohydrate	13 g	Sodium	250 mg

Per serving:			
Calories	130	Fat	6 g
Protein	3 g	Cholesterol	35 mg
Carbohydrate	16 g	Sodium	105 mg

Fluffy Corn Bread

This bread with its cracked top has a light texture, achieved by beating the egg whites separately. It is delightful warm or cold.

2 egg whites
¼ teaspoon cream of tartar
1 egg yolk
⅔ cup all-purpose flour
⅓ cup yellow cornmeal
⅔ cup skim milk
1 tablespoon vegetable oil
1½ teaspoons baking powder
¾ teaspoon dried cilantro leaves
¼ teaspoon salt
¼ teaspoon ground cumin
Yellow cornmeal

Heat oven to 425°. Spray round pan, 8 × 1½ inches, with nonstick cooking spray. Beat egg whites and cream of tartar in medium bowl on high speed until stiff but not dry. Mix egg yolk and remaining ingredients in medium bowl; beat vigorously 30 seconds. Fold yolk mixture into egg whites. Pour into pan; sprinkle with additional cornmeal. Bake until golden brown, 15 to 20 minutes. Serve warm.

8 SERVINGS

Almond Strips

Here is a reduced-calorie version of an old favorite, the Danish Puff. Graham crackers are a delicious, quick substitution for the usual calorie-rich butter pastry.

4 graham cracker rectangles, 5 × 2½ inches each
3 tablespoons reduced-calorie margarine
½ cup water
½ teaspoon almond extract
½ cup all-purpose flour
1 egg
1 egg white
2 tablespoons chopped toasted almonds
Powdered Sugar Glaze (page 203)

Heat oven to 350°. Arrange graham crackers with long sides touching on ungreased cookie sheet. Heat margarine and water to rolling boil in 2-quart saucepan; remove from heat. Quickly stir in almond extract and flour. Stir vigorously over low heat until mixture forms a ball, about 1 minute; remove from heat. Add egg and egg white; beat until smooth and glossy. Carefully spread over graham cracker rectangle, being certain topping comes to very edge of graham crackers. Sprinkle with almonds. Bake until topping is crisp and brown, about 30 minutes; cool. (Topping will shrink and fall, forming a custardy top.) Drizzle with Powdered Sugar Glaze.

8 SERVINGS, ABOUT 1¼-INCH STRIP EACH

Powdered Sugar Glaze

⅓ cup powdered sugar
⅛ teaspoon almond extract
1 to 2 teaspoons warm water

Mix all ingredients until smooth and of desired consistency.

Per serving:

Calories	115	Fat	4 g
Protein	2 g	Cholesterol	0 mg
Carbohydrate	17 g	Sodium	250 mg

Honey-drizzled Coffee Cake

Egg whites only are used in this coffee cake. Honey is drizzled over the batter before baking, giving this light coffee cake a pretty look when dusted with powdered sugar.

1⅓ cups variety baking mix
1 tablespoon honey
1 tablespoon vegetable oil
2 egg whites
⅓ cup water
¼ teaspoon ground nutmeg
1 tablespoon honey
Powdered sugar

Heat oven to 350°. Spray round pan, 8 × 1½ inches, with nonstick cooking spray. Mix baking mix, 1 tablespoon honey, the oil, egg whites and water; beat vigorously 30 seconds. Spread batter in pan. Sprinkle with nutmeg; drizzle with 1 tablespoon honey. Bake until wooden pick inserted in center comes out clean, 15 to 18 minutes. Cool 10 minutes; sprinkle with powdered sugar. Serve warm.

8 SERVINGS

Per slice:

Calories	80	Fat	2 g
Protein	1 g	Cholesterol	10 mg
Carbohydrate	15 g	Sodium	125 mg

Banana Bread

⅔ cup sugar
¼ cup reduced-calorie margarine, softened
1 egg
2 egg whites
1 cup mashed ripe bananas (about 2 large)
¼ cup water
1⅔ cups all-purpose flour
1 teaspoon baking soda
½ teaspoon salt
¼ teaspoon baking powder

Heat oven to 350°. Spray loaf pan, 8½ × 4½ × 2½ or 9 × 5 × 3 inches, with nonstick cooking spray. Beat sugar and margarine in medium bowl on medium speed, scraping bowl constantly until light and fluffy, about 30 seconds. Beat in egg, egg whites, bananas and water on low speed until well blended, about 30 seconds. Stir in remaining ingredients just until moistened. Pour into loaf pan. Bake until wooden pick inserted in center comes out clean, 8-inch loaf 60 minutes, 9-inch loaf 45 to 50 minutes; cool 5 minutes. Loosen sides of loaf from pan; remove from pan. Cool completely before slicing.

1 LOAF, 24 SLICES

Banana Bread (page 203), Almond Strips (page 202)
and Honey-drizzled Coffee Cake (page 203)

Parmesan Perch (page 43) and Confetti Wild Rice

Per serving:

Calories	90	Fat	2 g
Protein	4 g	Cholesterol	0 mg
Carbohydrate	14 g	Sodium	210 mg

Per serving:

Calories	95	Fat	4 g
Protein	9 g	Cholesterol	80 mg
Carbohydrate	6 g	Sodium	290 mg

Confetti Wild Rice

½ cup uncooked wild rice
1½ cups sliced mushrooms (about 4 ounces)
2 green onions (with tops), thinly sliced
1 tablespoon reduced-calorie margarine
1¼ cups water
½ teaspoon salt
¼ teaspoon pepper
1 package (10 ounces) frozen chopped broccoli, thawed and drained
1 tablespoon lemon juice

Cook and stir wild rice, mushrooms and onions in margarine in 10-inch nonstick skillet over medium heat until onions are tender, about 3 minutes. Stir in water, salt and pepper. Heat to boiling, stirring occasionally; reduce heat. Cover and simmer until rice is tender, 40 to 50 minutes; drain if necessary. Stir in broccoli and lemon juice; heat uncovered, stirring occasionally, until hot.

6 SERVINGS, ABOUT ½ CUP EACH

Rice and Cheese Casserole

To serve this as a main course, simply double the serving size (remember to double the calories).

2 cups water
1 cup uncooked regular rice
½ teaspoon salt
½ teaspoon dry mustard
⅛ to ¼ teaspoon red pepper sauce
¼ teaspoon pepper
½ cup chopped onion (about 1 medium)
1 cup chopped green bell pepper (about 1 medium)
2 eggs
2 egg whites
2 cups skim milk
1 cup shredded mozzarella cheese (4 ounces)
2 tablespoons grated Parmesan cheese

Heat water, rice, salt, mustard, pepper sauce and pepper to boiling, stirring once or twice; reduce heat. Cover and simmer 14 minutes. (Do not lift cover or stir.) Remove from heat. Fluff rice lightly with fork; cover and let steam 5 to 10 minutes. Stir in onion and bell pepper.

Heat oven to 325°. Pour rice mixture into rectangular baking dish, 11 × 7 × 1½ inches, sprayed with nonstick cooking spray. Mix eggs, egg whites and milk; pour over rice mixture. Sprinkle with cheeses. Bake uncovered until golden brown and set, 40 to 45 minutes. Let stand 10 minutes.

8 SERVINGS

Per serving:

Calories	35	Fat	0 g
Protein	1 g	Cholesterol	0 mg
Carbohydrate	7 g	Sodium	320 mg

Orange Rice Bake

1 teaspoon grated orange peel
¾ cup uncooked regular rice
2 teaspoons instant chicken bouillon
¼ teaspoon ground nutmeg
2 cups ¼-inch carrot slices (about 4 medium)
1½ cups boiling water
3 tablespoons orange juice
2 tablespoons snipped parsley

Heat oven to 350°. Mix orange peel, rice, bouillon (dry) and nutmeg in ungreased 1½-quart casserole. Add carrots and boiling water. Cover and bake until liquid is absorbed and carrots are tender, 30 to 35 minutes. Sprinkle orange juice over rice. Add parsley; toss until well mixed. Let stand 5 minutes before serving.

4 SERVINGS, ABOUT ⅔ CUP EACH

Per serving:

Calories	35	Fat	0 g
Protein	1 g	Cholesterol	0 mg
Carbohydrate	8 g	Sodium	150 mg

Crunchy Lemon Rice

Chopped water chestnuts add texture to this lemony dish. This is terrific with most any fish.

½ cup uncooked regular rice
1 cup water
1 tablespoon instant chicken bouillon
4 to 6 drops red pepper sauce
1 can (8 ounces) water chestnuts, drained and chopped
⅓ cup sliced green onions (with tops)
1 tablespoon finely shredded lemon peel

Heat rice, water, bouillon (dry) and pepper sauce to boiling, stirring once or twice. Cover and simmer 14 minutes. (Do not lift cover or stir.) Remove from heat. Stir in remaining ingredients. Cover and let stand 10 minutes.

6 SERVINGS, ABOUT ½ CUP EACH

Per serving:

Calories	60	Fat	0 g
Protein	0 g	Cholesterol	0 mg
Carbohydrate	15 g	Sodium	90 mg

Pineapple Rice

1½ cups uncooked instant rice
1 can (20 ounces) pineapple tidbits in juice, undrained
½ cup water
¼ teaspoon salt
¼ teaspoon ground nutmeg
¼ cup snipped parsley

Heat all ingredients except parsley to boiling; reduce heat. Cover and simmer until rice is tender, about 5 minutes. Stir in parsley.

6 SERVINGS, ABOUT ⅔ CUP EACH

MICROWAVE DIRECTIONS: Decrease hot water to ⅓ cup and use 1½-quart microwavable casserole. Cover tightly and microwave on high

(100%) until rice is tender and water is absorbed, 6 to 8 minutes. Stir in parsley.

Per serving:

Calories	160	Fat	7 g
Protein	10 g	Cholesterol	25 g
Carbohydrate	14 g	Sodium	360 mg

Mushroom- and Beef-stuffed Shells

This is a perfect family dish. Two shells are a satisfying, calorie-conscious serving, and heartier appetites can take it from there.

12 uncooked jumbo macaroni shells
1 can (16 ounces) Italian tomatoes, undrained and cut up
2 tablespoons tomato paste
¼ cup dry red wine
1 tablespoon cornstarch
1 tablespoon snipped fresh basil leaves or 1 teaspoon dried basil leaves
½ pound lean ground beef
3 cups sliced mushrooms (about 8 ounces)
½ cup chopped onion (about 1 medium)
½ cup chopped green bell pepper (about ½ medium)
2 cloves garlic, finely chopped
½ teaspoon salt
2 tablespoons grated Romano cheese

Cook macaroni shells as directed on package until almost tender; drain.

Heat tomatoes, tomato paste, wine, cornstarch and basil to boiling in 2-quart saucepan, stirring constantly. Boil and stir 1 minute until thickened and bubbly; reserve.

Heat oven to 350°. Cook and stir ground beef, mushrooms, onion, bell pepper and garlic in 10-inch nonstick skillet until beef is brown; drain. Stir in salt and about ⅓ cup of the tomato sauce. Spoon about ¼ cup of the beef mixture into each macaroni shell; arrange in ungreased rectangular baking dish, 10 × 6 × 1½ inches. Top with remaining tomato sauce; sprinkle with cheese. Cover and bake until hot, 20 to 25 minutes.

6 SERVINGS, 2 SHELLS EACH

Per serving:

Calories	175	Fat	5 g
Protein	5 g	Cholesterol	0 mg
Carbohydrate	28 g	Sodium	190 mg

Macaroni with Marinated Tomatoes

2 cups chopped tomatoes (about 2 medium)
2 green onions (with tops), chopped
2 cloves garlic, finely chopped
¼ cup snipped parsley
½ teaspoon salt
2 teaspoons snipped fresh basil leaves or ½ teaspoon dried basil leaves
⅛ teaspoon coarsely cracked pepper
2 tablespoons olive oil or vegetable oil
1 package (7 ounces) macaroni shells

Mix all ingredients except macaroni shells. Cover and refrigerate at least 2 hours but no longer than 24 hours.

Prepare macaroni as directed on package; drain. Immediately toss with tomato mixture.

6 SERVINGS, ABOUT ¾ CUP EACH

Per serving:			
Calories	125	Fat	1 g
Protein	5 g	Cholesterol	0 mg
Carbohydrate	24 g	Sodium	1640 mg

Barley Soup with Vegetables

2 cups frozen mixed vegetables
2 cups sliced mushrooms (about 5 ounces)
1 cup sliced celery (about 2 medium stalks)
½ cup quick-cooking barley
⅓ cup sliced green onions (with tops)
2 teaspoons snipped fresh thyme leaves or
   ½ teaspoon dried thyme leaves
1 teaspoon snipped fresh basil leaves or
   ½ teaspoon dried basil leaves
1 teaspoon garlic salt
5 cups chicken broth*

Heat all ingredients to boiling; reduce heat. Cover and simmer until barley and vegetables are tender, about 15 minutes.

6 SERVINGS, ABOUT 1 CUP EACH

*If using instant chicken bouillon to make broth, use 4 teaspoons with 5 cups water.

Per serving:			
Calories	35	Fat	1 g
Protein	2 g	Cholesterol	5 mg
Carbohydrate	4 g	Sodium	270 mg

Polenta with Tomatoes

½ cup yellow cornmeal
½ cup cold water
1½ cups boiling water
½ teaspoon salt
¼ cup chopped onion (about 1 small)
1 clove garlic, finely chopped
2 tablespoons snipped fresh marjoram leaves
   or 2 teaspoons dried marjoram leaves
1 medium tomato, cut into 6 slices
2 tablespoons finely crumbled Gorgonzola
   or blue cheese (1 ounce)

Mix cornmeal and cold water in 2-quart nonstick saucepan. Stir in boiling water and salt. Cook until mixture thickens and boils, stirring constantly; reduce heat. Cover; simmer 10 minutes, stirring occasionally. Remove from heat; cool to room temperature. Stir onion and garlic into cornmeal mixture. Spread in rectangular baking dish, 10 × 6 × 1½ inches, sprayed with nonstick cooking spray; sprinkle with half of the marjoram. Refrigerate at least 6 hours.

Heat oven to 425°. Cut cornmeal mixture into six rectangles and place on cookie sheet sprayed with nonstick cooking spray. Bake 5 minutes. Arrange tomato slices over top; sprinkle with remaining marjoram and the cheese. Bake until tomato is hot and cheese begins to melt, 5 to 7 minutes longer.

6 SERVINGS

Polenta with Tomatoes

Per serving:

Calories	130	Fat	3 g
Protein	5 g	Cholesterol	0 mg
Carbohydrate	21 g	Sodium	210 mg

Spaghetti with Broccoli and Mushrooms

1 package (10 ounces) frozen chopped broccoli
1 jar (4½ ounces) sliced mushrooms, drained
2 tablespoons reduced-calorie margarine
½ teaspoon salt
⅛ teaspoon pepper
1 package (7 ounces) spaghetti
¼ cup grated Parmesan cheese
1 tablespoon lemon juice

Cook broccoli as directed on package; drain. Stir in mushrooms, margarine, salt and pepper. Heat over low heat, stirring occasionally, until mushrooms are hot, about 5 minutes. Cook spaghetti as directed on package; drain. Toss spaghetti, broccoli mixture, Parmesan cheese and lemon juice.

8 SERVINGS, ABOUT ⅔ CUP EACH

Per serving:

Calories	110	Fat	2 g
Protein	3 g	Cholesterol	0 mg
Carbohydrate	20 g	Sodium	100 mg

German-style Pasta

These pasta spirals with a sweet-sour caraway dressing are delicious as a cold salad.

1 cup uncooked rotini or spiral macaroni (about 4 ounces)
2 teaspoons vegetable oil
4 cups shredded red cabbage (about 12 ounces)
1 tablespoon packed brown sugar
2 tablespoons vinegar
½ teaspoon caraway seed
¼ teaspoon salt
Freshly ground pepper

Cook rotini as directed on package; drain. Heat oil in 10-inch nonstick skillet; add cabbage. Cook and stir over medium heat 2 minutes. Stir in brown sugar, vinegar and caraway seed. Cover and cook, stirring occasionally, until crisp-tender, about 5 minutes. Stir in rotini; heat until hot. Sprinkle with salt and pepper.

6 SERVINGS, ABOUT ⅔ CUP EACH

Per serving:

Calories	130	Fat	1 g
Protein	5 g	Cholesterol	2 mg
Carbohydrate	25 g	Sodium	180 mg

Dijon Broccoli Pasta

1 cup uncooked tiny pasta rings (anelli) (about 4 ounces)
1 package (10 ounces) frozen chopped broccoli, cooked and drained
2 tablespoons reduced-calorie sour cream
2 teaspoons Dijon-style mustard
¼ teaspoon salt

Cook pasta rings as directed on package; drain. Toss all ingredients until well mixed.

4 SERVINGS, ABOUT ⅔ CUP EACH

Per serving:			
Calories	250	Fat	11 g
Protein	17 g	Cholesterol	90 mg
Carbohydrate	20 g	Sodium	780 mg

Vegetable Lasagne

There's a garden of vegetables in the sauce for this simple lasagne: fresh tomatoes, zucchini, bell pepper, onion and garlic. The pungent flavor of Romano makes it especially satisfying.

Vegetable Sauce (right)
1 container (15 ounces) part-skim ricotta cheese
¼ cup grated Romano cheese
2 tablespoons snipped parsley
1 egg
3 uncooked lasagne noodles
½ cup shredded mozzarella cheese (2 ounces)
2 tablespoons grated Romano cheese

Heat oven to 350°. Prepare Vegetable Sauce. Mix ricotta cheese, ¼ cup Romano cheese, the parsley and egg. Layer noodles, ½ of the Vegetable Sauce, ½ of the cheese mixture, the remaining sauce and cheese mixture in rectangular baking dish, 10 × 6 × 1½ inches, sprayed with nonstick cooking spray. Cover and bake until sauce is hot and bubbly, about 1 hour. Sprinkle with mozzarella cheese and 2 tablespoons Romano cheese. Bake uncovered until cheese is hot and bubbly, 10 to 15 minutes longer. Let stand about 15 minutes before serving.

6 SERVINGS

Vegetable Sauce

2 small zucchini
½ green bell pepper
1 small onion
3 medium tomatoes, seeded
1 can (8 ounces) tomato sauce
2 cloves garlic, finely chopped
1 tablespoon snipped fresh basil leaves or 1 teaspoon dried basil leaves
1 tablespoon snipped fresh oregano leaves or 1 teaspoon dried oregano leaves
1 teaspoon salt
¼ teaspoon fennel seed

Cut zucchini, bell pepper and onion into fourths; place in food processor workbowl fitted with steel blade. Process until mixture is coarsely chopped and well mixed, about 10 seconds; place in 2-quart saucepan. Cut tomatoes into fourths; place in food processor workbowl. Process until tomatoes are coarsely chopped, about 10 seconds. Stir tomatoes into vegetable mixture; heat to boiling. Reduce heat; simmer uncovered until vegetables are tender, 10 to 12 minutes. Drain well; stir in remaining ingredients.

Spaghetti with Squash

Per serving:			
Calories	115	Fat	4 g
Protein	3 g	Cholesterol	0 mg
Carbohydrate	17 g	Sodium	260 mg

Spaghetti with Squash

Spaghetti squash strands are easily removed if the squash is cut in half. To serve Spaghetti with Squash in the shell, the squash is halved lengthwise, rather than crosswise. A cross-wise cut usually gives longer strands, but a lengthwise cut makes serving easier.

1 medium spaghetti squash (about 3 pounds)
4 ounces uncooked spaghetti
¼ cup snipped parsley
2 tablespoons grated Parmesan cheese
2 tablespoons reduced-calorie margarine, melted
1 tablespoon snipped fresh oregano leaves or 1 teaspoon dried oregano leaves
½ teaspoon garlic salt

Heat oven to 400°. Prick spaghetti squash with fork; place in ungreased square baking dish, 8 × 8 × 2 inches. Bake uncovered until soft, about 1½ hours.

Break uncooked spaghetti into halves. Cook as directed on package; drain. Cut squash lengthwise into halves; remove seeds and fibers. Save one half for another use. Remove spaghettilike strands with 2 forks. Toss squash with pasta and remaining ingredients. To serve, return spaghetti mixture to squash shell.

6 SERVINGS, ABOUT ½ CUP EACH

MICROWAVE DIRECTIONS: Prick spaghetti squash with fork; place on microwavable paper towel in microwave oven. Microwave on high (100%) 8 minutes; turn squash over. Microwave until tender, 8 to 11 minutes longer; let stand 10 minutes. Continue as directed.

Per serving:			
Calories	70	Fat	2 g
Protein	2 g	Cholesterol	12 mg
Carbohydrate	10 g	Sodium	230 mg

Green Noodles and Vegetables

2 cups uncooked spinach noodles (about 3 ounces)
1 tablespoon reduced-calorie margarine
1 cup coarsely chopped zucchini (about 1 medium)
1 cup sliced celery (about 2 medium stalks)
1 cup frozen peas, thawed
½ teaspoon salt
¼ teaspoon lemon pepper
1 tablespoon grated Parmesan cheese

Cook noodles as directed on package; drain. Heat margarine in 10-inch nonstick skillet over medium heat until melted. Stir in remaining ingredients. Cover and cook until zucchini is crisp-tender, stirring occasionally, about 2 minutes. Stir in noodles; heat through. Sprinkle with Parmesan cheese.

6 SERVINGS, ABOUT ½ CUP EACH

Celebrate Something Special

....

Waldorf Chicken (page 82)

Mixed Green Salad with Sliced Mushrooms

Garlic Blue Cheese Dressing (page 195)

Popovers (page 201)

Sacher Cake Roll (page 222) or

Crunchy Pears (page 233)

DESSERTS

Crunchy Pears (page 233) and Sacher Cake Roll (page 222)

Healthy Hints

- Almost all of our desserts have fewer than 200 calories per serving. In many cases, the sugar and fat have been drastically reduced.
- If you are planning to entertain guests and dessert is in order, prepare only enough for the number of people you plan to serve. Always freeze any leftover dessert.
- Eat desserts slowly, so that the sensation lasts longer and you feel more full. You'll eat less if you eat slowly.
- Fresh fruit, cut up or sliced, makes an attractive and healthy dessert. Serve it plain or top it with nonfat yogurt or a splash of liqueur or brandy. Use higher-calorie fruits such as bananas, persimmons, mangoes and papaya in smaller amounts.
- Use canned fruit, packed in juice, or rinse syrup-packed canned fruit to remove as much of the syrup as possible.
- There are ways to have your dessert and eat it, too, without worrying about preparation and calories. A variety of delicious, reduced-calorie frozen desserts are available in most supermarkets. Many of them are individually packaged and calorie counts can be found on the labels.
- Almost nothing beats cool, refreshing ice cream for dessert, but there are healthier alternatives to the premium ice creams that top 200 calories per half cup. Ice milk, frozen yogurt and fruit ices contain, by comparison, almost half the calories per serving, and they are every bit as luscious.
- Enjoy the many specially flavored coffees and teas such as macadamia nut, hazelnut-chocolate or cinnamon-orange. These drinks, desserts in themselves, are available in special sections in most grocery stores. Use instant coffee mixes sparingly— they have added sugar.

Deli Counters

Those luscious pieces of cheesecake, chocolate layer cake, apple pie and cream puff that line the display counters come in at 400 to 600 calories apiece. Reward yourself occasionally, if you want to, but share the bounty with a friend or save half for a later date. Fresh fruit is the healthiest dessert at the deli counter. Top it with small dollops of pudding or mousse, or look for angel food cake or pound cake to accompany seasonal fruits.

Carrot Cake

At last, a truly moist carrot cake in a convenient size. Sugar and oil are significantly reduced as compared to traditional recipes.

1 can (8 ounces) crushed pineapple in juice, drained (reserve ¼ cup juice)
1 cup all-purpose flour
1 cup shredded carrots (about 2 small)
⅓ cup packed brown sugar
⅓ cup chopped walnuts
¼ cup vegetable oil
1 teaspoon vanilla
¾ teaspoon baking soda
½ teaspoon ground cinnamon
¼ teaspoon salt
¼ teaspoon ground cloves
¼ teaspoon ground ginger
1 egg
¾ cup thawed frozen whipped topping

Heat oven to 350°. Spray round pan, 8 × 1½ inches, with nonstick cooking spray. Reserve ¼ cup crushed pineapple. Blend ¼ cup of the crushed pineapple, the reserved juice and remaining ingredients except whipped topping in medium bowl on low speed, scraping bowl constantly, 1 minute. Beat on medium speed, scraping bowl occasionally, 2 minutes. Pour batter into pan. Bake until wooden pick inserted in center comes out clean, 25 to 35 minutes; cool. Fold remaining pineapple into topping until creamy; serve with cake.

8 SERVINGS, WITH 2 TABLESPOONS TOPPING EACH

MICROWAVE DIRECTIONS: Use round microwavable dish, 8 × 1½ inches. Microwave uncovered on medium (50%), rotating dish ¼ turn every 3 minutes, until surface is almost dry, 9 to 12 minutes. Let cool on heatproof surface (do not use rack). Continue as directed.

Creamy Strawberry Angel Cake

1 cup boiling water
1 package (0.3 ounce) sugar-free strawberry-flavored gelatin
½ cup cold water
1 pint strawberries
1 container (8 ounces) frozen whipped topping, thawed
10-inch angel food cake

Pour boiling water on gelatin in large bowl; stir until gelatin is dissolved. Stir in cold water. Refrigerate until thickened but not set, about 1 hour. Slice strawberries, reserving a few berries for garnish if desired. Fold in sliced strawberries and half of the whipped topping. Refrigerate until thickened but not set, about 15 minutes. Split cake horizontally to make 3 layers. (To split evenly, mark side of cake with wooden picks and cut with long, thin knife.) Fill layers with gelatin mixture. Spread remaining whipped topping over top. Garnish with reserved strawberries. Cut with long, thin knife or serrated knife.

12 SERVINGS

Gingerbread with Orange Sauce

Per serving:			
Calories	140	Fat	3 g
Protein	2 g	Cholesterol	0 mg
Carbohydrate	26 g	Sodium	120 mg

✓

Gingerbread with Orange Sauce

This ginger loaf is tender and moist. Orange is a delicious accompaniment.

1 cup all-purpose flour
¼ cup molasses
¼ cup hot water
2 tablespoons packed brown sugar
2 tablespoons shortening
½ teaspoon baking soda
½ teaspoon ground ginger
½ teaspoon ground cinnamon
⅛ teaspoon salt
1 egg white
Orange Sauce (right)

Heat oven to 325°. Spray loaf pan, 8½ × 4½ × 2½ inches, with nonstick cooking spray. Beat all ingredients except Orange Sauce on low speed 30 seconds, scraping bowl constantly. Beat on medium speed 3 minutes, scraping bowl occasionally. Pour into pan.

Bake until wooden pick inserted in center comes out clean, 30 to 35 minutes. Cool 10 minutes; remove from pan. Serve warm or cool with Orange Sauce.

8 SERVINGS, ABOUT 1-INCH SLICE GINGERBREAD AND 2 TABLESPOONS SAUCE EACH

Orange Sauce

3 tablespoons sugar
1 tablespoon cornstarch
1 cup water
1 tablespoon grated orange peel
1 tablespoon orange juice

Mix sugar and cornstarch in 1-quart saucepan. Gradually stir in water. Cook over medium heat until mixture thickens and boils, stirring constantly. Boil and stir 1 minute; remove from heat. Stir in orange peel and juice. Serve warm or cool.

Per serving:			
Calories	160	Fat	2 g
Protein	3 g	Cholesterol	70 mg
Carbohydrate	33 g	Sodium	170 mg

Per serving:			
Calories	180	Fat	2 g
Protein	3 g	Cholesterol	55 mg
Carbohydrate	38 g	Sodium	125 mg

Pineapple-Lemon Upside-down Cake

1 can (8¼ ounces) crushed pineapple in juice, drained (reserve juice)
1 package (0.3 ounce) sugar-free lemon- or orange-flavored gelatin
2 eggs
1 egg white
¾ cup sugar
1 teaspoon vanilla
¾ cup all-purpose flour
1 teaspoon baking powder
¼ teaspoon salt

Heat oven to 375°. Line round pan, 9 × 1½ inches, with waxed paper; spray with nonstick cooking spray. Spread pineapple evenly in pan; sprinkle with gelatin (dry).

Beat eggs and egg white in small bowl on high speed until very thick and lemon colored, about 5 minutes; pour into medium bowl. Gradually beat in sugar. Add enough water to reserved pineapple juice to measure ⅓ cup. Beat in pineapple juice and vanilla on low speed. Gradually add flour, baking powder and salt, beating just until batter is smooth. Pour into pan.

Bake until wooden pick inserted in center comes out clean, 25 to 30 minutes. Immediately loosen cake from edge of pan; invert pan on heatproof serving plate. Carefully remove waxed paper. Serve warm.

8 SERVINGS

Sacher Cake Roll

Sifted cocoa, rather than powdered sugar, is sprinkled on the towel before the cake is rolled, enhancing the deep chocolate flavor.

2 eggs
2 egg whites
¾ cup sugar
⅓ cup water
1 teaspoon vanilla
¾ cup all-purpose flour
3 tablespoons cocoa
1 teaspoon baking powder
¼ teaspoon salt
Cocoa
½ cup apricot preserves or jam
Chocolate Glaze (page 223)

Heat oven to 375°. Line jelly roll pan, 15½ × 10½ × 1 inch, with aluminum foil or waxed paper; spray with nonstick cooking spray. Beat eggs and egg whites in small bowl on high speed until very thick and lemon colored, about 5 minutes. Pour into medium bowl. Gradually beat in sugar. Beat in water and vanilla on low speed. Gradually beat in flour, 3 tablespoons cocoa, the baking powder and salt just until batter is smooth. Pour into pan.

Bake until wooden pick inserted in center comes out clean, 12 to 15 minutes. Immediately loosen cake from edges of pan; invert on towel sprinkled with cocoa. Carefully remove foil. Trim off stiff edges of cake if necessary. While hot, carefully roll cake and towel from narrow end. Cool on wire rack at least 30 minutes. Unroll cake; remove towel. Beat preserves with fork to soften; spread over top of cake. Roll up cake. Prepare Chocolate Glaze; immediately spread over cake roll.

10 SERVINGS, ABOUT ONE 1-INCH OR TWO ½-INCH SLICES EACH

Chocolate Glaze

⅓ cup powdered sugar
1 tablespoon cocoa
1½ to 2½ teaspoons hot water
¼ teaspoon vanilla

Mix all ingredients until smooth and of desired consistency.

Per serving:			
Calories	100	Fat	3 g
Protein	2 g	Cholesterol	0 mg
Carbohydrate	16 g	Sodium	215 mg

Strawberry Pie with Meringue Crust

Enjoy this pie the day it is made. Like all meringues, the filled shell here will lose some of its crisp, airy quality with time.

2 egg whites
⅛ teaspoon cream of tartar
¼ cup sugar
1 package (1.1 ounces) sugar-free vanilla instant pudding and pie filling
1 cup skim milk
1 cup thawed frozen whipped topping
1 pint strawberries, sliced
½ cup thawed frozen whipped topping

Heat oven to 275°. Spray pie plate, 9 × 1¼ inches, with nonstick cooking spray. Beat egg whites and cream of tartar in medium bowl until foamy. Beat in sugar, 1 tablespoon at a time; continue beating until stiff and glossy. Do not underbeat. Spread mixture evenly on bottom and halfway up side of pie plate. Bake 40 minutes. Turn off oven; leave meringue in oven with door closed 1 hour. Finish cooling meringue at room temperature.

Beat pudding and pie filling (dry) and skim milk about 45 seconds; fold in 1 cup whipped topping. Layer half of the pudding mixture and half of the strawberries in crust; repeat. Cover loosely and refrigerate until firm, at least 1 hour but no longer than 8 hours. Run knife around edge to loosen crust. Top each serving with whipped topping. Refrigerate any remaining pie.

8 SERVINGS, WITH ABOUT 1 TABLESPOON TOPPING EACH

Creamy Strawberry Angel Cake (page 219) and
Orange Trifle (page 232)

Per cookie:			
Calories	50	Fat	2 g
Protein	1 g	Cholesterol	10 mg
Carbohydrate	7 g	Sodium	50 mg

Quick Oatmeal Cookies

1½ cups quick-cooking oats
½ cup sugar
3 tablespoons reduced-calorie margarine, softened
1 teaspoon vanilla
½ teaspoon baking powder
½ teaspoon ground cinnamon
¼ teaspoon salt
1 egg

Heat oven to 350°. Spray cookie sheet with nonstick cooking spray. Mix all ingredients. If necessary, press dough together. Drop dough by rounded teaspoonfuls 2 inches apart onto cookie sheet. Bake until tops are dry and edges are light brown, 8 to 10 minutes. Cool slightly; remove from cookie sheet. Cool completely; store in airtight container.

ABOUT 2 DOZEN COOKIES

Per brownie:			
Calories	105	Fat	5 g
Protein	1 g	Cholesterol	15 mg
Carbohydrate	14 g	Sodium	130 mg

Brownies

These cocoa brownies have ⅓ fewer calories than our traditional cocoa brownies. Brownies made with unsweetened baking chocolate, may have up to 300 calories each.

⅔ cup packed brown sugar
⅓ cup reduced-calorie margarine, melted
1 teaspoon vanilla
1 egg
1 egg white
⅔ cup all-purpose flour
⅓ cup cocoa
⅓ cup chopped walnuts
½ teaspoon baking powder
½ teaspoon salt
Powdered sugar

Heat oven to 325°. Spray square pan, 8 × 8 × 2 inches, with nonstick cooking spray. Mix brown sugar, margarine, vanilla, egg and egg white. Stir in remaining ingredients except powdered sugar. Spread in pan.

Bake until wooden pick inserted in center comes out clean, about 20 minutes; cool. Cut into 2-inch squares; sprinkle with powdered sugar. Store tightly covered.

16 BROWNIES

Per cookie:			
Calories	30	Fat	1 g
Protein	0 g	Cholesterol	0 mg
Carbohydrate	5 g	Sodium	20 mg

Coconut-Almond Macaroons

3 egg whites
¼ teaspoon cream of tartar
⅛ teaspoon salt
¾ cup sugar
¼ teaspoon almond extract
2 cups flaked coconut
About 12 candied cherries, each cut into fourths

Beat egg whites, cream of tartar and salt in small bowl until foamy. Beat in sugar, 1 tablespoon at a time; continue beating until stiff and glossy. Do not underbeat. Pour into medium bowl. Fold in almond extract and coconut.

Heat oven to 300°. Drop mixture by teaspoonfuls about 1 inch apart onto aluminum foil-covered cookie sheet. Place a cherry piece on each cookie. Bake just until edges are light brown, 20 to 25 minutes. Cool 10 minutes; remove from foil.

ABOUT 4 DOZEN COOKIES

Per serving:			
Calories	130	Fat	3 g
Protein	6 g	Cholesterol	75 mg
Carbohydrate	18 g	Sodium	170 mg

Maple Custard

Use low-fat—not skim—for a sturdier custard.

1 egg
2 egg whites
3 tablespoons sugar
½ teaspoon maple flavoring
Dash of salt
1¾ cups low-fat milk, scalded
4 teaspoons maple-flavored syrup

Heat oven to 350°. Beat egg, egg whites, sugar, maple flavoring and salt. Gradually stir in milk. Pour into four 6-ounce custard cups. Drop 1 teaspoon maple-flavored syrup carefully onto center of each mixture (syrup will sink to bottom). Place cups in square pan, 9 × 9 × 2 inches, on oven rack. Pour very hot water into pan to within ½ inch of tops of cups.

Bake until knife inserted halfway between center and edge comes out clean, about 45 minutes. Remove cups from water. Let stand 15 minutes. Unmold and serve warm. Or cover, refrigerate and unmold at serving time. Refrigerate any remaining custards immediately.

4 SERVINGS

Per serving:			
Calories	85	Fat	1 g
Protein	2 g	Cholesterol	0 mg
Carbohydrate	16 g	Sodium	35 mg

Chocolate-Orange Bavarian

½ cup boiling water
1 package (0.3 ounce) sugar-free orange-flavored gelatin
2 tablespoons cocoa
2 tablespoons sugar
2 teaspoons grated orange peel
1 cup unsweetened orange juice
½ package (2.8-ounce size) whipped topping mix (1 envelope)
Skim milk

Pour boiling water on gelatin and cocoa in medium bowl; stir until gelatin is dissolved. Stir in sugar, orange peel and juice. Refrigerate until mixture mounds slightly when dropped from a spoon, stirring occasionally.

Prepare topping mix as directed on package except use skim milk. Beat gelatin mixture 3 minutes; fold in whipped topping. Pour into 6 dishes. Refrigerate until firm, at least 2 hours.

6 SERVINGS, ABOUT ½ CUP EACH

Per serving:			
Calories	155	Fat	3 g
Protein	6 g	Cholesterol	115 mg
Carbohydrate	26 g	Sodium	270 mg

Bread Pudding with Brown Sugar Meringue

1½ cups lukewarm skim milk
1 egg
2 egg yolks
¼ cup packed brown sugar
½ teaspoon ground cinnamon
1 teaspoon vanilla
¼ teaspoon salt
3 cups toasted bread cubes (4 slices bread)
Brown Sugar Meringue (below)

Heat oven to 350°. Spray 1½-quart soufflé dish or casserole with nonstick cooking spray. Mix milk, egg and egg yolks, brown sugar, cinnamon, vanilla and salt in large bowl; stir in bread cubes. Bake uncovered until knife inserted 1 inch from edge comes out almost clean, 30 to 35 minutes.

Prepare Brown Sugar Meringue; spoon onto hot bread budding. Spread over top, mounding to form peaks and carefully sealing meringue to edge of dish to prevent shrinking or weeping. Bake until peaks are golden brown, 12 to 15 minutes. Serve warm or cold. Refrigerate any remaining pudding.

6 SERVINGS, ABOUT 1 CUP EACH

Brown Sugar Meringue

2 egg whites
¼ teaspoon cream of tartar
3 tablespoons packed brown sugar
½ teaspoon vanilla

Beat egg whites and cream of tartar in small bowl until foamy. Beat in brown sugar, 1 tablespoon at a time; continue beating until stiff and glossy. Do not underbeat. Beat in vanilla.

Per serving:			
Calories	155	Fat	10 g
Protein	8 g	Cholesterol	55 mg
Carbohydrate	8 g	Sodium	145 mg

Almond Cheesecake

Whole-milk ricotta gives this cake a smooth richness. If you like, serve with fresh fruit.

¼ cup chopped toasted almonds
3 egg whites
¼ cup sugar
2 cups whole-milk ricotta cheese (16 ounces)
1 package (8 ounces) Neufchâtel cheese, softened
3 tablespoons skim milk
1 teaspoon almond extract
½ teaspoon vanilla
1 egg yolk

Heat oven to 275°. Spray springform pan, 9 × 3 inches, with nonstick cooking spray; sprinkle bottom with almonds. Beat egg whites in medium bowl until foamy. Beat in sugar, 1 tablespoon at a time; continue beating until stiff and glossy. Do not underbeat.

Beat remaining ingredients in large bowl until fluffy; fold into egg whites. Pour into pan. Bake 1 hour. Turn off oven; leave cheesecake in oven 30 minutes. Cool 15 minutes. Cover and refrigerate at least 2 hours but no longer than 48 hours.

12 SERVINGS

Almond Cheesecake

Pumpkin Squares and Chocolate Crème de Menthe Meringues

Calories	85	Fat	1 g
Protein	2 g	Cholesterol	0 mg
Carbohydrate	17 g	Sodium	20 mg

Per serving:			
Calories	205	Fat	5 g
Protein	4 g	Cholesterol	10 mg
Carbohydrate	36 g	Sodium	75 mg

Pumpkin Squares

Like miniature square Pumpkin Pies.

2 envelopes unflavored gelatin
¾ cup unsweetened apple juice
½ cup water
1 can (16 ounces) pumpkin
2 tablespoons packed brown sugar
½ teaspoon ground cinnamon
¼ teaspoon ground ginger
⅛ teaspoon ground cloves
½ package (2.8-ounce size) whipped topping mix (1 envelope)
Skim milk
¼ cup graham cracker crumbs

Sprinkle gelatin on apple juice in 1-quart saucepan to soften; add water. Heat over low heat until gelatin is dissolved, stirring constantly; remove from heat. Mix pumpkin, brown sugar, cinnamon, ginger and cloves in medium bowl; stir in gelatin mixture until smooth. Refrigerate until mixture mounds slightly when dropped from a spoon, stirring occasionally.

Prepare topping mix as directed on package except use skim milk. Reserve ½ cup topping. Beat pumpkin mixture until smooth and light; fold remaining topping into pumpkin mixture. Sprinkle crumbs in bottom of square pan, 9 × 9 × 2 inches, sprayed with nonstick cooking spray; spread pumpkin mixture in pan. Cover and refrigerate until firm, at least 2 hours. Top with remaining topping.

9 SERVINGS, WITH 1 TABLESPOON TOPPING EACH

Chocolate Crème de Menthe Meringues

Chocolate Meringues (below)
1 quart vanilla ice milk
3 tablespoons green crème de menthe

Prepare Chocolate Meringues. Fill each meringue with about ½ cup ice milk; drizzle with 1 teaspoon crème de menthe.

8 SERVINGS

Chocolate Meringues

3 egg whites
¼ teaspoon cream of tartar
¾ cup sugar
1 ounce unsweetened chocolate, coarsely grated

Heat oven to 275°. Cover cookie sheet with parchment paper or heavy brown paper. Beat egg whites and cream of tartar in medium bowl until foamy. Beat in sugar, 1 tablespoon at a time; continue beating until stiff and glossy. Do not underbeat. Fold in chocolate. Drop meringue by ⅓ cupfuls onto paper. Shape into circles with back of spoon, building up sides. Bake 1 hour. Turn off oven; leave meringues in oven with door closed 1½ hours. Finish cooling meringues at room temperature.

Per serving:			
Calories	175	Fat	4 g
Protein	4 g	Cholesterol	0 mg
Carbohydrate	31 g	Sodium	315 mg

Per serving:			
Calories	155	Fat	8 g
Protein	3 g	Cholesterol	90 mg
Carbohydrate	17 g	Sodium	65 mg

Orange Trifle

1 package (about 16 ounces) white angel food cake mix
1 package (1.1 ounces) sugar-free vanilla instant pudding and pie filling
Skim milk
1 tablespoon grated orange peel
1 container (4 ounces) frozen whipped topping, thawed
6 tablespoons orange juice
¼ cup sliced almonds

Heat oven to 350°. Prepare cake mix as directed on package except divide batter between 2 ungreased loaf pans, 9 × 5 × 3 inches. Bake until tops are deep golden brown and cracks feel dry, 45 to 50 minutes. Do not underbake. Immediately invert pans; cool cakes completely. Remove cakes from pans; freeze 1 cake for future use.

Cut remaining cake into 1-inch cubes. Prepare pudding and pie filling as directed on package except use skim milk. Fold orange peel and half of the whipped topping into pudding.

Place ⅓ of the cake cubes in 2-quart serving bowl; sprinkle with 2 tablespoons orange juice. Spread ⅓ of the pudding mixture over cake cubes; repeat twice. Spread remaining whipped topping over top. Cover and refrigerate at least 3 hours. Sprinkle with almonds before serving.

12 SERVINGS, ABOUT ⅔ CUP EACH

Cranberry-Orange Cream Puffs

½ cup water
2 tablespoons reduced-calorie margarine
½ cup all-purpose flour
2 eggs
⅛ teaspoon ground nutmeg
Cranberry-Orange Cream Filling (below)
Powdered sugar

Heat oven to 400°. Heat water and margarine to rolling boil in 1½-quart saucepan; stir in flour. Stir vigorously over low heat until mixture forms a ball, about 1 minute; remove from heat. Beat in eggs and nutmeg all at once; continue beating until smooth. Drop dough by scant ¼ cupfuls into 6 mounds about 3 inches apart onto ungreased cookie sheet.

Bake until puffed and golden, 35 to 40 minutes. Cool away from draft. Cut off tops; pull out any filaments of soft dough. Fill puffs with about ¼ cup Cranberry-Orange Cream Filling each. Replace tops; sprinkle with powdered sugar. Refrigerate any remaining puffs.

6 SERVINGS

Cranberry-Orange Cream Filling

1¼ cups thawed frozen whipped topping
¼ cup nonfat plain yogurt
¼ cup cranberry-orange relish
⅛ teaspoon ground nutmeg

Mix whipped topping and yogurt in medium bowl; fold in relish and nutmeg.

Crunchy Pears

Ripe pears are baked with a sweet, almond-crumb coating. Serve them standing in a shallow pool of orange sauce.

4 firm ripe large pears
¼ cup unsweetened orange juice
3 tablespoons orange marmalade
2 tablespoons vanilla wafer crumbs
2 tablespoons chopped almonds
½ cup nonfat plain yogurt

Place oven rack in lowest position. Heat oven to 350°. Carefully pare pears, leaving stems attached; place on large plate. Mix orange juice and marmalade; spoon over pears.

Mix wafer crumbs and almonds. Roll pears in crumb mixture and stand upright in pie plate, 9 × 1¼ inches, sprayed with nonstick cooking spray. Mix yogurt and remaining marmalade mixture from plate; cover and refrigerate. Bake pears until tender when pierced with fork, 35 to 45 minutes (baking time may vary due to size of pears). Serve warm with sauce.

4 SERVINGS, 1 PEAR AND ABOUT 3 TABLESPOONS SAUCE EACH

MICROWAVE DIRECTIONS: Prepare as directed except place pears on microwavable pie plate, 9 × 1¼ inches. Microwave uncovered on high (100%) 6 minutes; rotate pie plate ½ turn. Microwave until tender when pierced with fork, 4 to 7 minutes longer. Serve warm with sauce.

Butterscotch Peach Slices

⅓ cup packed dark brown sugar
1 tablespoon cornstarch
⅛ teaspoon salt
1½ cups low-fat milk
2 tablespoons reduced-calorie margarine
1 to 1½ teaspoons vanilla
3 peaches, cut into ½-inch slices

Mix brown sugar, cornstarch and salt in 2-quart saucepan. Gradually stir in milk. Cook over medium heat until mixture thickens and boils, stirring constantly. Boil and stir 1 minute; remove from heat. Stir in margarine and vanilla. Place ¼ cup sauce on each of 6 dessert plates; arrange ½ sliced peach on sauce.

6 SERVINGS

Raspberry Graham Cracker Torte

Raspberry Graham Cracker Torte

This show-stopping torte belies its easy assembly. It is pretty, perfect for special occasions.

1 cup raspberries
½ teaspoon almond extract
2½ cups thawed frozen whipped topping
7 graham cracker rectangles, 5 × 2½ inches each (about ¾ packet)

Place raspberries in workbowl of food processor fitted with steel blade or in blender container. Cover and process until smooth; reserve ¼ cup. Fold remaining raspberry purée and the almond extract into whipped topping until creamy.

Spread 1 cracker with about 2 tablespoons topping mixture; layer with a second cracker. Place on serving plate. Continue layering 5 more times. Gently press torte together. Using pancake turner, carefully turn torte on its side so crackers are vertical. Frost top and sides with remaining topping. Cover and refrigerate at least 6 hours (torte will mellow and become moist). Serve reserved raspberry purée with torte. Refrigerate any remaining torte.

6 SERVINGS, ABOUT ¾-INCH SLICE EACH

Chocolate-Cherry Cobbler

2 tablespoons packed brown sugar
2 tablespoons cornstarch
1 can (16 ounces) pitted red tart cherries packed in water, undrained
¼ teaspoon almond extract
6 drops red food color, if desired
2 tablespoons reduced-calorie margarine
½ cup all-purpose flour
1 tablespoon plus 1 teaspoon cocoa
1 tablespoon packed brown sugar
¾ teaspoon baking powder
⅛ teaspoon salt
⅓ cup skim milk
1 teaspoon vanilla

Heat oven to 375°. Mix 2 tablespoons brown sugar and cornstarch in 2-quart saucepan; stir in cherries. Cook over medium heat, stirring occasionally, until slightly thickened, 4 to 5 minutes. Stir in almond extract and food color. Pour into ungreased 1-quart casserole.

Cut margarine into flour, cocoa, 1 tablespoon brown sugar, the baking powder and salt until mixture resembles fine crumbs. Stir in milk and vanilla. Drop dough by 6 spoonfuls onto hot cherry mixture. Bake until topping is no longer doughy, 20 to 25 minutes. Serve warm.

6 SERVINGS, ABOUT ⅔ CUP EACH

Per serving:			
Calories	160	Fat	7 g
Protein	2 g	Cholesterol	0 mg
Carbohydrate	24 g	Sodium	80 mg

Almond Apple Crisp

1 tablespoon water
1 teaspoon almond extract
6 cups sliced unpared, tart eating apples
 (about 4 medium)
½ cup coarsely crushed zwieback crumbs
2 tablespoons all-purpose flour
2 tablespoons sugar
2 tablespoons chopped almonds
½ teaspoon ground cinnamon
3 tablespoons reduced-calorie margarine
Yogurt Topping (below)

Heat oven to 375°. Mix water and almond extract; toss with apples in 1½-quart casserole sprayed with nonstick cooking spray. Mix remaining ingredients except Yogurt Topping until crumbly; sprinkle over apples.

Bake until top is golden brown and apples are tender, about 30 minutes. Serve warm with Yogurt Topping.

6 SERVINGS, ABOUT ½ CUP AND 1 TABLESPOON TOPPING EACH

Yogurt Topping

½ cup nonfat plain yogurt
⅛ teaspoon almond extract
1 teaspoon sugar

Mix all ingredients.

MICROWAVE DIRECTIONS: Prepare as directed except use microwavable pie plate, 9 × 1¼ inches. Microwave uncovered on high (100%) 5 minutes; rotate pie plate ½ turn. Microwave until apples are tender, 4 to 7 minutes longer.

Per serving:			
Calories	115	Fat	3 g
Protein	2 g	Cholesterol	0 mg
Carbohydrate	20 g	Sodium	25 mg

Chocolate-laced Kiwifruit with Orange Sauce

½ cup nonfat plain yogurt
1 tablespoon partially thawed frozen
 unsweetened orange juice concentrate
4 large kiwifruit, pared and cut into ¼-inch
 slices
2 tablespoons semisweet chocolate chips
1 teaspoon shortening

Mix yogurt and orange juice concentrate; spoon 2 tablespoons onto each of 4 dessert plates. Arrange 1 sliced kiwifruit over yogurt mixture on each plate. Heat chocolate chips and shortening over low heat, stirring constantly, until chocolate is melted. Carefully drizzle chocolate in thin lines over kiwifruit.

4 SERVINGS

Chocolate-laced Kiwifruit with Orange Sauce

Honeydew Sorbet with Strawberry Purée

Per serving:			
Calories	50	Fat	0 g
Protein	0 g	Cholesterol	0 mg
Carbohydrate	13 g	Sodium	10 mg

Per serving:			
Calories	105	Fat	0 g
Protein	0 g	Cholesterol	0 mg
Carbohydrate	26 g	Sodium	5 mg

Honeydew Sorbet with Strawberry Purée

A food processor makes preparing refreshing sorbets a snap. Try to select ripe (sweet) fruit, as there is no added sweetening.

½ medium honeydew melon, pared and cut
   into 1-inch chunks
2 cups strawberries
1 teaspoon lemon juice
6 strawberries

Place melon chunks in ungreased jelly roll pan, 15½ × 10½ × 1 inch. Cover and freeze until hard, at least 2 hours.

Place 2 cups strawberries in workbowl of food processor fitted with steel blade. Cover and process until smooth. Place about 3 tablespoons strawberry purée on each of 6 plates.

Wash workbowl and blade. Place half of the frozen melon chunks and ½ teaspoon lemon juice at a time in workbowl of food processor. Cover and process until smooth. Scoop or spoon about ½ cup melon mixture over strawberry purée. (Melon mixture may be frozen up to 30 minutes before serving.) Garnish with remaining strawberries and serve immediately.

6 SERVINGS

NOTE: If sorbet is to be frozen longer than 1 hour, remove from freezer about 45 minutes before serving.

Peach Sorbet with Pineapple

Here is an astonishingly fresh-tasting and pretty dessert that can be made with frozen fruit. For best results, the freezer temperature should be 0° F.

1 package (16 ounces) frozen unsweetened
   peach slices
¼ cup unsweetened apple juice
6 slices pineapple*, ½ inch thick

Place half of the peaches and 2 tablespoons apple juice at a time in workbowl of food processor fitted with steel blade. Cover and process until smooth. Cover and freeze until icy, 2 to 4 hours. Scoop or spoon ⅓ cup sorbet onto pineapple slices.

6 SERVINGS

*Six canned pineapple slices in juice, drained, can be substituted for fresh pineapple slices.

NOTE: If sorbet is to be frozen longer than 1 hour, remove from freezer about 1 hour before serving.

MENUS FOR FOUR WEEKS

Menu planning can be difficult and time-consuming, particularly when you are trying to keep the calorie count low. These menus are your guide to good nutrition, at only 1200 calories or fewer per day. (Unlike adult women, children and men can increase their caloric intake, generally to as much as 1800 calories a day, and still lose weight.) Look to these menus as a guide to food combinations. You don't have to follow them in any particular order. Variety is the key, as well as adequate servings from the basic food groups (see the Basic Food Groups Chart, page 9).

These menus provide calorie counts, your guideline for total daily consumption. To check the calorie content of many common foods, and to calculate the calories of many foods you might want to substitute into the menus that follow, refer to the Calorie Chart on pages 260–264. In comparing calorie charts from different sources, it is possible to find slightly different calorie counts for the same item.

While the 1200-calorie daily menus could have been made up entirely from *Eat and Lose Weight* recipes, that would call for more preparation in the kitchen every single day. These menus show you how to use convenience foods for a plan that easily fits into your lifestyle. Not all menus come in right at 1200 calories per day. You are free to choose how you want to spend those extra calories, so choose wisely.

Menu 9, Dinner (page 246)

TIPS FOR *EAT AND LOSE WEIGHT* MENUS

- Preparation: Rather than indicate how vegetables and fruits should be served, we've left this to your imagination. If you ordinarily slice raw vegetables (or cooked meats, for that matter), try cutting them into strips, chunks, juliennes or cubes for variety. Fruits are meant to be unsweetened; fresh or frozen may be used. Often, fruit rather than fruit juice is suggested because of the importance of fiber in the diet.

- A mixed green salad (as large as you like) can be a fantasy of crisp greens: escarole, celery, cucumber, endive, alfalfa sprouts, lettuces, parsley and spinach. Add thinly sliced, low-calorie radishes for their peppery flavor and brilliant color. If you wash, dry and mix greens by the sinkful, you'll have them on hand throughout the week.

- Substitutions: Substitutions may be made if you dislike a particular food or don't have it on hand. Substitute another food from the same food category, with a similar calorie count. You may also eat foods at different times of the day than the menu suggests. For example, if you like your more substantial meal at noon, switch lunch and dinner menus; or, your lunchtime brownie can be enjoyed as an afternoon snack.

- Seasoning: Herbs fresh and dried, spices, garlic, fresh lemon and lime, and such no- or low-calorie condiments as hot sauce, chili peppers, horseradish, mustards and vinegars of all kinds add sensational flavor.

- Sweeteners: Sugar substitutes are allowed, as is table sugar in small amounts. Remember that when sugar is added, the calorie count increases. Commercial sugar substitutes vary, and you may want to try several to find the one you like best.

- Beverages: Coffee, teas and other noncaloric drinks in addition to water may be included with meals. Try some of the many flavored coffees and teas. For a change of pace, trade some of your snack calorie allotment for some sugar-free hot chocolate.

- Lunch away from home: Most of the lunch menus that follow pack well, and many reheat in the microwave oven.

- No time? For many of us, an active lifestyle doesn't allow as much time for cooking as we would like. Happily, most low-calorie cooking methods are relatively quick. Simple broiled and baked meats, poached and microwave-cooked fish and briefly steamed or stir-fried vegetables are as no-fuss as they are delicious. Feel free to pick up prepared foods from the delicatessen as part of a meal; make low-fat, low-calorie selections. In-store salad bars offer a wide variety.

Menu 1

	Calories
BREAKFAST	
½ medium grapefruit	50
1 slice raisin bread, toasted and	65
spread with 1 tablespoon peanut	
butter	95
1 cup nonfat plain yogurt mixed with	
sugar substitute and vanilla to taste	110
LUNCH	
2 ounces cooked white meat turkey	
(skin removed)	110
½ medium cucumber	10
1 medium tomato	40
1 cup skim milk	90
DINNER	
Vegetable Lasagne (page 213)	250
Mixed green salad with 1 tablespoon	
reduced-calorie Italian dressing	50
1 soft breadstick	100
Almond Cheesecake (page 228) with	155
¼ cup unsweetened blueberries	20
SNACKS	
1 frozen gelatin pop	30
1 medium carrot	25
TOTAL	1200

Menu 2

	Calories
BREAKFAST	
1 cup tomato juice	40
Mushroom Omelet (page 129)	170
½ whole wheat bagel, toasted	90
1 cup skim milk	90
LUNCH	
⅛ of 14-inch cheese pizza	145
1 medium carrot	25
1 cup skim milk	90
2 Marshmallow Squares (page 34)	50
DINNER	
Parmesan Perch (page 43)	145
½ cup cooked rice	115
Sliced medium orange and red onion	
on lettuce	80
½ cup sugar-free gelatin	10
2 vanilla wafer cookies	30
SNACK	
1 small apple	70
TOTAL	1150

Menu 3

	Calories
BREAKFAST	
1 small baked apple with cinnamon	70
1 cup unsweetened whole wheat or oat	110
flake cereal with 1 cup skim milk	90
LUNCH	
Barley Soup with Vegetables (page 210)	125
4 saltine crackers	60
1 medium carrot	25
2 Quick Oatmeal Cookies (page 226)	100
DINNER	
Chili-stuffed Peppers (page 91)	175
½ cup cooked pasta	75
½ cup cooked broccoli	20
1 small tomato	40
½ cup orange sherbet	130
SNACKS	
1 ounce pretzels	110
1 medium orange	65
TOTAL	1195

Menu 4

	Calories
BREAKFAST	
½ cup unsweetened blueberries	40
1 medium frozen buttermilk waffle,	
toasted	110
½ cup nonfat plain yogurt	45
LUNCH	
Mixed green salad with 1 tablespoon	
reduced-calorie French dressing	50
1 ounce string cheese, made with part-	
skim milk	120
1 Wheat Muffin (page 199)	90
1 cup skim milk	90
DINNER	
Oriental Vegetable Meat Roll	
(pages 108–109)	235
½ cup cooked rice	115
½ cup cooked green beans	15
½ cup sugar-free gelatin with	
unsweetened fruit cocktail	50
1 cup unsweetened strawberries	60
SNACKS	
2 cups hot-air-popped popcorn	50
1 banana (6-inch)	80
TOTAL	1150

Menu 5

	Calories
BREAKFAST	
¼ cantaloupe (5-inch)	30
1 slice whole wheat bread, toasted with 1 ounce Cheddar cheese melted on top	65
	115
1 cup skim milk	90
LUNCH	
1 cup vegetable beef soup	100
4 melba toast crackers	60
1 small tomato	40
1 medium orange	65
1 cup skim milk	90
DINNER	
Chutney Chicken (pages 74–75)	145
½ cup Crunchy Lemon Rice (page 208)	35
½ cup cooked carrots	25
Mixed green salad with 1 tablespoon reduced-calorie French dressing	50
Maple Custard (page 227)	130
SNACKS	
2 Marshmallow Squares (page 34)	50
½ cup tomato juice	20
TOTAL	1110

Menu 6

	Calories
BREAKFAST	
½ cup fresh pineapple chunks	40
1 Cranberry Muffin (page 201)	110
1 cup skim milk	90
LUNCH	
Chicken sandwich, made with 2 ounces chopped cooked chicken mixed with	95
1 tablespoon reduced-calorie mayonnaise and 1 teaspoon Dijon-style mustard	50
	5
1 English muffin	140
Raw vegetable sticks	25
1 cup skim milk	90
DINNER	
Red Snapper Stew (page 53)	140
Mixed green salad with 1 tablespoon reduced-calorie French dressing	50
1 slice French bread	60
1 teaspoon reduced-calorie margarine	15
Creamy Strawberry Angel Cake (page 219)	210
SNACK	
1 small apple	70
TOTAL	1190

Menu 7

	Calories
BREAKFAST	
4 medium prunes	70
¾ cup hot cooked oatmeal or oat bran	90
1 slice whole wheat bread, toasted	65
2 teaspoons reduced-calorie fruit preserves	30
1 cup skim milk	90
LUNCH	
1 cup vegetable-beef soup	100
1 hard breadstick	40
Mixed green salad with 1 tablespoon reduced-calorie buttermilk dressing	50
1 cup skim milk	90
1 medium orange	65
DINNER	
Crustless Tuna Quiche (page 49)	195
½ cup drained three-bean salad	50
½ cup cooked carrots	25
Almond Apple Crisp (page 236)	160
SNACK	
2 cups hot-air-popped popcorn	50
TOTAL	1185

Menu 8

	Calories
BREAKFAST	
1 banana (6-inch)	80
¾ cup cooked unsweetened oatmeal	90
or oat bran with 1 teaspoon brown sugar and 1 cup skim milk	15
	90
LUNCH	
2 ounces extra-lean ham with	120
lettuce, tomato, sprouts and mustard on 1 slice rye bread	70
½ cup drained three-bean salad	65
1 cup skim milk	90
1 nectarine	30
DINNER	
Easy Fish and Vegetable Packets (page 46)	190
Mixed green salad with 1 tablespoon Honey-Mustard Dressing (page 192)	50
Chocolate-laced Kiwifruit with Orange Sauce (page 236)	115
SNACKS	
1 frozen gelatin pop	30
1 cup Savory Popcorn Mix (page 31) or 3 cups hot-air-popped popcorn	85
TOTAL	1120

Menu 8, Lunch

Menu 9

	Calories
BREAKFAST	
1 cup unsweetened strawberries	60
1 slice Banana Bread (page 203)	80
1 cup nonfat plain yogurt topped with	110
1 teaspoon brown sugar	15
LUNCH	
Crustless Tuna Quiche (page 49) (left over from Menu 7)	195
Fresh spinach tossed with sliced mushrooms and 1 tablespoon reduced-calorie French dressing	50
1 cup skim milk	90
DINNER	
1 frozen 300-calorie dinner	300
Tarragon Tomato Slices (page 189)	35
1 small whole wheat dinner roll	60
2 teaspoons reduced-calorie margarine	30
½ cup ice milk	100
SNACK	
1 medium orange	65
TOTAL	1190

Menu 10

	Calories
BREAKFAST	
½ cup unsweetened orange juice	60
mixed with ½ cup buttermilk, sugar substitute and vanilla to taste	45
2 pancakes (4-inch)	120
2 tablespoons reduced-calorie maple-flavored syrup	60
LUNCH	
2 ounces cooked white meat turkey	110
Mixed green salad with 1 tablespoon reduced-calorie Italian dressing	50
1 Wheat Muffin (page 199)	90
1 cup skim milk	90
1 Brownie (page 226)	105
DINNER	
3 ounces broiled lean fish	145
Crunchy Lemon Rice (page 208)	35
1 cup cooked summer squash	30
1 slice fresh pineapple, 1 inch thick	80
SNACKS	
1 frozen gelatin pop	30
1 banana (6-inch)	80
TOTAL	1130

Menu 11

	Calories
BREAKFAST	
1 banana (6-inch)	80
1 cup unsweetened wheat or oat flake cereal	110
1 cup skim milk	90
LUNCH	
3 ounces cooked shrimp on a mixed green salad with 1 tablespoon	100
reduced-calorie Italian dressing	50
2 crisp rye crackers	50
3 ounces frozen yogurt	90
1 medium pear	100
DINNER	
3 ounces broiled chicken breast, without skin	100
Rice and Cheese Casserole (page 207)	95
½ cup cooked broccoli	20
Spiced Apples and Pears (page 190)	55
¹⁄₁₂ angel food cake (10-inch)	135
SNACKS	
2 tablespoons Herbed Yogurt Cheese (page 24)	50
4 melba toast crackers	60
TOTAL	1185

Menu 12

	Calories
BREAKFAST	
½ cup tomato juice	20
Zucchini Frittata (page 129)	245
1 cup skim milk	90
LUNCH	
1 cup chicken rice soup	100
1 slice whole wheat bread	65
1 tablespoon Herbed Yogurt Cheese (page 24)	25
3 medium celery stalks	15
1 small apple	70
DINNER	
Indian Beef with Cucumber Rice (page 103)	330
1 sliced medium orange and red onions on lettuce with 1 tablespoon Honey-Mustard Dressing (page 192)	50
½ cup sugar-free pudding	80
SNACK	
1 ounce pretzels	110
TOTAL	1200

Menu 13

	Calories
BREAKFAST	
½ cup unsweetened orange juice	60
¾ cup cooked unsweetened oatmeal	
or oat bran	90
1 cup skim milk	90
1 Wheat Muffin (page 199)	90
LUNCH	
Tuna sandwich, made with	
2 ounces water-packed tuna and	70
1 tablespoon reduced-calorie	
mayonnaise on 2 slices reduced-	50
calorie whole wheat bread	80
1 medium pear	100
1 cup skim milk	90
DINNER	
Pork Chops with Rhubarb Sauce	
(page 113)	285
½ cup cooked cabbage	15
½ cup cooked pasta	75
Mixed green salad with 1 tablespoon	
reduced-calorie Italian dressing	50
SNACK	
1 reduced-calorie frozen yogurt bar	50
TOTAL	1195

Menu 14

	Calories
BREAKFAST	
¼ cantaloupe (5-inch)	30
1 cup unsweetened wheat or oat flake	110
cereal with 1 cup skim milk	90
LUNCH	
Gorgonzola–White Bean Soup	
(page 146)	155
2 rice cakes spread with	60
2 tablespoons Herbed Yogurt Cheese	
(page 24)	50
1 small carrot and 1 medium stalk celery	25
1 cup skim milk	90
DINNER	
Plum-barbecued Chicken (page 78)	150
½ cup cooked brown rice with pimiento	115
½ cup cooked Brussels sprouts	30
Spicy Mushrooms (page 187)	20
Raspberry Graham Cracker Torte	
(page 235)	165
SNACKS	
1 reduced-calorie frozen yogurt bar	50
½ cup tomato juice	20
TOTAL	1160

Menu 15

	Calories
BREAKFAST	
1 medium orange	65
1 scrambled egg	80
1 Almond Strip (page 202)	130
1 cup skim milk	90
LUNCH	
Turkey sandwich, made with	
2 ounces cooked white meat turkey,	110
Dijon-style mustard and lettuce on	5
2 slices reduced-calorie whole	
wheat bread	80
½ medium cucumber	10
1 cup skim milk	90
DINNER	
3 ounces broiled lean beef sirloin steak	180
½ cup cooked carrots	25
Mixed green salad with 1 tablespoon	
reduced-calorie French dressing	50
Pineapple-Lemon Upside-down Cake	160
(page 222)	
SNACKS	
2 tablespoons Mock Guacamole	
(page 23)	15
Crisp Tortilla Chips (page 31)	75
TOTAL	1165

Menu 16

	Calories
BREAKFAST	
1 small baked apple with cinnamon	70
1 slice raisin bread, toasted	65
1 tablespoon peanut butter	95
1 cup skim milk	90
LUNCH	
1 Bean and Cheese Taco (page 148)	300
1 cup skim milk	90
Gazpacho Mold (page 190)	40
½ cup canned unsweetened peaches	40
DINNER	
Mushroom-Cheese Soufflé (page 138)	200
1 cup cooked broccoli and cauliflower	40
1 Cranberry Muffin (page 201)	110
SNACK	
2 cups hot-air-popped popcorn	50
TOTAL	1190

Menu 19, Dinner

Menu 17

	Calories
BREAKFAST	
¼ honeydew melon (5-inch)	35
Eggs Benedict (page 133)	215
1 cup skim milk	90
LUNCH	
Small chef's salad: 1 ounce each ham, turkey and low-fat cheese; ½ hard-cooked egg; 2 tablespoons reduced-calorie salad dressing tossed with mixed greens	300
2 melba toast crackers	30
1 cup skim milk	90
DINNER	
3 ounces sliced lean roast pork loin	215
1 small baked potato	80
1 medium tomato	40
½ cup unsweetened blueberries with 1 tablespoon nonfat plain yogurt	50
1 Coconut-Almond Macaroon (pages 226–227)	30
SNACK	
1 medium carrot	25
TOTAL	1200

....

Menu 18

	Calories
BREAKFAST	
½ cup tomato juice	20
1 medium frozen buttermilk waffle, toasted	110
½ cup nonfat plain yogurt mixed with	55
½ cup unsweetened strawberries	30
1 cup skim milk	90
LUNCH	
1 cup minestrone soup	100
2 melba toast crackers	30
1 Brownie (page 226)	105
1 cup skim milk	90
DINNER	
Savory Pork Stew (page 116)	215
1 cup cooked green beans marinated in 2 tablespoons reduced-calorie Italian dressing	60
Pumpkin Squares (page 231)	85
SNACK	
1 small apple	70
TOTAL	1180

Menu 19

	Calories
BREAKFAST	
1 cup tomato juice	40
1 cup unsweetened wheat or oat flake cereal	110
1 cup nonfat plain yogurt	110
LUNCH	
1 beef frankfurter with ketchup and mustard, on 1 frankfurter roll	140 / 100
1 small carrot and 1 medium celery stalk	25
1 cup skim milk	90
DINNER	
Turkey Pasta with Pesto (page 93)	315
1 medium tomato	40
Peach Sorbet with Pineapple (page 239)	105
SNACK	
3 ounces frozen yogurt	90
TOTAL	1165

....

Menu 20

	Calories
BREAKFAST	
½ cup unsweetened orange juice	60
1 slice Banana Bread (page 203) with	80
1 tablespoon Neufchâtel cheese	70
1 cup skim milk	90
LUNCH	
Cheese sandwich, made with 2 ounces low-fat Cheddar cheese and mustard on 2 slices reduced-calorie whole wheat bread	140 / 80
1 medium carrot	25
1 cup skim milk	90
DINNER	
Mushroom- and Beef-stuffed Shells (page 209)	160
½ cup cooked peas and carrots	50
Mixed green salad with 1 tablespoon reduced-calorie Italian dressing	50
1 small baked apple with 1 tablespoon nonfat plain yogurt and 1 teaspoon brown sugar	100
4 ounces white wine	100
SNACKS	
¼ cup Tangy Yogurt Dip (page 23)	40
1 medium cucumber	20
1 frozen gelatin pop	30
TOTAL	1185

Menu 21

	Calories
BREAKFAST	
½ cup unsweetened apple juice	60
1 whole wheat English muffin, toasted,	140
with 1 ounce water-packed tuna	35
and 2 teaspoons reduced-calorie	
mayonnaise	30
1 cup skim milk	90
LUNCH	
2 ounces cooked white meat turkey,	110
tossed with mixed green salad with	
1 cup sliced fresh mushrooms and 2	
tablespoons Garlic Blue Cheese	
Dressing (page 195)	85
1 slice Banana Bread (page 203)	80
1 cup skim milk	90
DINNER	
3 ounces broiled or baked lean fish	145
Orange Rice Bake (page 208)	35
½ cup cold cooked asparagus tossed	
with 2 tablespoons reduced-calorie	
French dressing	50
Chocolate Crème de Menthe Meringues	
(page 231)	205
SNACKS	
1 frozen gelatin pop	30
3 medium celery stalks	15
TOTAL	1200

Menu 22

	Calories
BREAKFAST	
½ medium grapefruit	50
Quick Chili-Cheese Puff (page 133)	200
1 slice whole wheat bread, toasted	65
2 teaspoons reduced-calorie fruit	
preserves	30
1 cup skim milk	90
LUNCH	
Turkey Taco Salad (page 180)	345
1 cup skim milk	90
DINNER	
3 ounces broiled lean fish	145
Confetti Wild Rice (page 207)	90
½ cup cooked green beans	15
Honeydew Sorbet with Strawberry	
Purée (page 239)	50
SNACK	
1 frozen gelatin pop	30
TOTAL	1200

Menu 23

	Calories
BREAKFAST	
½ cup unsweetened orange juice	60
1 slice whole wheat bread, toasted,	65
topped with ¼ cup low-fat cottage	
cheese mixed with sugar substitute,	
vanilla and cinnamon to taste	60
1 cup skim milk	90
LUNCH	
2 ounces cooked shrimp on a	
mixed green salad with 2 tablespoons	
reduced-calorie Blue Cheese dressing	65
1 soft breadstick	65
1 Brownie (page 226)	105
DINNER	
3 ounces lean cooked roast beef	180
Vegetable-stuffed Potatoes (page 169)	100
1 cup sliced mushrooms and green	
onion, tossed with 2 tablespoons	
reduced-calorie Russian dressing	70
Chocolate-Cherry Cobbler (page 235)	135
SNACKS	
4 ounces wine	100
1 medium pear	100
TOTAL	1195

Menu 24

	Calories
BREAKFAST	
1 cup unsweetened strawberries	60
1 cup nonfat plain yogurt	110
1 piece Honey Drizzled Coffee Cake	
(page 203)	115
LUNCH	
2 ounces shaved lean roast beef rolled	120
in 1 flour tortilla (8-inch) with	130
2 tablespoons taco sauce	10
1 bell pepper, cut into strips	15
1 cup skim milk	90
DINNER	
1 frozen 300-calorie dinner	300
Mixed green salad with 2 tablespoons	
Curry Dressing (page 195)	50
½ cup ice milk	100
SNACKS	
½ cup sugar-free gelatin	10
2 wheat crackers	30
TOTAL	1140

Menu 25

	Calories
BREAKFAST	
1 cup unsweetened strawberries	60
Huevos Rancheros (page 131)	210
1 cup skim milk	90
LUNCH	
1 cup chicken noodle soup	100
Mixed green salad with 1 tablespoon reduced-calorie Thousand Island dressing	50
2 crisp rye crackers	50
1 cup skim milk	90
DINNER	
Fish with Green Chilies (page 62)	170
½ cup Mexican-style corn	85
Beans and Rice (pages 142–143)	70
¼ honeydew melon (5-inch) with lime	35
SNACKS	
2 rice cakes	60
1 medium orange	65
TOTAL	1135

Menu 27

	Calories
BREAKFAST	
¼ cantaloupe (5-inch)	30
¾ cup cooked unsweetened oatmeal or oat bran	90
2 tablespoons raisins	60
1 cup skim milk	90
LUNCH	
Salmon-topped Rice Cakes (page 53)	220
1 small carrot and 1 medium celery stalk	25
1 cup skim milk	90
DINNER	
3 ounces broiled chicken breast, without skin	100
½ cup cooked pasta with herbs	75
½ cup Brussels sprouts	30
Marinated Cauliflower Salad (page 186)	60
Carrot Cake (page 219)	220
SNACK	
1 small apple	70
TOTAL	1160

Menu 26

	Calories
BREAKFAST	
½ cup unsweetened orange juice	60
1 slice whole wheat bread, toasted	65
1 tablespoon peanut butter	95
1 cup skim milk	90
LUNCH	
Egg salad sandwich, made with 1 hard-cooked egg, chopped, mixed	80
with 1 tablespoon reduced-calorie mayonnaise, with 2 slices reduced-	50
calorie whole wheat bread	80
1 medium apple	70
1 cup skim milk	90
DINNER	
Pork Chops with Vegetables (page 110)	360
1 medium tomato	40
Chocolate-Orange Bavarian (page 227)	85
SNACK	
1 frozen gelatin pop	30
TOTAL	1195

Menu 28

	Calories
BREAKFAST	
1 medium orange	65
1 Wheat Muffin (page 199)	90
1 cup unsweetened wheat or oat flake cereal	110
1 cup skim milk	90
LUNCH	
1 cup vegetable beef soup	100
2 corn cakes	60
1 small apple	70
1 cup skim milk	90
DINNER	
1 frozen 300-calorie dinner	300
Creamy Cucumbers (page 187)	20
1 Wheat Muffin (page 199)	90
SNACK	
½ cup unsweetened strawberries mixed with ½ cup nonfat plain yogurt, sugar substitute and vanilla to taste	85
TOTAL	1170

THE *EAT AND LOSE WEIGHT* WORKBOOK

Don't forget to photocopy worksheets and diaries to have on hand as you need them.

MEASUREMENT RECORD

Before you begin Betty Crocker's Five-Point Program, take your measurements and record them here. Take them every four weeks. As your measurements change, relate your eating habits and exercise to the results.

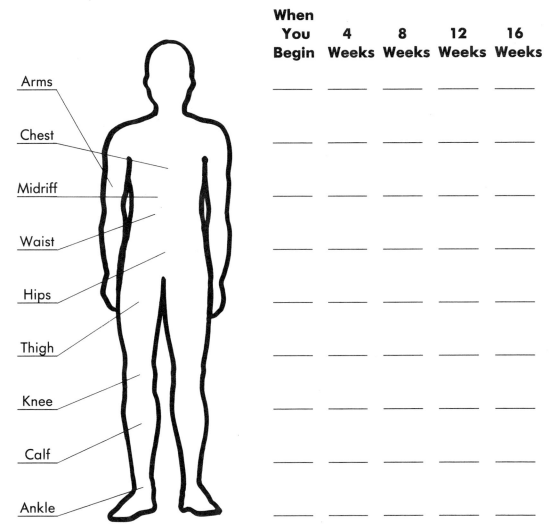

	When You Begin	4 Weeks	8 Weeks	12 Weeks	16 Weeks
Arms	___	___	___	___	___
Chest	___	___	___	___	___
Midriff	___	___	___	___	___
Waist	___	___	___	___	___
Hips	___	___	___	___	___
Thigh	___	___	___	___	___
Knee	___	___	___	___	___
Calf	___	___	___	___	___
Ankle	___	___	___	___	___

Source: General Mills, Inc.

Daily Exercise Diary

A regular exercise program of at least 5 workouts per week for a minimum of 30 minutes is necessary for weight loss and maintenance. Keep track of your daily exercise by referring to Calories Burned in Various Physical Activities.

Date	Activity	Time (in minutes)	Calories × per = Minute	Calories Burned	How You Felt Before	How You Felt After

Total Calories Burned = _____

Source: General Mills, Inc.

CALORIES BURNED IN VARIOUS PHYSICAL ACTIVITIES

Activity	Calories per Minute	Activity	Calories per Minute	Activity	Calories per Minute
Aerobics		road/field		Shoveling (depends	
Low-intensity	3.0–4.0	(3.5 mph)	5.6–7.0	on weight of	
High-intensity	8.0–10.0	snow, soft-hard		load, rate of	
Archery	5.2	(2.5–3.5 mph)	10.0–20.0	work height of lift)	5.4–10.5
Badminton		uphill		Showering	3.4
recreation	5.2	5–15 percent		Singing in loud	
competition	10.0	grade (3.5 mph)	8.0–15.6	voice	0.9
Baseball (except		Hill climbing (100		Sitting quietly	0.5
pitcher)	4.7	feet/hour)	8.2	Skipping rope	10.0–15.0
Basketball		Hockey	12.0–15.0	Skiing (snow)	
half court	6.0	Horseback riding		moderate to	
fastbreak	9.0	trot	5.0	steep	8.0–12.0
Bowling (while active)	7.0	walk	1.6	downhill racing	16.5
Calisthenics	6.0–8.0	Horseshoes	3.8	cross-country	
Canoeing		Ironing clothes	4.2	(3.8 mph)	11.0–20.0
(2.5–4.0 mph)	3.0–7.0	Jogging alternated		Sleeping	0.5–1.2
Carpentry	3.8	with walking, 5		Snowshoeing	
Cleaning windows	3.7	minutes each	10.0	(2.5 mph)	10.0
Clerical work	1.2–1.6	Judo and karate	13.0	Soccer	9.0
Cycling		Knitting or		Standing, light	
fast (12 mph)	8.0–10.0	crocheting	0.5–0.8	activity	2.6
slow (6 mph)	4.0–5.0	Making beds	3.4	Standing, relaxed	0.6
10-speed bicycle		Meal preparation	2.5	Sweeping with:	
(5–15 mph)	4.0–12.0	Mopping floors	4.9	broom	1.6
Dancing (moderate		Mountain climbing	10.0	vacuum cleaner	3.2
to vigorous)	4.2–7.7	Piano playing	1.6	Swimming	
Dishwashing	1.2	Plastering walls	4.1	pleasure	6.0
Dressing	3.4	Pool or billiards	1.8	backstroke,	
Driving car	2.8	Racquetball		breaststroke,	
Driving motorcycle	3.4	recreation	8.1	crawl (25–50	
Dusting	2.5	competition	11.5	yard/minute)	6.0–12.5
Eating	2.5	Reclining		butterfly (50	
Farming chores		(watching TV)	1.5	yard/minute)	14.0
haying	6.7	Roller skating		Table tennis	5.1
planting	4.7	(moderate to		Talking	1.0–1.2
Football (while		vigorous)	5.0–15.0	Tennis	
active)	13.3	Rowing		recreation	7.0
Gardening		pleasure	5.0	competition	11.0
digging	8.6	vigorous	15.0	Tree felling (ax)	8.4–12.7
weeding	5.6	Running		Truck and auto	
Golf		12-minute mile		repair	4.2
foursome	2.7	(5 mph)	9.0	Typing (rapidly)	1.2
twosome	3.0	8-minute mile		Volleyball	
Gymnastics		(7.5 mph)	11.0	recreation	3.5
balancing	2.5	6-minute mile		competition	8.0
abdominal	3.0	(10 mph)	20.0	Walking	
trunk bending	3.5	5-minute mile		3 mph	4.0–5.0
hopping	6.5	(12 mph)	25.0	4 mph	6.0–7.0
Handball	10.0	Sawing		downstairs	4.0
Hiking		chain saw	6.2	upstairs	8.0–10.0
downhill, 5–10		crosscut saw	7.5–10.5	Washing and	
percent grade		Sewing (hand or		dressing	2.6
(2.5 mph)	3.5–3.6	machine)	0.6	Washing clothes	3.1
downhill, 15–20		Shining shoes	3.2	Water skiing	8.0
percent grade				Wrestling	14.4
(2.5 mph)	3.7–4.3			Writing	0.5

Source: General Mills, Inc.

SAMPLE OF COMPLETED RECORD OF BEHAVIOR PATTERNS AND COPING SKILLS

Behavior Patterns	Coping Skills
Eating too fast	Allow 25–30 minutes per meal. Take small bites and chew slowly. Put utensils down between mouthfuls.
Impulsive eating	Have preplanned daily menu. Wait at least 10 minutes before eating any unplanned food. Don't skip meals. Shop only from a prepared list. Shop when I am not hungry. QUIT THE CLEAN PLATE CLUB.
Nibbling on leftovers	Throw them out. Store them out of sight as soon as possible.
Evening or night eating	Plan activity for specific "problem times." Include appropriate snacks in my diet plan.
Eating while reading or watching TV	Limit all eating to one location (table) at home. Do not do any other activity while eating.
Eating because I am depressed bored anxious frustrated tired excited in crisis alone	Become aware of my feelings and learn to cope without food. Get involved in a new activity. Learn relaxation techniques. Share my feelings with my support person.
Problem events: holidays, trips, parties	Plan ahead for these events—then enjoy the party. Contract to eat only a predetermined amount. Concentrate on improving my interaction with people.

Source: General Mills, Inc.

RECORD OF BEHAVIOR PATTERNS AND COPING SKILLS

Behavior Patterns   **Coping Skills**

_____   _____
_____   _____
_____   _____
_____   _____
_____   _____
_____   _____
_____   _____
_____   _____
_____   _____
_____   _____
_____   _____
_____   _____
_____   _____
_____   _____
_____   _____
_____   _____
_____   _____
_____   _____
_____   _____
_____   _____
_____   _____
_____   _____
_____   _____
_____   _____
_____   _____
_____   _____

EAT AND LOSE WEIGHT PROGRESS CHART

Starting date _____   Weight goal _____   "Alert" weight _____

Enter starting weight at top of left column. Record decreasing weight in that column and graph your progress from week to week in pounds lost, beginning at the initial dot. Weigh in weekly, using the same scale and at the same time of day. Set an "alert" weight of 5 to 7 pounds above your goal weight; reevaluate your eating and exercise habits when you reach your "alert" weight. Plan your rewards.

Weeks

Starting weight:	1	2	3	4	5	6	7	8	9	10	11	12	13	14	15	16	17	18	19	20	21	22	Rewards

Each Square = ½ Pound

Source: General Mills, Inc.

EAT AND LOSE WEIGHT

DAILY FOOD DIARY

Date _____

By tracking what you eat, you will be able to discover patterns and make changes in the future. Be aware of where you are, what you are doing and who is with you. Note foods you could have eliminated with an asterisk(*).

Time	Food Eaten	Amount	Calories	How I Felt	What I Was Doing and Where

Total calories = _____

Source: General Mills, Inc.

CALORIE CHART

Beverages	Calories	Breads, Cereal and Grain Products (cont.)	Calories
Alcoholic		Croissant (1 plain)	170
beer (8 ounces)	115	Dried beans and lentils	
liquor (1 ounce)	75	(½ cup cooked)	105
mixed drinks	155	English muffin (1 plain)	140
wine (4 ounces)	100	Flour, all-purpose (1 tablespoon)	30
Carbonated (8 ounces)		Muffin (2½-inch)	190
cola	95	Pancake (4-inch)	60
ginger ale	75	Pasta (½ cup cooked)	75
lemonade	110	Rice (½ cup cooked)	115
sugar-free	5	Rice cake (4-inch)	30
tonic water	80	Rolls (1 average)	
Coffee (8 ounces)		frankfurter or hamburger	120
black	5	hard	155
with cream and sugar	35	sweet	180
Milk-type (8 ounces)		Tortilla (8-inch)	130
cocoa with milk	245	Waffle (7-inch)	210
eggnog	290	Wheat germ (3 tablespoons)	100
malted milk shake, chocolate	500	Zwieback (1 piece)	30
milk			
buttermilk, skim	90	**Cheese**	
evaporated	345	American (1 ounce)	105
low-fat, 2 percent	120	Cheddar (1 ounce)	115
skim	90	Cottage (¼ cup)	60
whole	160	Cream (1 ounce)	105
Tea (8 ounces)	2	Mozzarella, part-skim (1 ounce)	70
		Neufchâtel (1 ounce)	70
Breads, Cereal and Grain Products		Parmesan (1 ounce)	130
Bagel (1 plain)	165	Parmesan (1 tablespoon grated)	25
Biscuit (2-inch)	140	Spread (1 ounce)	80
Breads (1-ounce slice raisin, white or whole wheat)	65	Swiss (1 ounce)	105
reduced-calorie, thinly sliced	40	**Desserts**	
Cereals		Apple Betty (½ cup)	210
cooked (½ cup)		Brownies (2-inch square)	145
cornmeal	60	Cake	
oatmeal	65	angel food (10-inch, 1/12, plain)	135
dry (1 cup)		chocolate/chocolate icing	
flaked cereal, bran, corn and wheat	100	(2-layer, 1/16)	235
puffed cereal, rice and wheat	60	cupcake, plain (2½-inch)	90
wheat, shredded (1 biscuit)	90	pound (½-inch slice)	140
Cornbread (2-inch square)	110	Cheesecake	
Crackers		cake, from mix (⅛)	300
graham (2½-inch square)	30	New York-style (1/20)	410
saltine (2-inch square)	15	Cookies	
		chocolate chip (3-inch)	90
		ginger snap (1½-inch)	20
		oatmeal with raisins (3-inch)	65
		sandwich (1½-inch)	50
		shortbread (1½-inch square)	35

Desserts (cont.)	Calories	Fats and Oils (cont.)	Calories
sugar (3-inch)	90	Salad dressings	
vanilla wafer (1½-inch)	15	blue cheese	
Custard (½ cup)	150	reduced-calorie	40
Doughnuts		regular	75
cake-type, plain	125	French	
raised	125	reduced-calorie	25
raised, jelly center	225	regular	65
Eclair, custard filling,		mayonnaise	
chocolate icing	315	reduced-calorie	50
Gelatin (½ cup)		regular	100
regular, fruit-flavored	70	Thousand Island	
sugar-free, fruit-flavored	8	reduced-calorie	30
Gingerbread (2-inch square)	205	regular	80
Ice cream (½ cup)			
regular	140	**Fruits and Fruit Juices**	
premium	200	Apple (2½-inch)	70
Ice milk (½ cup)		Apple juice (½ cup)	60
hardened	100	Applesauce (½ cup)	
soft-serve	135	canned, sweetened	115
Pies (9-inch, ⅛)		canned, unsweetened	50
fruit, 2-crust	315	Apricots	
custard	260	canned, sweetened	
lemon meringue	285	(½ cup)	110
pecan	430	canned, unsweetened	
pumpkin	240	(½ cup)	40
Pudding (½ cup)		fresh (3 medium)	55
bread with raisins	210	Avocado (3½ × 4 inches, ½)	165
chocolate, regular with		Banana (6 inches)	80
whole milk	195	Blackberries, fresh (½ cup)	40
chocolate, sugar-free with		Blueberries, fresh (½ cup)	40
skim milk	80	Cantaloupe (5-inch, ½)	60
rice with raisins	140	Cherries	
tapioca	110	canned, sweetened (½ cup)	90
Sherbet (½ cup)	130	canned, unsweetened	
Shortcake, strawberry	380	(½ cup)	50
		fresh (½ cup)	60
Eggs		maraschino (1 large)	10
Cooked, hard or soft	80	Coconut, shredded, firmly	
Fried or scrambled	110	packed (½ cup)	225
		Cranberry sauce, sweetened	
Fats and Oils (1 tablespoon)		(½ cup)	200
Butter	100	Dates (3 medium)	80
Cream		Fig, dried (1 large)	60
coffee	30	Fruit cocktail, sweetened	
half-and-half	20	(½ cup)	75
sour	25	Grapes, green seedless	
whipping	55	(½ cup)	50
Lard	115	Grape juice, canned (½ cup)	80
Margarine		Grapefruit (½ medium)	50
reduced-calorie	50	Grapefruit juice, canned (½ cup)	50
regular	100	Honeydew melon (5-inch, ¼)	35
Oil, vegetable	125	Lemon juice (1 tablespoon)	5

Fruits and Fruit Juices (cont.)	Calories
Nectarine (2-inch)	30
Orange (2⅝-inch)	65
Orange juice, unsweetened (½ cup)	60
Peach	
canned, sweetened (½ cup)	100
canned, unsweetened (½ cup)	40
fresh (2-inch)	35
Pear	
canned, sweetened (½ cup)	100
canned, unsweetened (½ cup)	40
fresh (3 × 2½ inches)	100
Pineapple	
canned, sweetened (1 large slice)	90
fresh (½ cup)	40
juice, unsweetened (½ cup)	70
Plum, fresh (2-inch)	25
Prunes (4 medium)	70
Prune juice (½ cup)	100
Pumpkin, canned (½ cup)	40
Raisins, dry (2 tablespoons)	60
Raspberries, fresh (½ cup)	35
Rhubarb, stewed, sweetened (½ cup)	190
Strawberries (½ cup)	
fresh	30
frozen, sweetened	140
Tangerine (2½-inch)	40
Watermelon (4 to 8-inch wedge)	115

Meats (lean, well-trimmed, 3 ounces cooked)

	Calories
Beef	
chuck	200
corned	215
ground beef	
grilled, regular	245
grilled, lean	230
liver, fried	185
roast	
rib	200
rump	180
steak	
flank	210
porterhouse	185
round	165
sirloin	180
T-bone	180
Lamb	
chop, loin	160

Meats (cont.)	Calories
roast	
leg	160
shoulder	175
Pork	
chop, loin	230
ham	
cured	160
fresh	185
roast, loin	215
tenderloin	205
Veal	
chop, loin	175
cutlet	185
roast	145
Miscellaneous	
bacon (2 medium slices)	90
bologna (3 inch × ⅛-inch slice)	80
Braunschweiger (2 inch × ¼-inch slice)	65
frankfurter (2 ounces)	170
pork link (3 × ½ inches)	125

Nuts

	Calories
Almonds (¼ cup)	215
Brazil (4)	95
Cashews (¼ cup)	195
Hazelnuts (6)	50
Peanuts (¼ cup)	210
Pecans (¼ cup)	185
Walnuts (¼ cup)	200

Poultry (3 ounces cooked)

	Calories
Chicken	
breast, broiled	100
breast, fried, with bone	140
drumstick, fried, with bone	130
roasted, no skin	145
Goose, roasted, no skin	275
Turkey, roasted, no skin	165

Sauces (2 tablespoons)

	Calories
Butterscotch	205
Cheese	65
Chili	35
Chocolate	85
Hollandaise	95
Lemon	65
Tartar	150
Tomato	40
White	50

Seafood (3 ounces)	Calories	Sweets (cont.)	Calories
Clams, canned	85	Sugars (½ cup)	
Cod, broiled	145	brown	410
Crabmeat, canned	85	granulated	385
Fish stick, batter-dipped	250	powdered	230
Halibut, broiled	145		
Lobster, canned	80	**Vegetables**	
Oysters, raw	60	Asparagus, cooked (½ cup)	20
Salmon, pink, canned	120	Bamboo shoots (½ cup)	20
Sardines, canned in oil	175	Beans (½ cup)	
Scallops, steamed	95	baked, no pork	150
Shrimp		green, cooked	15
canned	100	kidney, cooked	115
French fried	190	lima, cooked	95
Tuna		Bell pepper, raw (1 medium)	15
canned in oil	170	Beets, cooked (½ cup)	25
water-packed	110	Beet greens, cooked (½ cup)	20
		Broccoli, cooked (½ cup)	20
Soups (made with water, 1 cup)		Brussels sprouts, cooked (½ cup)	30
Bean with pork	170	Cabbage (½ cup)	
Beef noodle	70	cooked	15
Bouillon	30	raw	10
Clam chowder	80	Carrots, raw or cooked (½ cup or one, 5½ × 1 inch)	25
Cream of chicken	95	Cauliflower, cooked (½ cup)	15
Cream of mushroom	135	Celery (8 × ½-inch stalk)	5
Oyster stew	120	Corn	
Split pea	145	canned, whole kernel (½ cup)	85
Tomato	90	cob (5 × 1¾-inch ear)	70
Vegetable-Beef	80	Cucumber (12 slices)	10
		Eggplant, raw (2 slices)	25
		Kale, cooked (½ cup)	15
Sweets		Lettuce, iceberg (5-inch, ¼)	15
Candies		Mushrooms, canned (¼ cup)	10
caramel (1 medium)	40	Okra, cooked (3 × ⅝ inches, 8 pods)	25
chocolate		Onions	
bar, plain (1 ounce)	150	cooked (½ cup)	30
kisses (7)	150	green (6 small)	20
fudge (1-inch square)	105	Parsnips, cooked (½ cup)	50
gumdrops (1 large or 8 small)	35	Peas, cooked (½ cup)	60
jelly beans (10)	65	Potato	
lollypop (2¼-inch)	110	baked (2¼-inch)	80
marshmallow (1 large)	25	French fried (2 × ½ inches, 10 pieces)	155
peanut brittle (2½-inch piece)	110	sweet (½ cup)	120
Jams and preserves (1 tablespoon)	55	Radishes (4 small)	5
Jellies (1 tablespoon)	50	Rutabagas, cooked (½ cup)	35
Syrups (1 tablespoon)		Sauerkraut (½ cup)	20
chocolate-flavored	50	Spinach, cooked (½ cup)	20
corn	60	Squash, cooked (½ cup)	
honey	65	summer	15
maple	50	winter	65
molasses	50		

Vegetables (cont.)	Calories	Unclassified (cont.)	Calories
Tomato		Olives	
canned (½ cup)	25	green (4 medium)	15
fresh (3-inch)	40	ripe (3 small)	15
Tomato juice (½ cup)	20	Peanut butter (1 tablespoon)	95
Turnips, cooked (½ cup)	20	Pickles	
Water chestnuts (4)	20	dill (3¾ × 1¼ inches)	10
		relish (1 tablespoon)	20
		sweet (2½ × ¾ inches)	20
Unclassified		Pizza, cheese (14-inch, ⅛)	185
Catsup (1 tablespoon)	15	Popcorn (1 cup)	
Cocoa (1 tablespoon)	20	added oil	40
Chocolate, bitter (1 ounce)	145	hot-air-popped	30
Gelatin, unflavored		Popsicle	70
(1 envelope)	25	Potato chips (10)	115
Gelatin pop, frozen	30	Pretzels (3 inches, 5 sticks)	10
Gravy (1 tablespoon)	40	Vinegar (2 tablespoons)	5
Herring, pickled (1 × ½ inch)	50	Yeast, dry, active	
Ice cream bar, chocolate-		(1 package)	20
covered	145	Yogurt (1 cup)	
Mustard, prepared		made from skim milk	125
(1 teaspoon)	5	made from whole milk	150
		nonfat plain	110

Source: General Mills, Inc.

INDEX

Alcoholic beverages, 12
Almond(s)
  Crisp, Apple, 236
  Cheesecake, 228
  Macaroons, Coconut-, 226–227
  Strips, 202
  -Cheese Sandwich, Toasted, 139
Appetizers
  Carrots and Jícama, Spicy, 27
  Dip
    Pimiento Cheese, 23
    Tangy Yogurt, 23
  Eggs, Deviled, with Vegetables, 28
  Guacamole, Mock, 23
  Meatballs, Curried, with Chutney Sauce, 26
  Minibites, Peppery, 28
  Mushrooms, Savory Stuffed, 27
  Spread
    Dilled Cucumber–Shrimp, 24
    Mushroom, Smoky, 26
    Yogurt Cheese, Herbed, 24
Apple(s)
  Cider, Lemony, 34
  Cornish Hens with, Curried, 97
  Crisp, Almond, 236
  Medley, Cabbage-, 160
  and Pears, Spiced, 190
  -stuffed Sole, 56
  Sauce, Swordfish with Thyme- 49
Apricot Chicken, 75
Artichoke Hearts, Creole, 155
Asparagus
  Roulades, Chicken and, 81
  with Toasted Cashews, 157

Baked Eggplant with Curry Sauce, 164

Baked Fish with Summer Vegetables, 41
Banana Bread, 203
Barley Soup with Vegetables, 210
Basil
  Chicken, Lemon-, 71
Bean(s)
  and Cheese Tacos, 148
  Garbanzo, with Spinach, 143
  and Rice, 142–143
  Soup, Black, 146
  Soup, Gorgonzola–White, 146
  Soup, Red Kidney, 143
  and Squash, Skillet, 144
Beef
  Casserole, and Bulgur, 108
  Casserole, Easy, 105
  with Cucumber Rice, Indian, 103
  Liver Italiano, 109
  Meatballs in Dijon Sauce, 107
  with Pea Pods, 104
  with Peppers, Garlicky, 104
  Roll, Oriental Vegetable Meat, 108–109
  Salad, Spicy, 181
  Sandwiches, Pocket, Roast, 109
  Shells, -stuffed, Mushroom- and, 209
  Steak, with Dilled Vegetables, 101
  Steak, Mexican Flank, 101
  Stroganoff, 105
Beets, Sweet and Sour, 157
Behavior patterns, 256–257
Beverages
  Apple Cider, Lemony, 34
  Tomato Drink, Hot, 34
Black Bean Soup, 146
Blue Cheese Waldorf Salad, 192

Bok Choy Stir-Fry, 159
Bread(s)
  Banana, 203
  Corn, Fluffy, 202
  Muffins
    Cranberry, 201
    Wheat, 199
  Popovers, 201
  Rolls, Easy Herb, 199
Bread Pudding with Brown Sugar Meringue, 228
Broccoli
  and Corn, Festive, 158
  Pasta, Dijon, 212
  Risotto, Pork and, 116
  Spaghetti with, and Mushrooms, 212
  with Mushrooms and Thyme, 158
Brownies, 226
Brussels Sprouts, Savory, 159
Butterscotch Peach Slices, 233

Cabbage
  -Apple Medley, 160
  Oriental Pork and, 122
Cake(s)
  Angel, Creamy Strawberry, 219
  Carrot, 219
  Gingerbread with Orange Sauce, 221
  Sacher Cake Roll, 222
  Upside-down, Pineapple-Lemon, 222
Calorie Chart, 260–264
Calories, activity and, 8, 15, 255
Carrot(s)
  Cake, 219
  Honey-Mint, 160
  and Jícama, Spicy, 27

Cashews, Asparagus with Toasted, 157
Catfish
  Smoky, 39
  Stew, 41
Cauliflower
  with Cheeses, 162
  Salad, Marinated, 186
  Wedges with Salsa, 162
Cellulite, 17
Cheese(s)
  Casserole, Rice and, 207
  Cauliflower with, 162
  Chicken with Fruit and, 87
  Dip, Pimiento, 23
  Dressing, Garlic Blue, 195
  Drumsticks, Spicy, with Blue Cheese Sauce, 87
  Perch, Parmesan, 43
  Potatoes, Ham- and Swiss-topped, 122–123
  Puff, Gruyère, in Mushroom Crust, 142
  Puff, Quick Chili-, 133
  Quiche, Smoky Beef and, 134
  Salad, Blue Cheese Waldorf, 192
  Sandwich, Toasted Almond-, 139
  Soufflé, Mushroom-, 138
  Soup, Gorgonzola–White Bean, 146
  Soup with Popcorn, Vegetable-, 139
  Strata, Gouda, 144
  Tacos, Bean and, 148
Chicken
  Apricot, 75
  and Asparagus Roulades, 81
  Breasts Dijon, 81
  Chutney, 74–75
  Curried, Spicy, with Couscous, 78–79
  Drumsticks, Spicy, with Blue Cheese Sauce, 87
  with Fruit and Cheese, 87
  Kiev, Garlic, 79
  Lemon, 85
  Lemon-Basil, 71

with Peppers and Onions, 71
Plum-barbecued, 78
Poached, Cold, with Two Sauces, 76
Salad, Raspberry, 177
Satay, 74
Sherried Orange, 84–85
on Skewers, Ginger, 90
Soup with Leeks, 73
Soup, -Vegetable, 73
Stir-Fry, Italian, 90
with Vegetables, 84
Waldorf, 82
Chili(es)
  Fish with Green, 62
  -Cheese Puff, Quick Chili, 133
  -stuffed Peppers, 91
  Turkey-Vegetable, 92
Chocolate
  -Cherry Cobbler, 235
  -laced Kiwifruit with Orange Sauce, 236
  Meringues, Crème de Menthe, 231
  -Orange Bavarian, 227
Cholesterol, 8, 10
Chutney
  Chicken, 74–75
  Curried Meatballs with Chutney Sauce, 26
Citrus Salad, 191
Cobbler, Chocolate-Cherry, 235
Coconut-Almond Macaroons, 226–227
Cod, Hot Salsa, 42
Cold Poached Chicken with Two Sauces, 76
Coleslaw, Creamy, 186
Colorful Pepper Skillet, 165
Confetti Wild Rice, 207
Coping, 15
Coping skills, 256–257
Corn
  Broccoli and, Festive, 158
  Pudding, Fluffy, 163
Cornish Hens
  Curried, with Apples, 97
  Herbed, 97

Couscous, Spicy Curried Chicken with, 78–79
Cranberry
  Muffins, 201
  -Orange Cream Puffs, 232
Creamy
  Coleslaw, 186
  Cucumbers, 187
  Fish Chowder, 61
  Fruit Dressing, 195
  Garlic Dressing, 194
  Smoked Ham, 123
  Strawberry Angel Cake, 219
Creole Artichoke Hearts, 155
Crisp Tortilla Chips, 31
Crunchy Baked Fish, 40
  Ham Salad, 180–181
  Lemon Rice, 208
  Pears, 233
Crustless Tuna Quiche, 49
Cucumber(s)
  Creamy, 187
  Dressing, 194
  Rice, Indian Beef with, 103
  Salad, Salmon-Rice, with Dilled Dressing, 179
  Sandwiches, Dilled, 140
  Soup, Cold, -Yogurt, 163
  Spread, Dilled, –Shrimp, 24
Curry
  Curried Chicken with Couscous, Spicy, 78–79
  Eggplant with Curry Sauce, Baked, 164
  Curried Cornish Hens with Apples, 97
  Curried Eggs and Vegetables on Rice, 138–139
  Curried Meatballs with Chutney Sauce, 26
  Curried Scallop Kabobs, 66
  Dressing, 195
Custard, Maple, 227

Dessert(s) See also Cakes
  Bavarian, Chocolate-Orange, 227
  Brownies, 226
  Cheesecake, Almond, 228

Cobbler, Chocolate-Cherry, 235
Cookies, Oatmeal, Quick, 226
Cream Puffs, Cranberry-
    Orange, 232
Crisp, Almond Apple, 236
Custard, Maple, 227
Kiwifruit, Chocolate-laced, with
    Orange Sauce, 236
Macaroons, Coconut-Almond,
    226
Meringues, Chocolate Crème
    de Menthe, 231
Peach Slices, Butterscotch, 233
Pears, Crunchy, 233
Pie, Strawberry with Meringue
    Crust, 223
Pudding, Bread, with Brown
    Sugar Meringue, 228
Sorbet
    Honeydew, with Strawberry
        Purée, 239
    Peach, with Pineapple, 239
Trifle, Orange, 232
Torte, Raspberry Graham
    Cracker, 235
Deviled Eggs with Vegetables,
    28
Diary, daily
    exercise, 254
    food, 259
Dijon-style mustard
    Chicken Breasts, Dijon, 81
    Meatballs in Dijon Sauce,
        107
    Pasta, Dijon Broccoli, 212
    Poached Fish Dijon, 40
Dill
    Dilled Cucumber Sandwiches,
        140
    Dilled Cucumber-Shrimp
        Spread, 24
    Dilled Steak with Vegetables,
        101
    Salmon-Rice Salad with Dilled
        Cucumber Dressing, 179
Dips. See also Dressings
    Mock Guacamole, 23
    Pimiento Cheese, 23
    Tangy Yogurt, 23

Dressings. See also Dips
    Cucumber, 194
    Curry, 195
    Fruit, Creamy, 195
    Garlic, Creamy, 194
    Garlic Blue Cheese, 195
    Honey-Mustard, 192
    Mexican-style Salad, 194
    Mock Mayonnaise, Rich, 195

Easy
    Beef Casserole, 105
    Fish and Vegetable Packets,
        46
    Herb Rolls, 199
    Spinach Soup, 167
Egg(s)
    Benedict, 133
    Curried, and Vegetables on
        Rice, 138–139
    Deviled, with Vegetables, 28
    Foo Yong, 130–131
    Frittata, Zucchini, 129
    Huevos Rancheros, 131
    Omelet, with Tomato Sauce,
        Fluffy, 130
    Omelets, Mushroom, 129
    Scrambled Eggs Mélange, 134
Eggplant with Curry Sauce,
    Baked, 164
Exercise, 15–17
    diary, 254

Fast food, 18
Fat, avoiding, 8, 10
Festive Broccoli and Corn, 158
Fiber, 10
Fish
    Baked, Crunchy, 40
    Baked, with Summer Vegeta-
        bles, 41
    Catfish, Smoky, 39
    Cod, Hot Salsa, 42
    Chowder, Creamy, 61
    Flounder with Mushrooms and
        Wine, 43
    with Green Chilies, 62
    Grouper, Steamed, with
        Spinach, 54

Halibut
    Mediterranean, 47
    Stir-Fry, 47
Mahimahi with Pineapple
    Sauce, 55
Orange Roughy
    with Red Peppers, 44
    with Tarragon Sauce, 46
    Packets, Easy, and Vegetables,
        46
Perch, Parmesan, 43
Pike Fillets, Piquant, 44
Poached, Dijon, 40
Red Snapper, Zesty, with
    Mushrooms, 54
Salmon-topped Rice Cakes, 53
Shark Steaks, Marinated, 56
Sole
    Apple-stuffed, 56
    Gratin, 58
    Steamed with Vegetables,
        59
Soup, Oriental Seafood, 59
Steaks, Mustard, 55
Stew
    Catfish, 41
    Red Snapper, 53
Sweet and Sour, 58
Swordfish with Thyme-Apple
    Sauce, 49
Tuna
    Casserole, Southern, 50
    -filled Tomatoes, 50
    Quiche, Crustless, 49
Five-Point Program
    Design Your Lifestyle, 19
    Eat Smart, 8–15
    Exercise, 15–17
    Keep Good Records, 18
    Set Goals, 17–18
Flounder with Mushrooms and
    Wine, 43
Fluffy
    Corn Bread, 202
    Corn Pudding, 163
    Omelet with Tomato Sauce, 130
Food diary, 259
Food groups, basic, 9, 13
Food shopping, 19

Fruit. *See also* types of
Chicken with Fruit and Cheese, 87
Citrus Salad, 191
Dressing, Creamy, 195
Kabobs with Pineapple Dip, 30

Garbanzo Beans with Spinach, 143
Garden Potato Salad, 187
Garlic
Beef with Peppers, 104
Blue Cheese Dressing, 195
Chicken Kiev, 79
Dressing, Creamy, 194
Shrimp, Stir-fried, 63
Garlicky Beef with Peppers, 104
Gazpacho Mold, 190
German-style Pasta, 212
Ginger
Chicken on Skewers, 90
Gingerbread with Orange Sauce, 221
Ginger, Spinach, 168
Pork on Pineapple, 118–19
Gorgonzola–White Bean Soup, 146
Gouda Strata, 144
Graham Cracker Torte, Raspberry, 235
Green Beans and Tomatoes, Italian, 155
Green Noodles and Vegetables, 215
Grouper with Spinach, Steamed, 54–55
Gruyère Puff in Mushroom Crust, 142
Guacamole, Mock, 23

Halibut
Mediterranean, 47
Stir-Fry, 47
Ham
Creamy Smoked, 123
Salad, Crunchy, 180–181
and Swiss-topped Potatoes, 122–123
Height tables, 11

Herb(s)
Cheese Yogurt, 24
Cornish Hens, 97
Rolls, 199
Sauce, 170
Vegetables and Lentils, 149
Vegetables, Steamed, with Herb Sauce, 170
Honey
-drizzled Coffee Cake, 203
-Mint Carrots, 160
-Mustard Dressing, 192
Honeydew Sorbet with Strawberry Purée, 239
Hot
German Vegetable Salad, 189
Salsa, 42
Salsa Cod, 42
Tomato Drink, 34
Huevos Rancheros, 131

Indian Beef with Cucumber Rice, 103
Italian
Chicken Stir-Fry, 90
Green Beans and Tomatoes, 155
Sausage and Vegetables, 123

Kiwifruit with Orange Sauce, Chocolate-laced, 236

Lamb Paprikash, 124
Lamb Patties with Fresh Mint Sauce, 124
Lasagne, Vegetable, 213
Leek(s)
and Chèvre Pizza, 140
Chicken Soup with, 78
Lemon
Cake, Upside-down, Pineapple-, 222
Chicken, 85
Chicken, -Basil, 71
Cider, Apple, 34
Rice, Crunchy, 208
Salad, Greek, 184
Vegetables, -Pepper, 165
Lentils, Herbed Vegetables and, 149

Liver Italiano, 109

Macaroni with Marinated Tomatoes, 209
Mahimahi with Pineapple Sauce, 55
Maple Custard, 227
Marinated Cauliflower Salad, 186
Marinated Shark Steaks, 56
Marshmallow Squares, 34
Mayonnaise, Rich Mock, 195
Measurement record, 253
Meatballs
Curried with Chutney Sauce, 26
in Dijon Sauce, 107
Mediterranean Halibut, 47
Melon Salad with Tea-flavored Cream, 191
Menus, 240–251
Meringues, Chocolate Crème de Menthe, 231
Metabolism, defined, 16
Mexican Flank Steak, 101
Mexican-style Salad Dressing, 194
Middle Eastern Stew, 149
Mock Guacamole, 23
Mock Hollandaise Sauce, 133
Mushroom(s)
and Beef-stuffed shells, 209
Broccoli with, and Thyme, 158
Flounder with, and Wine, 43
Gruyère Puff in Mushroom Crust, 142
Omelets, 129
Pita Pizzas, 33
Red Snapper, Zesty, with, 54
Savory Stuffed, 27
Soufflé, -Cheese, 138
Spaghetti with Broccoli and, 212
Spicy, 187
Spread, Smoky, 26
Stir-Fry, Triple, 169
Mussels with Mustard Sauce, 62

Mustard. *See also* Dijon-style
  mustard
  Dressing, Honey-, 192
  Fish Steaks, 55
  Mussels with Mustard Sauce,
    62

Oatmeal Cookies, Quick, 226
Oils, types of, 10
Onion(s)
  Chicken with Peppers and, 71
  Pork with Squash and, 110
  Tart, and Pepper, 167
Orange
  Bavarian, Chocolate-, 227
  Chocolate-laced Kiwifruit with,
    Sauce, 236
  Cream Puffs, Cranberry-, 232
  Gingerbread with, Sauce,
    221
  Rice Bake, 208
  Trifle, 232
  Yogurt Salad, 192
Orange Roughy
  with Red Peppers, 44
  with Tarragon Sauce, 46
Oriental
  Pork and Cabbage, 122
  Seafood Soup, 59
  Vegetable Meat Roll, 108–109

Parmesan Perch, 43
Pasta
  Green Noodles and Vegeta-
    bles, 215
  Primavera, Turkey-, 93
  Salad, Pimiento, 186
  Salad, Tangy Shrimp Noodle,
    177
  Spaghetti with Broccoli and
    Mushrooms, 212
  Spaghetti with Squash, 215
  Stir-Fry, Pork and, 119
  Turkey, with Pesto, 93
Peach
  Slices, Butterscotch, 233
  Sorbet with Pineapple, 239
Pears
  Apples and, Spiced, 190

Crunchy, 233
Peas
  Beef with Pea Pods, 104
  in Tomato Shells, 164
Pepper(s)
  Beef, Garlicky with, 104
  Chicken with, and Onions, 71
  Chili-stuffed, 91
  Orange Roughy with Red, 44
  Skillet, Colorful, 165
  Tart, Onion and, 167
  Vegetables, Lemon-, 165
Peppery Minibites, 28
Perch, Parmesan, 43
Pike Fillets, Piquant, 44
Pimiento
  Cheese Dip, 23
  Pasta Salad, 186
Pineapple
  Fruit Kabobs with, 30
  Cake, -Lemon Upside-down,
    222
  Ginger Pork on, 118–19
  Mahimahi with Pineapple
    Sauce, 55
  Peach Sorbet with, 239
  Pork Chops, 114–115
  Rice, 208–209
Piquant Pike Fillets, 44
Pizza(s)
  Leek and Chèvre, 140
  Mushroom Pita, 33
  Scallop, 66
Plum-barbecued Chicken, 78
Poached Fish Dijon, 40
Polenta with Tomatoes, 210
Popcorn
  Mix, Savory, 31
  Mix, Sweet, 30
  Soup, Vegetable-Cheese with,
    139
Popovers, 201
Poppy Seed Squash, 170
Pork
  Chops, Pineapple, 114–115
  Chops with Rhubarb Sauce,
    113
  Chops with Vegetables, 110
  Fajitas, 115

Florentine, 118
Ginger, on Pineapple,
  118–19
Oriental, and Cabbage,
  122
Pretzel, with Sauerkraut
  Relish, 114
Risotto, and Broccoli, 116
with Squash and Onions, 110
Stir-Fry, and Pasta, 119
Stew, Savory, 116
Potato(es)
  Ham- and Swiss-topped,
    122–123
  Salad, Garden, 187
  Snacks, 33
  Vegetable-stuffed, 169
Pretzel Pork with Sauerkraut
  Relish, 144
Progress Chart, 254
Pumpkin Squares, 231

Quiche, Crustless Tuna, 49
Quiche, Smoky Beef and
  Cheese, 134
Quick Chili-Cheese Puff, 133
Quick Oatmeal Cookies, 226

Raspberry
  Chicken Salad, 177
  Torte, Graham Cracker, 235
Ratatouille, 173
Red Kidney Bean Soup, 143
Red Snapper with Mushrooms,
  Zesty, 54
Red Snapper Stew, 53
Rice
  Bake, Orange, 208
  Beans and, 142–143
  Cakes, Salmon-topped, 53
  Casserole, and Cheese, 207
  Crust, Seafood Pie with, 63
  Cucumber, Indian Beef with,
    103
  Lemon, Crunchy, 208
  Pineapple, 208–209
  Salad, Salmon, with Dilled
    Cucumber Dressing, 179
  Wild, Confetti, 207

Rich Mock Mayonnaise, 195
Roast Beef Pocket Sandwiches,
    109

Sacher Cake Roll, 222–223
Salad
    Apples and Pears, Spiced, 190
    Beef, Spicy, 181
    Citrus, 191
    Cauliflower, Marinated, 186
    Coleslaw, Creamy, 186
    Cucumbers, Creamy, 187
    Gazpacho Mold, 190
    Ham, Crunchy, 180
    Lemon Greek, 184
    Melon, with Tea-flavored
        Cream, 191
    Mushrooms, Spicy, 187
    Orange Yogurt, 192
    Pimiento Pasta, 186
    Potato, Garden, 187
    Raspberry Chicken, 177
    Salmon-Rice, with Dilled
        Cucumber Dressing, 179
    Spinach with Sprouts, 184
    Tangy Shrimp Noodle, 177
    Tomato Slices, Tarragon, 189
    Turkey Taco, 180
    Vegetable, Hot German, 189
    Waldorf, Blue Cheese, 192
Salad bar strategy, 7
Salmon
    -Rice Salad with Dilled
        Cucumber Dressing, 179
    -topped Rice Cakes, 53
Salsa, Cauliflower Wedges with,
    162
Salsa, Cod, Hot, 42
Saturated fat, 8, 10
Sausage and Vegetables, Italian,
    123
Savory
    Brussels Sprouts, 159
    Popcorn Mix, 31
    Pork Stew, 116
    Stuffed Mushrooms, 27
Scallop Kabobs, Curried, 66
Scallop Pizza, 66
Scrambled Eggs Mélange, 134

Seafood Pasta with Vegetables,
    67
Seafood Pie with Rice Crust, 63
Shark Steaks, Marinated, 56
Shellfish
    Mussels with Mustard Sauce,
        62
    Salad, Tangy Shrimp Noodle,
        177
    Scallop
        Kabobs, Curried, 66
        Pizza, 66
    Seafood
        Pasta with Vegetables, 67
        Pie with Rice Crust, 63
        Shrimp, Stir-fried Garlic, 63
        Spread, Dilled Cucumber–
            Shrimp, 24
Sherried Orange Chicken, 84–85
Shopping Smart, 15
Shrimp
    Noodle Salad, Tangy, 177
    Spread, Dilled Cucumber–, 24
    Stir-fried Garlic, 63
Skillet Beans and Squash, 144
Smoky
    Beef and Cheese Quiche, 134
    Catfish, 39
    Mushroom Spread, 26
Sodium, avoiding, 11–12
Sole
    Apple-stuffed, 56
    Gratin, 58
    Steamed with Vegetables, 59
Sorbet
    Honeydew, with Strawberry
        Purée, 239
    Peach, with Pineapple,
        239
Soup
    Chicken
        With Leeks, 73
        -Vegetable, 73
    Chowder, Creamy Fish, 61
    Cold Cucumber-Yogurt, 163
    Seafood, Oriental, 59
    Spinach, Easy, 167
    Vegetable-Cheese with Pop-
        corn, 139

Southern Tuna Casserole, 50
Spaghetti
    with Broccoli and Mushrooms,
        212
    with Squash, 215
Spicy
    Beef Salad, 181
    Carrots and Jícama, 27
    Chicken, Curried, with Cous-
        cous, 78–79
    Drumsticks with Blue Cheese
        Sauce, 87
    Mushrooms, 187
Spinach
    Garbanzo Beans with, 143
    Gingered, 168
    Grouper with, Steamed, 54
    Mélange, 168
    Soup, Easy, 167
    with Sprouts, 184
Squash
    Beans and, Skillet, 144
    Poppy Seed, 170
    Pork with, and Onions, 110
    Spaghetti with, 215
Starch, 10
Steamed Grouper with Spinach,
    54
Steamed Vegetables with Herb
    Sauce, 170
Stir-fried Garlic Shrimp, 63
Strawberry
    Angel Cake, Creamy, 219
    Honeydew Sorbert with Straw-
        berry Purée, 239
    Pie with Meringue Crust, 223
Sugar, avoiding, 10–11
Sweet Popcorn Mix, 30
Sweet and Sour Beets, 157
Sweet and Sour Fish, 58
Swordfish with Thyme-Apple
    Sauce, 49

Tacos
    Bean and Cheese, 148
    Salad, Turkey, 180
Tangy Shrimp Noodle Salad,
    177
Tarragon Tomato Slices, 189

Toasted Almond-Cheese Sandwich, 139
Tomato(es)
    Drink, Hot, 34
    Fluffy Omelet with Tomato Sauce, 130
    Green Beans and, Italian, 155
    Macaroni with Marinated, 209
    Polenta with, 210
    Shells, Peas in, 164
    Slices, Tarragon, 189
    Tuna-filled, 50
Tortilla Chips, Crisp, 31
Triple Mushroom Stir-Fry, 169
Tuna
    Casserole, Southern, 50
    -filled Tomatoes, 50
    Quiche, Crustless, 49
Turkey
    with Chipotle Sauce, 94
    -Pasta Primavera, 93
    Pasta with Pesto, 93
    Pie, 92
    Salad, Taco, 180
    -Vegetable Chili, 92
    with Wine, 91

Vegetable(s). *See also types of*
    Chicken with, 84
    Chili, Turkey-, 92
    Curried Eggs and, on Rice, 138–139
    Deviled Eggs with, 28
    Fish, Baked, with Summer, 41
    Fish and Vegetable Packets, Easy, 46
    Green Noodles and, 215
    Lasagne, 213
    Lemon-Pepper, 165
    and Lentils, Herbed, 149
    Meat Roll, Oriental, 108–109
    Pasta with, Seafood, 67
    Pork Chops with, 110
    Potatoes, -stuffed, 169
    Ratatouille, 173
    Salad, Hot German, 189
    Sausage and, Italian, 123
    Sole Steamed with, 59
    Soufflé Roll, -filled, 137
    Soup with, Barley, 210
    Soup, Chicken-, 73
    Soup with Popcorn, -Cheese, 139
    Steak, Dilled, with, 101

    Steamed, with Herb Sauce, 170

Waldorf Chicken, 82
Water, importance of, 12
Weight tables, 11
Wheat Muffins, 199
Wine
    Flounder with Mushrooms and, 43
    Turkey with, 91
    Zucchini in, 173

Yogurt
    Cheese, Herbed, 24
    Dip, Tangy, 23
    Salad, Orange, 192
    Soup, Cold Cucumber-, 163

Zesty Red Snapper with Mushrooms, 54
Zucchini
    Frittata, 129
    in Wine, 173

CREDITS

PRENTICE HALL

Vice-President and Publisher: Anne M. Zeman
Senior Editor: Rebecca W. Atwater
Art Director: Laurence Alexander
Designers: Patricia Fabricant, Frederick J. Latasa
Prop Stylist: Janice Ervin

GENERAL MILLS, INC.

Editor: Jean E. Kozar
Test Kitchen Home Economists: Pat Little, Mary E. Petersen, Joyce Gauck
Recipe Copy Editor: Deb Hance
Nutrition Department Consultant: Nancy Holmes, R.D.
Administrative Assistant: Phyllis Weinbender
Food Stylists: Cindy Lund, Katie McElroy, Carol Grones
Photographer: Nanci E. Doonan
Photography Assistant: Chuck Carver
Director, Betty Crocker Food and Publications Center: Marcia Copeland
Assistant Manager, Publications: Lois Tlusty

The following plates are courtesy of: A. Mallory
California (pages 72, 117, 145, 147, 237), Haviland and
Company (pages 124 and 245) and Dan Levy (page 80).